AF863609

THE RIGHT TO EDUCATION IN INDIA

Law, Policies and its Governance

THE RIGHT TO EDUCATION IN INDIA

Law, Policies and its Governance

Dr.Ashok Kumar

Dr. Rajeev Sagar

NAMYA PRESS.com

Published by

Namya Press

Address
India : 213, Vardaan House, 7/28 Ansari Road Daryaganj Delhi- 110002
USA : 10685-B Hazlehurst Dr. # 31013 Houston, Texas- 77043

Email : namyapress@gmail.com
Website : https://namyapress.com

Edition : First Published in 2021 (Namya Press)
Title : The Right To Education In India
Author : Dr.Ashok Kumar
ISBN : 978-93-91010-39-3
Copyright : © Dr.Ashok Kumar 2021 All rights reserved

This book is being sold on the condition that it cannot be used commercially or in any other form without the prior written permission of the publisher. This book cannot be republished or sold or rented. And it cannot be operated among readers in book-binding or any other form. All these conditions will also apply to the buyer of the book. All rights of copyright are reserved in this context.

This book has been published with all efforts taken in making the material error-free after the consent of the author. However, the author and the publisher do not assume and hereby disclaim any liability of any part for loss, damage, or disruption caused by error or omissions.

Preface

Education is indispensable for everyone. It is the level of education that helps people earn respect and recognition. In my opinion, it is a requisite part of life both personally and socially. However, the unequal criterion of education is still a major problem that needs to be solved.

The significance of education is unquestionable for every single person. It goes without saying that education has a positive effect on human life. , education plays such an elementary role on our society that we cannot even imagine a life without it. It is an unwavering element for the development of human civilization. Education in its general sense is a form of learning in which the knowledge, skills, and habits of a group of people are transferred from one generation to the next through teaching, training, or research. Education frequently takes place under the guidance of others, but may also be auto didactic. Any experience that has a formative effect on the way one thinks, feels, or acts may be considered educational.

Education is the most powerful tool which can shape the destiny of an individual as well as the whole nation. As we know education is the most powerful tool which can shape the destiny of an individual as well as the whole nation. If we look at the reasons responsible for demarcating the boundaries between developed and under-developed nations, education emerges as the single most vital factor spinning the wheel of progress in the developed nations. It has been established that an educated citizen not only improve the economic and social status of the nation but political scenario also. The Indian Constitution has recognized the importance of education for social transformation and is committed to social justice. The Preamble determines, to secure liberty of thought, expression, belief, faith and worship and equality of status and opportunity and to promote amongst the people a feeling of fraternity, ensuring the dignity of the individual and the unity of the nation. Literacy forms the foundation stone for making the provision of equality of opportunity a reality. The objective specified in the Preamble contains the basic structure of the Constitution, which cannot be amended, and the preamble may be invoked to determine the ambit of Fundamental Rights and Directive Principles of State Policy.

Education is the manifestation of the divine perfection, already existing in man. It is misfortune that our country is unsuccessful to eliminate the menace of illiteracy even after 6 decades of independence and our legislators have abandoned this prime area of human resource development for such a lengthy time. Because, It is and should be the prime duty of the state and Union governments to provide free Education and Health facilities to all the citizens of the country without any sort of prejudice. Anyway, because of the efforts made by our worthy educationists, academicians, NGO'S and civil society groups who followed a rights based approach that resulted in the passing of 86th constitutional amendment by the parliament and Article 21A in the year of 2002 which made Right to Education a fundamental right. One of the essential rights of human being is their right to be educated. Right to education is a fundamental right that cannot be alienate, thus, it is an absolute right essential for humans. Since it is very essential right, other rights cannot be enjoyed in the absence of this right to education. The continuum of subjects covered wide range from development of right to Education to constitutional mandate, International scenario Governance and mechanism of Right to Education and related Issues.

This book will be an essential reading those who are connected and concerned with Right to Education. We hope that it will be beneficial for researcher, Policy Makers and Readers.

Dr. Rajeev Sagar
Dr. Ashok Kumar

Content

Chapter I
Introduction

I. Introduction: Origin, concept and aspects of right to Education

A. Origin of Right to education and Right to Quality Education
B. Concepts of Right to education
C. Aspects of right to education

Everyone has the right to education. Education shall be free, at least in the elementary and fundamental stages. Elementary education shall be compulsory. Education is a human right and has been since 1948. When the Universal Declaration on Human Rights proclaimed in Article 26 that 'everyone has the right to education', it became enshrined in international law that states are obligated to provide education for their citizens. Since then, a number of legal instruments have been developed by the United Nations to facilitate the realization of the right to education, including the International Covenant on Economic, Social and Cultural Rights, the Convention on the Rights of the Child and the UNESCO Convention against Discrimination in Education. The right to education for all has also been reaffirmed in numerous global and regional treaty bodies covering specific marginalized groups and contexts and has been preserved in many national constitutions including India.

Origin of Right to Education

The word "Education" is derivative of the Latin word ēducātiō ("A breeding, a bringing up, a rearing") from ēducō ("I educate, I train") which is related to the homonym ēdūcō ("I lead forth, I take out; I raise up, I erect") from ē- ("from, out of") and dūcō ("I lead, I conduct"). Education began in prehistory, as adults trained the young in the knowledge and skills deemed necessary in their society. In pre-literate societies, this was achieved orally and through imitation. Story-telling passed knowledge, values, and skills from one generation to the next. As cultures began to extend their knowledge beyond skills that could be readily learned through imitation, formal education developed. Schools existed in Egypt at the time of the Middle Kingdom. Education is the process of facilitating learning, or the acquisition of knowledge, skills, values, morals, beliefs, and habits. Educational methods include teaching, training, storytelling, discussion and directed research. Education frequently takes place under the guidance of educators; however learners can also educate themselves. Education can take place in formal or informal settings and any experience that has a formative effect on the way one thinks, feels, or acts may be considered educational. The methodology of teaching is called pedagogy. Formal education is commonly divided formally into such stages as preschool or kindergarten, primary school, secondary school and then college, University, or apprenticeship. The role of education is also that it promotes virtues and good ideas. Education is a laudable achievement of humanity and the main role of education lies in solving the complexities of the country, society and humanity. Education should be seen as the right of everyone more than business. Because of being a human, the poor student has the same right over quality education as a student of a wealthy family. Education is not only the fundamental right of the person, but also his human rights. According to the 86th Amendment Act 2000 of the Constitution, free and compulsory education was made a fundamental right for all children in the age group of 6-14 years. Our society and government are also aware of the advancement of education. For this purpose, the government also participates in many associations and conferences from the state to the international level. Therefore, it can be said that society and education are complementary to each other.

A right to education has been recognized by some governments and the United Nations. In most regions, education is compulsory up to a certain age. There is a movement for education reform and in particular for evidence-based education with global initiatives aimed at achieving the Sustainable Development Goal 4, which promotes quality education for all.

The idea of free and compulsory education as a fundamental right initially came up for discussion during the Constituent Assembly debates. Although there was general clarity as to there being two separate categories of rights: justiciable and non-justiciable, the actual placement of the right to edu-cation became a contentious issue.[1] The members of the Constituent Assembly argued that it would be inappropriate in both form and substance to word the provision in such a manner so as to convey a constitutional guarantee towards the right to education.[2] It was understood to be a mere policy intended to guide future governments. The importance of education in the holistic development of the nation was, however, acknowledged and the Constitution accordingly obli-gated the

---

[1] B. ShIva Rao, The Constitution of India 174 (2004) (The right to education was initially placed as a justiciable right in the Report of the Sub-Committee on Fundamental Rights, 1947. This was however, rejected during subsequent discussions mainly apprehending the lack of government funds for its implementation and the inability of courts to properly adjudicate on it)

[2] Constituent assembly debates 538 (1989). (Pandit Lakshmi Kanta Maitra, member of the Constituent Assembly remarked that "Part IV deals with the directive principles of State policy, and the provisions in it indicate, the policy that is to be pursued by the future governments of the country. Unfortunately, in Art. 36, this directive principle of State policy is coupled with a sort of a fundamental right, i.e. "that every citizen is entitled.....etc.". This cannot fit in with the others.")

State to provide, within a period of ten years from the commencement of the Constitution, free and compulsory education to all children until they com-pleted the age of fourteen years. The RTE Case centres on whether the constitution permits burden sharing with non-state actors in the realisation of socio-economic rights. It is therefore imperative to analyse Art. 21A, from which the RTE Actflows,in order to deter-mine first, the nature and scope of the provision and second, the validity of the RTE Act itself. Art. 21A reads:"The State shall provide free and compulsory education to all children of the age of six to fourteen years in such manner as the State may, by law, determine."

The Right of Children to Free and Compulsory Education Act' or 'Right to Education Act also known as RTE'. Right to education is an Act of the Parliament of India enacted on 4 August 2009, which describes the modalities of the importance of free and compulsory education for children between 6 and 14 in India under Article 21A of the Indian Constitution.

India became one of135 countries to make education a fundamental right of every child when the act came into force on 1 April 2010. Present Act has its history in the drafting of the Indian constitution at the time of Independence. As for as Quality Education is concerned It lays down the norms and standards relating inter alia to Pupil Teacher Ratios (PTRs), buildings and infrastructure, school-working days, teacher-working hours. It provides for rational deployment of teachers by ensuring that the specified pupil teacher ratio is maintained for each school, rather than just as an average for the State or District or Block, thus ensuring that there is no urban-rural imbalance in teacher postings. It also provides for prohibition of deployment of teachers for non-educational work, other than decennial census, elections to local authority, state legislatures and parliament, and disaster relief. It provides for appointment of appropriately trained teachers, i.e. teachers with the requisite entry and academic qualifications. It prohibits (a) physical punishment and mental harassment; (b) screening procedures for admission of children; (c) capitation fee; (d) private tuition by teachers and (e) running of schools without recognition. It provides for development of curriculum inconsonance with the values enshrined in the Constitution, and which would ensure the all-round development of the child, building on the child's knowledge, potentiality and talent and making the child free of fear, trauma and anxiety through a system of child friendly and child centered learning.

Right to Quality Education

Every Child in India has the fundamental right to enjoy eight years of quality education, one that helps them acquire basic literacy and numeracy, enjoy learning without fear, and feel valued and included irrespective of where they come from. However, the quality of education remains one of the biggest challenges. There is a need to shift from the Right to Education to the Right to Learn: children learn the basics of literacy and numeracy; schools are child friendly for conducive learning, and there are adequate teachers with professional qualifications for teaching.

CHILD FRIENDLY SCHOOLS AND SYSTEMS: The RTE Act makes child friendly quality education the fundamental right of every child. A child-friendly school (CFS) ensures every child an environment that is physically safe, emotionally secure and psychologically enabling. A child-friendly school with improved quality of education results in children staying in schools and thus accelerated realization of the RTE.

PUPIL TEACHER RATIO: The RTE Act maintains that Pupil - Teacher ratio should be one teacher for every 30 students at the primary level and one teacher for every 35 children at the upper primary level. Forty one per cent schools at the primary level and 31 per cent schools at upper primary level meet the norm.

Quality education enables people to develop all of their attributes and skills to achieve their potential as human beings and members of society. In the words of the Delors Commission (UNESCO, 1996): "Education is at the heart of both personal and community development; its mission is to enable each of us, without exception, to develop all our talents to the full and to realize our creative potential, including responsibility for our own lives and achievement of our personal aims." Quality education is a human right and a public good. Governments and other public authorities should ensure that a quality education service is available freely to all citizens from early childhood into adulthood. Quality education provides the foundation for equity in society. Quality education is one of the most basic public services. It not only enlightens but also empowers citizens and enables them to contribute to the maximum extent possible to the social and economic development of their communities. The right to education entails an inclusive and holistic approach to education, as demonstrated in Article 26 of the UN Declaration of Human Rights: "Education shall be directed to the full development of the human personality and to the strengthening of respect for human rights and fundamental freedoms".

Concept of Right to Education

Education is a powerful tool by which economically and socially marginalized adults and children can lift themselves out of poverty and participate fully as citizens." Education is a fundamental human right and essential for the exercise of all other human rights. It promotes individual freedom and empowerment and yields important development benefits. Yet millions of children and adults remain deprived of educational opportunities, many as a result of poverty.

Everyone naturally has a desire to know the past. History makes humans see the realities of the past. Mankind commissions the knowledge of the consequences of many events that have taken place in the past in order to make its present and future superior. It would be logical to look at the history of Indian education in an effort to study the current education system and find solutions to its burning problems. The development of Indian education is old as human civilization.Education is a social activity, so in ancient times, education was also guided by religion. The main object of Education are:

- character building
- Attainment of nirvana
- social development
- Personality development
- Protection and dissemination of national culture
- Education should be self-reliant.

Education in which all the physical, mental and spiritual powers of the child are all-round development, literacy is neither the end of education nor the beginning. This cable is one of many means by which people can be educated. An important and popular education system to educate children is the Montessori education system. The credit for introducing and popularizing this system is to Madame Maria Montessori. In the new settlements of Rome, Mandam Maria established an institution called Children's House. After this, this teaching system started becoming popular and related books were also published and this system Adopted in India in 1939. The mai focus of this education system on :

- Education for development
- Complete freedom
- Self-education
- Self-expression
- Self-modification

- Teaching by play
- Self-reliance
- Education of senses

The National Education Policy 1986 emphasized on providing educational opportunities mainly in rural areas, development of national unity, equity and social justice and giving opportunities to students from backward classes to get education and to manage common grounded ghost courses. It was decided to end illiteracy within 10 years by giving compulsory and free education to all students. The National Education Policy 1968, whose main points are as follows -

- Provision of free and compulsory primary education
- Improvement in the position of teachers
- Development of languages
- Provision of equal opportunities for education
- Emphasis on talent recognition
- Production and production of books
- System of Examinations
- Improvement and progress in secondary education
- Dissemination of literacy and adult education
- Sports promotion
- Promotion of education of minorities
- Changes in the structure of education

Normative instruments of the United Nations and UNESCO lay down international legal obligations for the right to education. These instruments promote and develop the right of every person to enjoy access to education of good quality, without discrimination or exclusion. These instruments bear witness to the great importance that Member States and the international community attach to normative action for realizing the right to education. It is for governments to fulfill their obligations both legal and political in regard to providing education for all of good quality and to implement and monitor more effectively education strategies.

Education is a powerful tool by which economically and socially marginalized adults and children can lift themselves out of poverty and participate fully as citizens. The right to education is a universal entitlement to education. This is recognized in the International Covenant on Economic, Social and Cultural Rights as a human right that includes the right to free, compulsory primary education for all, an obligation to develop secondary education accessible to all, in particular by the progressive introduction of free secondary education, as well as an obligation to develop equitable access to higher education, ideally by the progressive introduction of free higher education.

The right to education also includes a responsibility to provide basic education for individuals who have not completed primary education. In addition to these access to education provisions, the right to education encompasses the obligation to rule out discrimination at all levels of the educational system, to set minimum standards and to improve the quality of education. The right to education is a human right covered and guaranteed by international law; and in committing to the right to education, states do so legally, through the ratification of human rights instruments3 and the adoption of relevant national legislation. While SDG4-Education 2030 does not establish legal obligations, states, through their political commitment, are expected to take ownership and establish requisite national frameworks, including laws, policies, plans, and programmes, for the effective implementation of the Education Agenda (UNESCO, 2015).

The Right to Education: Both an Empowerment Right and a Right That Needs Empowerment Education is recognized as 'a human right in itself and an indispensable means of realizing other human rights', because of its 'empowerment' potential (UNESCO & United Nations' Economic and Social Council, 2003). The right to education of all individuals calls for a renewed and broadened understanding in an age where individuals are increasingly encouraged and expected to learn throughout life. The right to education has been an increasingly central part of discussions concerning what constitutes sustainable development amidst deep global inequalities. Human rights concepts have influenced international discussions and policymaking related to education, delineating three relationships: 1) education as a human right 2) education with human rights: and 3) education for human rights.

The child is the future of every nation. In a democratic and welfare state like India, it's the duty of the state to raise the level of nutrition and the standard of dwelling and to enhance public fitness because schooling and health are two basic wants for human well-being. Food crisis also creates difficulties in achieving other social benefits. Therefore, it appears as one of the basic means for capacity building. Food is a means to achieve other ends in life.

India provides free and compulsory elementary education to all children in the age group of 6 years to 14 years of the country. As per Article 21 and the Right of Children to Free and Compulsory Education (RTE) Act, 2009, the Government is obliged to provide necessary infrastructure and ecosystem for completion of elementary education by all children in the country. Mid-Day Meal Scheme (MDMS) is one of the welfare schemes run by the government to encourage enrolments in the elementary sections in Government, Government aided, Local body schools recognized supported under Sarva Shiksha Abhiyan (SSA), Education Guarantee Scheme (EGS) and Alternative & Innovative Education (AIE) centers across the country. The concept of mid-day meal scheme is not new in India as its roots can be traced back to pre-independence era when British administration initiated a Mid-Day Meal Programme for disadvantage children in Madras Municipal Corporation in

1925.Like this many such programmes were initiated in different states. In 1953, Government of Uttar Pradesh started another such scheme. Tamil Nadu became the first state in India to introduce a noon meal programme in primary schools. In 1984 this scheme was introduced in Gujarat. From time to time the meal scheme was taken up by different states and later on it was taken up as a national scheme. Government of India launched National Programme of Nutritional Support to Primary Education (Commonly known as Mid-Day Meal Scheme) on August 15, 1995 to provide mid-day meal to the children studying at primary stage2. In 2002, the Supreme Court directed the Government to provide cooked Mid-Day Meals (as opposed to providing dry rations) in all Government and Government aided primary schools3.It was revised in September 2004 and in September2006.

Related to MDMS is the right to quality education. In this context of substantive civil rights, the MDMS was introduced to realize the goal of education for children without any kind of economic constraint. Both 'right to food' and 'right to education' appears to be fundamental objectives. This scheme, regarded as a significant social welfare scheme in the country in view of its objective to ensure the protection of two fundamental rights (education and food) necessitates effective performance by the government through good governance.

When most people hear the word, "Governance" they think of "Government" but Governance implies more than a formal government. The Governance is the process by which governments are selected, monitored and replaced. In practice, good governance involves promoting the rule of law, tolerance of minority and opposition groups, transparent political processes, an independent judiciary, an impartial police force, and a military that is strictly subject to civilian control. Above all, good governance means respect for human rights. MDM scheme is a testimony to assess the ability of the government agencies as well as their political will to abide by these principles and objectives of governance.

Primary education is far from universal and the Millennium Development Goals (MDGs) remains elusive. UNICEF (2008), the agency responsible for tracking progress on this MDG, estimates a net primary school enrollment rate in developing countries of 84%; this is also its estimated average for India. In view of this, governments across the developing world have instituted a wide range of policies aimed at encouraging school enrollment.

The National Programme of Nutritional Support to Primary Education (NP-NSPE) which is popularly known as the MDMS was introduced by the Indian Government on 15th August 1995 initially in 2408 blocks in the country and in 1997-98 the NP-NSPE was introduced in all blocks of the country."[3] NP-NSPE states that it aims to address "classroom hunger" and encourage terrible children, belonging to deprived sections, to attend school frequently and assist them to concentrate on lecture room activities. The MDMS is a multi-faceted programme of the Indian Government that, amongst other things, additionally seeks to tackle problems of food safety and facilitating education, lack of nutrition and access to schooling on a nationwide scale. The objective of the MDMS is to improve the academic standards in the schools.

Historically, the MDMS was introduced before the independence in 1925 for disadvantaged and underprivileged children (children of poor socio-economic status) in Madras Municipal Corporation. Tamil Nadu had launched a cooked MDMS in the 1950s and expanded it significantly in 1982, and Gujarat introduced MDMs in the 1980s. Besides this, the entire state of Kerala, and some

---

[3] Accessed 24 Jan. 2014, 8:17 pm URL: http://mdm.nic.in/aboutus.html

pockets of Madhya Pradesh and Orissa, began providing cooked meals in 1995.[4] (SWNMP Department, Secretariat, Chennai, 2012)

On 28 November 2001, the Indian Apex Supreme Court approved an order directing all the state government to apply MDM. Very few states, however, introduced cooked meals in primary schools before the Supreme Court's initial deadline of February 28, 2002. The primary schools are taking initiative with reference to this order, several states of the Union have provided for MDMs at different levels of education, covering a large population of children. Along with this, several NGOs and different other organizations also aid this scheme, throughout the nation. (Khera, 2005).

The aim of the MDMS is to improve the nutritional status of poor children. The main aim is also to attract them to schools. Along with this, this programme also aids in the eradication of child labor in a way that children who previously used to invest their energy in labor now focus on education. This makes the MDM programme a very important scheme in building India. The nutritional programme in schools is popular in developing countries for both education and nutritional benefits. The purpose of the MDM Scheme was to enhance enrolment, retention, and participation of children in primary schools, simultaneously improving their nutritional status. In order to ensure the fulfillment of this purpose, there is also a mechanism to maintain transparency in the system. The quantity and quality of food-grains are specified and there is also a body (School Management Committee) to keep a proper check in the proceedings.

This program has been beneficial in generating employment among females of the unprivileged classes and promoting gender equality. This scheme has helped in enhancing the attendance of

[4] Social Welfare and Nutritious Meal Programme Department, Secretariat, Chennai, Letter No19869/ NMP.1/2012-4 Dated : 18.04.2012

children to schools and played a very necessary position in imparting schooling and diet to the economically and at times, the socially backward class, too. This makes MDMS a welfare scheme. According to the Planning Commission Report, 06th October 2009 on performance evaluation of MDM programme in the Uttar Pradesh, MDM programme is being applied to see that September 2004 and is monitored by means of MDM Authority.

The food grain is the most vital element of the MDMS. The food grain requirement is ascertained through the state government.[5](Fifth Review Mission Uttar Pradesh , 2013-2014). The food grain for MDM is provided by the Food Corporation of India. (Fifth Review Mission Uttar Pradesh , 2013-2014).

Theoritical Intervention: Governance And Welfare

Since the early stage of the Third Wave of democratization now more than a generation ago, there is a visible inference of comparative politics on democracy, transitions to democracy, human rights and transitional justice, all of these unmark "Good" or "democratic" governance which is said to exist when the authority of the Government is based on the will of the people and is responsive to them. In view of this, a responsible and a welfare government is one that makes and implements public policies. (Governance for Sustainable Human Development, 1997).

In 21st Century India's moving rapid growing economy in the world, one cannot undermine the importance of education and here education is considered as an investment. People realize today the money that is spent education is a significant contribution to the national economy. The pace with which technological change is taking place all over the world has revolutionized every aspect of human life. In order to cope up

[5] Fifth Review Mission Uttar Pradesh 2013-14, pp 26-27

with such change, education is a must. But lack of education needs to be understood in the context of other bottlenecks like poverty, food insecurity, unemployment and the overall developmental inadequacies in the present day society. The scheme is often seen to be significant in view of it producing a quantitative jump on literacy rates. However, its inherent aim is also to promote social democracy by addressing the needs of economically marginalized sections at the grass-root level.

Arvind Sivaramakrishnan in Public Policy and Citizenship[6]

analyzes the two dominant public-policy approaches in India—managerialism, and neoliberalism—and argues that they have had a profoundly damaging impact. Drawing upon a substantial body of published work, the book shows how managerial and free-market systems are fundamentally incoherent and destructive. The discussion in this volume revolves primarily around Indian public policy on health, agriculture, and education. The author argues that the condition of these areas, and therefore the condition of hundreds of millions of people, is worse than many analysts claim it to be. Using examples and evidence from a range of countries and public-policy systems, the book also shows the ways in which the managerial application of public policies founded on neoliberal terms undermines the idea of citizenship in a democracy. The strength of the book is that it demonstrates links between public policy, the philosophy of the social sciences, and political philosophy, all in the light of everyday issues and concerns.

Dr. Sivramakrishnan rightly expressed the concern and says the Indian democracy is not a real democracy but mere

[6] Sivaramakrishnan, Arvind (2011), *Public Policy and Citizenship*, Sage publication, New Delhi, pp 55

symbolic democracy due to less participation of citizen and decision-making process. And a proverb says India is rich but Indian people are poor because of no links between managerialism, neoliberalism and the crisis of Indian democracy.

In an Uncertain Glory: India and Its Contradictions,

two of India's leading economists[7] argue that the country's important troubles lie elsewhere, especially in the lack of interest paid to the fundamental needs of the people, specifically the poor. The deep inequalities in Indian society tend to constrict public discussion in India's vibrant media to the lives and worries of the relatively affluent. One of the biggest disasters has been the very insufficient use of the public sources generated by monetary growth to make bigger India's lagging bodily and social infrastructure (in sharp contrast, for example, to what China has done): there is a continued inadequacy both social services such as schooling, medical care and immunization, and of bodily offerings such as the provision of protected water, electricity, drainage, and sanitation. Even as India has overtaken a large number of other international locations in the rate of financial growth, it has, due to the fact of these inadequacies, fallen at behind of many of the same nations.

Because of the importance of democracy in India, addressing these disasters will require no longer only enormous policy rethinking by using the government but also a better public perception of the abysmal extent of social and financial deprivations. The deep inequalities in Indian society tend to constrict public dialogue in India's brilliant media to the lives and issues of the enormously affluent. This book makes an effective contribution to that understanding.

---

[7] Sen, Amartya and Jean Draze (2013), *"An Uncertain Glory: India and Its Contradictions"*, New Delhi: Thomson Press India, pp 72-73.

The authors of this book provide a theoretical framework to understand problem-related with the governance of welfare programmes. They analyze the hierarchical chain of the government system in India and discuss the problem of poor accountability and corruption. In the absence of effective accountability, there may not only be rampant neglects of duties, but much temptation for officials to deliver at high 'prices' what they are actually supposed to deliver freely, as part of their job.[8] Corruption is fostered and nurtured by the absence of effective accountability. This creates predicaments of governance of welfare programmes like the MDMS, Serva Shiksha Abhiyan, and other healthcare schemes (Sen & Draze , 2013).

The authors of this book rightly analyze and evaluate the problem of Indian common people particularly socially and economically poor society, because the root problem of Indian democracy is social exclusion.

Amartya Sen in Development as Freedom

quotes the eighteenth-century poet William Cowper on freedom. Sen explains how, in a world of unprecedented increase in overall opulence, millions of people living in rich and poor countries are still unfree. Even if they are not technically slaves, they are denied elementary freedom and remain imprisoned in one way or the other way by economic poverty, social deprivation, political tyranny or cultural authoritarianism. The main purpose of development is to protect freedom and its 'thousand charms' to the unfree citizens.

Sen persuasively argues that at once the ultimate goal of social and economic arrangements and the most efficient means of realizing general welfare Social institutions like markets, political parties,

---

[8] Amartya Sen and Jean Draze, "*An Uncertain Glory: India and Its Contradictions*" Princeton University Press pp. 94

legislatures, the judiciary, and the media contribute to development by enhancing individual freedom and are in turn sustained by social values. Values, institutions, development and freedom are all closely interrelated, and Sen links them together in an elegant analytical framework. There are many new problems as well as old ones, including persistence of poverty and unfulfilled elementary needs, occurrence of famines and widespread hunger, violation of elementary political freedoms as well as of basic liberties, extensive neglect of the interests and agency of women and worsening threats to our environment and to the sustainability of our economic and social lives.

However, if increasing incomes in a country are not accompanied by the other factors that define a high standard of living then the country is not only getting richer but also not happier. It is not "developing" in the truest sense. The real meaning of development gets right to education, right to nutritious food, right to well live and the right to social equality etc. According to Sen, these above rights are necessary for the overall well-being of the people.

The MDMS has been quietly feeding more than 10 crore children every day for more than 10 years. Unfortunately, this popular and relatively successful programme makes it to the headlines only when things go wrong - this time following the tragic death of 23 children in Bihar after eating at school on 16 July 2013. Recent economic research clearly documents the positive impact of the scheme on enrolment, attendance, retention, and nutrition.[9] The MDMS is meant to boost children's participation. So it helps realize freedom and hence development. The existence of local power structures and social prejudices impose constraints on effective participation and responsive leadership that further impedes the successful implementation of welfare schemes like

---

[9] Ritika Khera (2013), *"MDMs: Looking Ahead"* Economic & Political Weekly, vol xiviii (32), 10 August 2013, pp 35.

MDM. This further interrogates the failures of implementation that arise out of curtailment of freedom (Khera R. , 2013).

MDM in Uttar Pradesh: A brief Rview

The main area of concern of the review report of 5th joint review mission on MDMS in Uttar Pradesh is low coverage of children, lack of community involvement, poor inspection, the poor nutritional status of children on hygienic toilets and drinking water, lack of security in school (The review report of 5th joint review mission on MDMS in Uttar Pradesh).

Generally, the bags of Foodgrains supplied by the FCI are less than 50Kg. In many states like Tamil Nadu, the Civil Supplies Department reweigh the bags and make it 50Kg and supply to the schools. It has been suggested that a similar practice may also be followed by the Government of Uttar Pradesh. The Team observed that the Pradhan/Mahila Samkhya are not maintaining any records of the Food Grains received and there is a gap in the records of the food grains supplied by the Kotedar and received/Utilized by the school. They suggested that there needs to be a more stringent monitoring mechanism to ensure that food grains are lifted by Kotedars.

There is a need to take very strict action against the officials was felt at all levels. Social audit of Mid-Day Scheme has already started. Increased involvement of SMCs in the conduct of Social Audit will facilitate its smooth functioning. Considerable disruption was found in the schools due to lack of food grains and the same could have been avoided if regular inspections had taken place by block level officials. Hence there is a need for strengthening the field level monitoring system and ensuring that monitoring takes place, the State government may consider the involvement of ABRCs (Assistant Block Resource Coordinator) to report on 10 schools in a month.

Awareness may be spread by adding more vegetables to MDM to meet the food norms and to improve the nutritional status of children. Kitchen gardens may be developed including plantation of fruit-bearing trees like banana, guava, mango, papaya, etc. All assets under the MDM scheme should be recorded in the stock register maintained in schools. As MDM is a major contributor of nutrition for primary and upper primary school children it is recommended that MDM should be supplemented with pulses, green leafy vegetables, and soybean. The weekly inclusion of milk and egg in the MDM is also recommended. The State government officials looking after MDMS may join the Review Mission in other states under exchange scheme. Orientation visits to other states will also widen the horizon of the officials.

For effective implementation of MDM, all the functionaries are involved in the scheme need to be aware of nutrition, health, hygiene and safety of foods. It was recommended that in different states Agricultural Universities, Foods and Nutrition Department and Horticulture Department can develop model schools in their districts by providing training to the BRC coordinators, teachers and cook-cum-helpers regarding nutrition, health, hygiene and food safety. Horticulture Department can also help in growing vegetables in model schools. It can be later followed by other districts.

The MDM programme suggests that at each level there should be effective mechanism and system of the social audit must be developed. The MDMS is an essential ingredient for attaining the goal of education for all and eradicate classroom hunger as well as enhance the rate of enrolment. The MDM programme can play an important role by the multidimensional impact (Draze and Goel: 01, 2003) - individual, health and social rights enhancement.[10] The basic issue is whether it is quality of education is another benefit that motivates the parent to send their children to school. And another basic question is why poor students are not attending the school and why there is a massive dropout at the school level? Here is an important distinction between the quality and quantity of the education. As Amartya Sen describes in Development as Freedom that what people can positively achieve is influenced by economic opportunity, social empowerment, enabling condition of good health and basic education. The institutional arrangements for these opportunities are also influenced by the exercise of people's freedom through the liberty to participate in social choice and in the making of public decisions (Draze & Goe, 2003).

The causes of failure in implementation of MDM could be stated as follow:

1. **Institutional Failure:** It is found that there is a lack of coordination among Gram Pradhans, Kotedar, principal of the schools and local administrator (Block Development Officer). The Rasoiya's are not provided proper training regarding cooking, estimating and managing relatively a huge quantity of food. Gram Pradhans being the leader of the village is also entitled to lead the MDM scheme in their villages but they are incapable of doing so because of illiteracy, lack of knowledge and confidence, lack of willingness and prejudices of kotedar.

2. **Participation:** Every villager is entitled to participate as custodian as he/she can inspect the food every day and if some deficiency regarding quality and quantity in food is found, he can make necessary complaints. But generally, no villager is interested in doing so.

---

[10] Jean Draze and Aprajita Goel Describe in article *future of MDM*, Economic & Political Weekly Nov. 01, 2003 pp 67

3. **The communication gap between local Government and State Government:** There is a lack of communications between the local and state government regarding the various problem.

4. **Supply-side Constraints:** This is the most important concern about the proper implementation of the scheme as the food grains are not supplied on time. Quality food grains are also exchanged by inferior quality by the kotedar. Conversion cost and wages of Rasoiyas are not paid timely by the state government. Therefore, this serves as a reference point to understand the causes of failure in governance.

The Book is classified following chapters, Chapter first deals with the introduction of the MDMS and different related issues. Chapter second explores & discusses the MDMS in the context of inclusive development and the welfare state. Chapter third describes the initiatives taken by the national and international regime in an objective manner. Chapter fourth explores and analyzes the problem and prospect of MDM in Uttar Pradesh. Chapter five deal with governance infrastructure of MDM. Chapter sixth discuss with participatory democracy and accountability of MDM scheme. Finally, the last chapter seven concludes with the conclusion and suggestions.

Chapter II
The right to education under Indian Constitution and its implication in the Framework of Welfare State and Inclusive Development

A. Theoretical Analysis
B. Functional Analysis

The state has two basic components are primary and secondary. The primary component is human created the secondary components like family, class, and society. In the words of Aristotle, he defined, "State came into existence for the sake of life and it continues to exist for the sake of good life." In the context of welfare, State undertakes the main responsibilities for providing the social, economic liberty and security for its citizens and upholds the principles of equality of opportunity, equitable distribution of wealth, and public responsibility for those who lack the minimal provisions for a good life. The term may be applied to a variety of economic and social organization. A key feature of the welfare state is social insurance intended to provide benefits during periods of greatest need. Harold L. Wilensky has given a classical definition of Welfare State in which he described "The essence of the welfare state as government-protected minimum standards of income, nutrition, health, housing, and education assured to every citizen as a political right, not charity." (Wilensky 1975: 1)

The Welfare State provides the citizen with free education and protects them against extreme poverty. Beyond this minimum social protection, welfare states differ with respect to the generosity and the scope of social protection against the risks of sickness, invalidity, unemployment and old age. Scharpf and Schmidt have stated that welfare states to provide social assistance to avoid extreme poverty. Beyond that the 'golden age' models differ fundamentally from one another along two dimensions.: the extent to which welfare goals are pursued through the regulation of labor markets and employment relations or through the 'formal welfare state' of publicly financed transfers and services and the extent to which 'caring' services are expected to be provided informally in the family or through professional services." (Scharpf and Schmidt 2000: 7).

The welfare state represents the single most important transformation of advanced capitalist democracies in the period after the Second World War. In welfare countries, inclusive development is a tool to achieve the well-being of individual. In a nutshell inclusive development is the intrinsic tool of the welfare state. (Masayuki 2000: 9):

A welfare state is contigent upon certain conditions like good governance, equal education, social-political-economic rights, population, and good health. A few think that it is an institutional arrangement for the solution of poverty. If one has to talk about the actual origin of the welfare state, it is neither wholly inspired by capitalism nor by socialism (Sakhder 1980: 26-34).

In the United Kingdom, the inadequacy of private charity, philanthropy and poor law led to the emergence of welfare state to meet the pressing demands of the poor people who acquired the new voting power. Welfare state helps both in the formulation and solutions of the felt and publicized problems of the want in the backdrop of the widespread fear of an impending revolution. The rise of the trade union movement, the political consciousness of the people, and the inadequacy of private charity added welfare and service functions to the administrative state.

The welfare state in India assumes qualitatively, a new form from the Western model. At the same time, the social contradictions are so sharp that urgent socio-economic reforms by the state. Land reforms, development of the public sector, provide free compulsory education to the children below the 14 years of age, and various concessions to the working class as well as weaker sections are some of the glaring examples of the responsive role of the contemporary welfare state. This role is expressed through formulation of various public policies. These are not mere superficial measures but necessarily substantive ones, because, without these changes, the state's legitimacy gets weakened. These policies, however, do not replace the contradictions which threaten to affect the domination of the ruling class; the coercive instruments freely intervene.

In the present time, the Union government regulates social policies transmission, while the states exercise exclusive authority over intrastate distribution, generation, and transmission siting. In an interconnected system, however, each state's social policies and infrastructure investments inevitably affect operations and costs throughout the entire social network by good governance which prepares strong social and administrative pillar for the welfare state. In this regard, governance becomes government's ability to create welfare policies for well-being and implement rules, to provide services, regardless of whether that government is democratic or not.

Governance is about the performance of agents in carrying out the wishes of principals, and not about the goals that principals set. "The government is an organization which can perform its functions better or worse; governance is thus about execution, or what has traditionally fallen within the domain of public administration, as opposed to politics." (Wilson 1887: 197-222). As

Bo Rothstein has pointed out, "it is not so easy to separate governance as implementation from the normative ends that government is meant to serve. It is not clear that a well-governed state is one that has ruthlessly efficient concentration camp guards as opposed to bribable ones. "The Governance is the process by which governments are selected, monitored and replaced. In practice, good governance involves promoting the rule of law, tolerance of minority and opposition groups, transparent political processes, an independent judiciary, an impartial police force and a military that is strictly subject to civilian control. Above all, good governance means respect for human rights." (Kofi Annan 1999). With economic, political and ideological conditions after the Second World War, the transition to the welfare state system grew to be a comparatively simple mission in developed nations.

Most of the democratic countries in the world adopt social democratic ideology including Scandinavian countries as well as India. In the 20th century, the democratic country has marked a shift from a child-centric approach to community development approach to mark a shift in education scenario. The MDMS or School Lunch is one of the most inclusive children development centric schemes adopted by the Scandinavian democratic counties.

Conceptualizing Welfare State in a Comparative Context:

In the modern welfare state suffers under pressures like population ageing, sluggish economy growth, mass unemployment, changing family structure, the transformation of life cycle patterns, post-industrial labour markets, the erosion of systems of interest intermediation and collective bargaining, the rise of new risks and needs, and international pressures (globalization) (see for a particularly enlightening overview

Schwartz 2001). There are two hypothesis with respect to impact of globalization on welfare:

1. Efficiency hypothesis:

"The Internationalized market and the intensified economic competition it triggers has rendered high levels of welfare spending unsustainable. International Competition forces national governments to reduce costs by scaling down taxes and social policies. Of more consequence for social policy is that globalization increases the power of capital over labor and national government because of the credible threat of investment strike by the exit.

2. Compensation hypothesis:

"The welfare state compensation for those who lose from economic openness has historically been a social and political precondition for the liberal post-war trade regime. This hypothesis says that the markets tend to disrupt traditional forms of social security and create a need for new compensatory policy that the government may supply. Social policies can also be fecund assets as they foster a better educated, trained and healthier workforce and contribute to the development of a more equal and less conflictual society. (Rodrik 1996; Rieger and Leibfried 1998, 2001; Glatzer and Rueschemeyer 2005)

The valuables dispensed by Government take many forms, but they all share one characteristic. They are steadily taking the place of traditional forms of wealth. These valuables which derive from relationships to Government are of many kinds like leases, licenses, contracts and so forth. There is a common perception in everyday discussions, political discourse, as well as academic literature that welfare states were invented in Europe. This perception is shaped by the North's welfare state history. For example, in Germany, social policy reforms by Chancellor **Bismarck** in the 1870s are often portrayed as establishing the first welfare state, although his reforms were undemocratic and driven entirely by nation-building and economic development concerns, and were accompanied by a dismantling of trade unions and an undermining of the social democratic movement. The British model was deeply influenced by the work of the economist **John Maynard Keynes**, whose ideas also permeated social policy in Northern and Southern Europe, where different forms of welfare states were put in place in the 1950s.

The New Deal in the United States (US) is also often identified as an early welfare state. As is well known, in response to the Great Crash and the massive economic depression of 1929 and the years that followed, the US government introduced in the 1930s a broad range of social policies to redress unemployment and poverty. Latin America had welfare state elements as early as the 1910s in Uruguay, Argentina, Chile, Brazil, and Costa Rica, among others.

Japan represents an interventionist welfare state in the phase immediately following World War II when provisions were made for social security and free education, as well as for an organized health system. Also in the post-war era, the United Kingdom (UK) introduced **the Beverage Plan** in the early 1950s, with an emphasis on income support and free and universal access to health care services.

In South Asian perspective, Sri Lanka is a model welfare state with its three pillars education, health and welfare. In the sense of poverty alleviation programme in Sri Lanka, was launched in the 1930s (Jayasuriya 2014:35). The concept of a welfare state has strong normative connotations. It is conceptually associated with a commitment to both democracy and social justice. Democracy, which encompasses human rights, citizen's voice and participatory decision-making power, freedom of information and many other factors, is a prerequisite to striving for and genuinely accepting social justice. It is also necessary to create the societal and political coalitions necessary to achieve at least acceptable levels of social justice, and at the practical level to finance and accept the institutions, policies and patterns that enable welfare state to function. In terms of its commitment to social justice, the welfare state can be defined as guaranteeing universal access to social services, making provisions for access to employment and decent work, offering a set of social assistance and social security provisions, as well as overseeing regulatory systems to safeguard the environment. In this mix, social protection takes on a role of income smoothing, as well as serving as a tool for income redistribution via the mechanics of tax policy but also taking responsibility for the sustainable functioning of the system.

The potential for income redistribution and environmental regulation are important elements with regard to social justice, and has become especially important in the current discourse on gender equality, social inclusion, and intergenerational justice because of the increasing intensity of vulnerability, income and multidimensional poverty, employment informality, income inequality, and ecological degradation observed in all countries. (Kohler, 2014: 2).

A comprehensive understanding could include five components of welfare state functions, where the service or provision considered needs to be a public good, a citizen's right, universally accessible, and financed from tax revenue. (Kohler, 2014: 2). A basic list might include, "education, at least for primary and secondary level's health access for all, in terms of services and funding mechanisms; social protection in its components of contributory social security and tax-funded social assistance; active labor market policies to generate employment, as well as microcredit and insurance provisions for the enterprise sector; and family policy, such as child-related policies and welfare services. Recently, environmental policies and measures that address environmental sustainability - has been seen as integral to welfare state policy (UNRISD 2014), so would conceivably constitute a sixth component (Kohler, 2014: 2)".

In a liberal interpretation of these criteria, most countries display some form of welfare state functions, with policies covering the areas of education and health, social protection, labor market schemes, and family policy. Compulsory primary education is now the norm globally, even if it is not free in many countries. Health services delivery and health insurance are being reorganized in several countries with a view to making access more secure and affordable. Social protection measures in the form of direct cash transfers, or school meals, have been introduced or enhanced in at least 50 countries (United Nations 2013: 33) (Kohler, 2014: 2). Many analysts, therefore, speak of a developmental welfare state. (Ehmke 2012 and Koehler 2014: 2). One can distinguish five types of developmental welfare states in Asia, "which all have in common a response however varied to poverty, vulnerability, social exclusion, demographic challenges, ecological stress, and to a lesser extent to income disparities (Porsche-Ludwig 2013, Lippl 2008 and Kohler, 2014: 2)".

Historically, the first group is developmental welfare states that intervened in the economy with a deliberate industrial policy to raise productivity in agriculture and trigger new branches of manufacturing production, or facilitate a shift into the services industry. However, social policy was subordinate to economic development, as evidenced by low levels of government spending dedicated to the social sectors, and a form of social protection that was means tested, and frequently conditional on behaviors. They could be classified as instrumentalist developmental welfare states. Examples include Japan in the 1950s, or South Korea, Taiwan, Hong Kong, Singapore, and Malaysia during the 1960s; a group of countries that have sometimes been labelled.

The second type of developmental welfare state emerged in Asia in the late 1990s. In these countries such as South Korea or Thailand, the Asian financial crisis led to considerable GDP growth cuts or even decreases and resulted in unemployment affecting all social strata. At the same time, democracy movements, led by trade unions and student movements, established claims on the state to provide public goods to its citizens. In that sense, a new social contract emerged in these countries after 1997. In South Korea, for example, the National Basic Livelihood Security Act was adopted in 1999. The Act introduced a right to social assistance, which was universal for all citizens, and designed to guarantee a social minimum. Democracy emerged in this period and became a constituent element (Ringen 2011; Kohler, 2014: 4). This type two developmental welfare state mischaracterized by a social contract, and could perhaps be classified as an emerging developmental welfare democracy.

In China, The Minimum Subsistence Guarantee, the dibao, for urban populations was introduced in 1999. This was a response to the impact of the market reforms introduced from the 1980s under Deng Xiaoping, which brought huge income disparities within and among economic classes and regions. The dibao was a selective - i.e., not universal - transfer, and was extended to rural populations only in 2008. It does not cover migrants. The Rural Cooperative Medical Insurance Scheme was universalized in 2013. Policy changes, such as an abolition of the **'Hukou System'**[11], were announced very recently. If that latter reform were to materialize, it would make all citizens eligible for the same type of social services - education, health, social assistance transfers - regardless of their status as rural or urban, migrant or resident. So far, however, the social contract is restrictive, and democracy

---

[11] The 'Hukou System' is the obligatory household registration certificate, Citizens have access to social services only in the place where they are registered, and registration cannot be transferred from rural to urban areas.

lacking, but there is a state commitment to universalize welfare state functions, thus constituting a third form.

The fourth type of developmental welfare state can be discerned for example in South Asia. Social policy in the realms of education, health, employment, and social protection is - notionally - based on norms of social justice, deducted from the country's constitutions and development plans and there is an explicit language of rights. Drivers have been various social movements such as that of the informal sector post-conflict situations with a need for social healing, as well as pressure from the emerging middle classes, either stemming from an enlightened commitment to improving social justice, or a concern over the impact of social disruptions on their security. The welfare functions are becoming justifiable: in at least one country, citizens can claim their entitlements in court. In several countries in South Asia, civil society organizations are in a position to monitor delivery and performance.

The social transfers are in principle universal, such as social pensions. Many are categorical - such as child benefits or education grants for girl children or children in disadvantaged castes - thus contain a strong social inclusion angle. Some social assistance transfers are means-tested. Access to food is an additional function, going beyond the five welfare state functions listed above. Outcomes in South Asia, on the other hand, are poor, with human development indicators still among the lowest in the world; there is a disconnection between design and welfare state performance. This form of the developmental welfare state is found in varying formats and qualities in Bangladesh, India, and the Maldives. It could perhaps be classifieds as emerging rights-based developmental welfare state.

There is a fifth type, or phase, of the developmental welfare state - those that are in regress. In some of the older developmental welfare states in Asia, one observes continuous dismantling of welfare provisions. There is a partial deterioration of entitlements and rights. Behavioral conditionality's and rigid forms of means-testing are being introduced. Finally, it is necessary to examine these welfare states outcomes. To do this, one needs to examine human development indicators and rankings and look at efforts in terms of expenditures. Regarding human development outcomes, it is well known that across Asia, despite its image as a highly successful region, individuals and communities face severe deprivations at many levels.

Classification of Welfare state:

Gosta Esping-Andersen's (1990) famously produced a threefold typology of social democratic, conservative and liberal welfare regimes.[12] These theories correspond to 'Titmus Welfare models'. They are described as follows:

1. The Social Democratic Welfare State:

In a social democratic welfare concept the state assumes primary responsibility for the welfare of its citizens. Social welfare now receives recognition in terms of the idea of a safety net against poverty rather than a means to social transformation and reduction of inequality Schooling, in particular, primary schooling, public health care and provide security of its citizens, has been a minimum program central to welfare claims of any government. In this regime schemes are predominantly tax-financed as well, but in contrast to the residual-liberal model, benefits are granted without means testing. They are a citizen's right and benefit levels tend to be much more generous, it is 'a welfare state that would promote an equality of the highest standards' (Esping-Andersen 1990: 28). Social Democratic regime

---

[12] Powell, Martin (2004) "*Welfare regimes and the welfare mix*"European Journal of Political Research 43: 83–105, 2004

provide a lot of welfare services in care, health and education, the welfare state itself becomes a major employer emphasizing mainly female employment (Huber and Stephens 2000) (Caramani 2014: 532) This responsibility in a theory ought to be comprehensive because all aspects of welfare is considered universally applied to citizens as guaranteed benefits and service as a right. Thee regimes exist in Sweden and Norway.

2. The Conservative Welfare State Theory:

The notion of the conservative welfare state depends upon 'let do' but it broadly implies 'leave it alone'. The insurance principle is advocated by this theory as dominant in Germany, Austria, France, Italy, the Netherlands, and Spain. In the conservative continental regime, social right is not based on citizen status but on employment relation. The welfare state is contribution financed rather than tax-financed. Those not dependently employed are covered via their employed spouse or relatives. Welfare benefits are differentiated according to income and record of contributions to the social insurance fund. Being based on occupational principles, conservative welfare states display a high degree of programme fragmentation. (Esping-Andersen 1990: 26-28). The welfare states in continental Europe as *conservative* regimes. Conservative regimes are characteristic for their blend of status segmentation, and the role of the family and church for promoting welfare. These regimes were never obsessed with market efficiency - in many instances, the market is displaced as a welfare provider. Instead, a statist and corporatist legacy is reflected in the attachment of social rights to class and status rather than citizenship. Furthermore, Christian democratic parties' role in the expansion of conservative welfare states is reflected in church and religious organizations expanded role for provision of especially social-service arrangement as day-care, kindergarten, health, and education (Esping-Andersen, 1990: 27, 1999: 83) (Caramani 2014: 532).

3. The Liberal Democratic Welfare State Theory:

This theory is primarily concernd with directing the resources to people most in need. This requires tight bureaucratic control over people concern. The unintended result is that there is a sharp divided between the receiver and producer of social welfare between country and its people. In a liberal welfare state regime, benefits tend to be the low and flat rate. They are means tested or targeted at clearly delineated groups in society. The state gives welfare benefits to the most destitute and needy. This model is dominating is the United States, the United Kingdom, and Australia also known as means-tested benefit policy. (Esping-Andersen, 1990: 26-28) (Caramani 2014: 532).

Above these theories shows three worlds of welfare capitalism, this has been shown in table 2.1.

Table 2.1 Esping-Andersen's Three Worlds of Welfare Capitalism

Esping-Andersen's welfare regimes (Titmus' welfare models)	**'Liberal' (residual Model)**	**'Conservative' (achievement performance model)**	**'Social Democratic' (institutional redistributive model)**
Prime example	US, UK	Germany	Sweden
Decommodification	Low	Medium	High
Social rights	Need-based	Employment-related	Universal

Welfare provision	Mixed services	Transfer payments	Public services
Benefits	Flat benefits	Contribution-related	Redistributiv e

Source: *Ebbinghaus and Manow, 2001: 9 (Caramani, 2014: 533)*

India after independence has been moving gradually along the line of welfare state based on the principle of equal opportunity and equitable distribution of wealth. It focuses on the government guarantee of social wellbeing and good life. Accordingly to the constitution of India has extensive provision to ensure the social welfare of the people of India.

(a) The welfare state in Scandinavian Countries:

In the twentieth century, the scope of social planning in Scandinavia countries continuously expanded, with the aim of achieving balanced economic and social development, that is to say, economic growth as well as social justice. Thus, fighting poverty went hand in hand with state institution building for social and economic growth as well as political democracy, and was pioneered by broad-based popular social movements. In 1950 and 1960s, the expansion of "the public sector", comprehensive state education as well as public health that a thoroughly coherent developmental perspective on economic prosperity and social change became part and parcel of welfare state philosophy.

Thus, at least since the last quarter of the twentieth century, this has characterized social welfare state theory and practice in general from child to disability policy—or "from the cradle to the grave", as the saying goes, about the universal Scandinavian welfare model. Moreover, during the rather painful reconstruction of the welfare state during the last decades of the twentieth century, the relationship between economic growth and social development was an important topic on the public agenda throughout Scandinavia. So far, however, the policy balance and conflict between efficiency and equality have in most cases been resolved and maintained in the five Scandinavian countries-Sweden, Norway, Denmark, Finland, and Iceland.

The Scandinavian type welfare state, those cores has been characterized as lying in "broad public participation in various areas of economic and social life, the purpose of which is to promote ability of society to master its problems, to enrich and equalize the living conditions of individuals and families. In social policy, the cornerstone of the model is universalism". Universalism is meant that the Scandinavian countries have set out to develop a welfare state that includes the entire population.

The hallmark of the contemporary Scandinavian institutional welfare state is expressed in terms of three essential features: a comprehensive social policy; a social entitlement principle that has been institutionalized (social rights); and social legislation that is solidaristic and Universalist in character.

Two characteristics of the Scandinavian type of welfare state are of prime importance and were visible from early on: public responsibility for welfare provision and the principle of universal coverage based on the idea of social rights. If we consider education as part of the welfare state, the Nordic countries stand out as relatively early proponents of a universal education. An early step toward democratization and universalization of education was the demand for general literacy for all—women as well as men. This "need" or "demand" was in principle created in the sixteenth century when, with the coming of the Reformation, the then two Nordic kingdoms of Denmark-Norway-Iceland and Sweden-Finland became Evangelical Lutheran, and the church took responsibility for making the population literate.

The introduction of a general and compulsory system of elementary education came in the nineteenth century; it was partly influenced by the ideas behind the American and French revolutions. Elementary schools became the responsibility of local authorities and every citizen had the right to an elementary education of a certain length and of a broader secular content than the former church schools had offered. Denmark was first, with its Public Education Act of 1814, which introduced seven years of compulsory education and obliged all municipalities to set up primary schools. Sweden followed, introducing a law covering compulsory elementary education of an unspecified length, in 1842. Next came Norway with compulsory education for all children from seven to the age of confirmation (about 14), legislated in 1848. Finally, in principle, a system of general elementary schools was established by legislation in Finland in 1866.

Locating welfare in India - Is India a welfare State?

The welfare state is a thinking of government where the state plays a vital role promotion, protection of social, socio-political, and the wellness of its citizens. The welfare kingdom offers education, sustain, health care, insurance etc. It also offers toddler care, social facilities such as libraries, public parks as nicely as many different freedom and rights guaranteed to citizens.

With the advent of the twenty-first century, it can also be stated that the welfare states is at crossroads. But socialism is on decline even in the present socialist/communist state. As a long way as India is a challenge that one of the salient points of Indian charter imposed responsibilities upon states to establish a welfare state. The preamble, the directive principle of state policy and imperative rights make it expressly clear that our aim is welfare and develop socialist economy through democratic capacity, as well as warranty quintessential to all citizens. It is yet to be seen how it will hasten in the right direction the convergence of education and health for the rural poor.

The welfare regime and social policy in India today have to be viewed in the context of the overall orientation of and shifts in state policy and government since 1947. With Independence, an interventionist and developmental state were seen as essential to achieving the stated aims of the 'Directive Principles' of State Policy[13] - the removal of poverty, social justice, self-reliance, and growth. Different recipes and structures were debated and concretized in successive Five-Year Plans.

The principles formulated included free and compulsory education to children, a public health care system and higher education system, economic and social rights to women, as well as Scheduled Castes, Scheduled Tribes, and Other Backward Classes and religious minorities along with adequate means of livelihood for all citizens linked to industrialization and agrarian reform, equal pay for equal work for men and women, proper working conditions, protection against exploitation, reduction of the concentration of wealth and means of production and economic inequality. The model of working conditions and social security that the new state enunciated for its employees was to act as a standard as well as to ensure the loyalty of the emerging middle class to the new state.

The Second Five Year Plan recognized the determinant influence of education and the rate of economic development. It laid emphasis on:

1. Basic education;
2. Elementary education;
3. Diversification of curricula at the secondary level;
4. Improvement of the standard of education at the college and university level;

---

[13] These were formulated by the Constituent Assembly as guidelines for governance which should aim to give substance to the fundamental rights given in the Constitution.

5. Development of professional and technical education;
6. Development of social education and cultural programme (Second Five Year Plan, 1956).[14]

Educational planning in the Third Five Year Plan stated that in the field of general education, as distinguished from technical education, the government laid major emphasis on the provision of facilities for the education of all children in the age group of 6 to 11 (Third Five-Year Plan, 1960).[15] The Fifth Five Year plan1974-79 emphasized four issues of educational development. These are the Equalization of educational opportunities for social justice. Coordination between various educational levels with employment and economic development, Quality improvement, Co-operation of the intelligentsia, including students, in it also stressed on the professionalization of education at secondary level and reorganization of curricula (Fifth Five-Year Plan, 1974).[16]

The Sixth Five Year Plan, 1980-85 emphasized on the development and consolidation of facilities within the twisting higher educational institutions and also on organizing an information system for technical manpower (Sixth Five-Year Plan,, 1983).[17]

In all the previous Five Year Plans, education was considered as a social service, rather than an input in the development process. The idea that education is some kind of social service performed by the welfare state, and substitute it with the idea that education is the most critical input into the entire process of social, economic, political and cultural transformation of India, the so-called

---

[14] *Second Five Year Plan*, Planning Commission, GOI, New Delhi: 1956, pp. 509-521.

[15] *Third Five-Year Plan*, Planning Commission, GOI, New Delhi: 1960, pp.98-105.

[16] *Fifth Five-Year Plan*, Planning Commission, GOI, New Delhi: 1974, pp. 88-89.

[17] *Sixth Five-Year Plan*, Planning Commission, GOI, New Delhi: 1983, pp. 91-98.

educational reforms would predictably produce explosive social tensions in our country.

In the Indian context, formulation of different educational policies, based on the recommendations of different commissions constituted by the government, came as a response to the changes at socio-economic and political level. National Policy on Education (NPE 1986) was formulated by the government (without constituting a commission) based on a public debate only. Subsequent chapters discuss the evolution of educational policy in India, the role of multiple agencies in the formulation of the educational policy, the comparative analysis of the document 'Challenge of Education: A Policy Perspective 1985' and the NPE 1986, the responses of the state governments and public on the NPE 1986.

As the dropout rate is also linked with the nutritional status of the children and their mothers, the mother's education level, as well as the prevalence of child labor, the National Literacy Mission has been reoriented to focus mainly on female literacy through the launch of the Sakshar Bharat campaign. While concerted efforts need to be made to improve infrastructure and access to schools, the links between teacher absenteeism, dropouts and learning at the elementary level also need to be explored. Other areas that demand the urgent attention of educationists and policymakers are

- Childcare;
- Education of adolescents and youth, which is as important as education for the 6-14 year age group, as all stages are interdependent;
- The issue of child labor;
- Convergence of SSA with development initiatives like MGNREGS;

- Systemic issues like financing and increasing investment on education, and apathy reflected in the preference for 'tweaking' the system to achieve goals, among other things.
- Educational needs of children with special cognitive abilities (for example, dyslexia, autism, and attention deficit disorder);
- Governance reform in the form of the genuine district and block level planning at the elementary education level to bring governance closer to schools, and
- Increasing the role of private schools in capacity building for ensuring 'quality' education.

These issues are compounded by the lack of motivation on the part of the child for undergoing 6-14 years of schooling as there are no economic incentives during these years of education. This makes elementary education an unattractive option for the poor as livelihood struggles take primacy over education. The education policy must be viewed in tandem with the labor market policy. Besides, there is also a need for some standardization in school education, with the mechanical provisioning of all core inputs and a well-developed pedagogy. The main issue that needs to be addressed in this area is the lack of an appropriate academic culture/environment in the existing institutions and systems. Further, it is important to link the District Institutes of Education and Training (DIETs) with other rungs in order to bring in professionalism. The poor learning outcomes at the elementary level also necessitate a national monitoring system to ensure the translation of efforts into outcomes.

The focus of the education policy must shift from enrolment to education improvement. The SSA framework has two components that are especially focused on individual schools, namely, school-specific grants provided to each school, and individual teacher grant. These interlinked investments must be utilized from the long-term perspective of improving the quality of every school. While SSA has, in recent years, laid an emphasis on quality enhancement, the scheme needs to devise direct strategies for changing the way in which schools function so that the outcome is an enhancement in learning outcomes rather than just the mechanical supply of teaching inputs.

Social and economic barriers, which impede effective participation in the learning process, should be essentially removed if the momentum of the movement towards Universal Elementary Education has to be maintained. Towards this end, the currently adopted generic strategies of promoting access to education and participation for all needs to be replaced by a more nuanced and differentiated strategy that directly targets the marginalized groups.

As things stand today, the illiterate population in the country is largely concentrated in seven states. Special strategies must, therefore, be devised to improve the outreach of the school system to the disadvantaged groups in these states. A more systematic school mapping exercise would be useful in order to ensure that access is gained not just lower primary classes but also the upper primary classes. Further, the location of facilities needs to be based on equity considerations that would help overcome both distance and social barriers. Education is not just about studying, but also about health and nutrition, as these ensure the students' ability to make full use of educational facilities. Malnutrition limits the capacity to learn by drastically affecting the motor, sensory, cognitive, social and emotional development of children. The age of six years, the formal age of entry to primary education, may be too late to act in the context of health issues. In this context, the convergence of education with other development initiatives must be emphasized to facilitate the sustainability of gains in the education sector.

Education of adolescents and young adults has to be pushed center-stage to help break the vicious cycle of illiteracy, lack of productive skills and poverty. High levels of non-enrolment and dropouts lead to large numbers of uneducated youth entering the world of work as unskilled laborers. The need of the hour is to equip this section of the population with productive skills so as to enhance their economic prospects and in the long term, also to ensure better education opportunities for the children of these young adults. Inclusive development can be seen in terms of progress in economic and social inclusion. Despite more than six decades of planning in India, the fruits of development have not reached the desired segments of the population who suffers from social and financial exclusion. The wide-ranging reforms have induced greater efficiency and competitiveness in all spheres of economic activities; however, its performance in the form of Human Development Indicators has been unsatisfactory. Indicators like education, health, family welfare, employment, women empowerment, rural infrastructure etc. have lagged behind in the race for a better standard of living (Savagaon).

MDM is the world's largest school feeding programme involving the preparation of a hot meal every day. The centrally sponsored MDM Scheme was revised and universalized at primary level with effect from September 2004 to make a provision for providing cooked meals to children of classes I-VIII studying in Government, Government-aided, and Local body schools, Madarsas and EGS, and AIE centers. Besides providing food grains free of cost to the States/UTs, and food grains transportation subsidy, the central government provides assistance for converting food grains into a cooked meal at a rate of Rs. 1/per child per day. The elementary sector faces numerous problems such as inadequate school infrastructure, presence of single-teacher schools, no schools at nearby place, high teacher absenteeism, poor drinking water, and toilet facilities, ill-equipped and ill-functioning government schools, large-scale teacher vacancies, inadequate equipment etc. in addition, education not considered as useful by many poor parents.

The poor quality of schooling to disadvantaged sections whose reliance on publicly provided facilities is greater, and poverty in backward regions and rising demand for labor in developed regions are also the reasons for non-enrolment and dropouts. The indirect cost of education viz. uniforms, books, transport, etc. also dampens the demand for education. NSS 52nd Round provides three reasons for never enrolled and reasons for dropout from school. They are lack of interest, direct school-related factors, and direct economic factors. A recent ASER study found that only 53.4% children in Standard V could read a standard II level text. 38% of the children who have completed four years of schooling cannot read a small paragraph with short sentences meant to be read by a student of class II. About 55% of such children cannot divide a three digit number by a one digit number. On an average, there has been a decrease in children's ability to do simple mathematics. Thus, dissatisfaction with the school functioning may induce the child and parents to forego education enforcing them to start earning. Thus, the schooling system is partly responsible for the persistence of child labor MDM Scheme can help increase attendance, improve nutrition reduce dropout rates.

Basic education is the primary agent either to improve the immediate living condition or to increase the potential for future living. The Millennium Development Goals has emphasized to ensure that all girls and boys must complete a full course of primary education and that gender disparity is eliminated at all levels of education by 2015. As a natural follow-up action, the Parliament of India enacted The Child Right to Free and Compulsory Education Act 2009 (RTE Act 2009) and it came into force on April 1, 2010.

India is considered to be the largest democracy in the world, which is governed by an elaborate and detailed written constitution. The Preamble of the Constitution has used the terms like "Socialist", "Social and Economic Justice", "Equality" etc., these terms indicate that the state would extensively involve in social welfare of people, and would try to establish an egalitarian society. Moreover, a separate chapter of the Directive Principles of State Policy has been devoted to the welfare responsibilities of the government, which lays down the norms of ideal governance for people's welfare. The current economic policies of the government, which are largely influenced by globalization and capitalism, are not in conformity with its welfare obligations. On the one hand, the economy is growly very fast but its benefit is confined to 10-15% population; the rich-poor divide is increasing continuously; the agriculture sector is neglected from the focus of economic development; the small scale industries have been devastated by the impact of neo-liberal policies; the regional disparities have been increased substantially.

India is considered to be a welfare state and moreover the largest democracy in the world. The people in India have been considered as the supreme authority in our country, as it is declared by the Preamble of Indian Constitution that sovereignty vests not in the Parliament but in the people of Union of India. "Social Welfare" has been (at least theoretically) at the center of our policy making from the time of independence itself. From the "First Five Year Plan" itself Programmes and schemes have been launched related to social welfare issues as like agriculture and rural development, employment and labor welfare, healthcare, education, etc. Indeed in the initial 20-25 years in spite of the scarcity of economic means, the government was focussed on the welfare policies and inclusive development.

In today's time, it seems that the concept of social welfare has not been taken by the government as sincerely, as it must have. The attitude of the government is not very friendly and cooperative towards the people. The government does not seem to be sincere about its responsibility towards serving the people as many scams and irregularities have come up in the central and state governments.

Committed to equality and welfare, the government is required to take steps to ensure that the minimum facilities of life are provided to every person, and there are equalities of income and material resources as far as democratically possible. The government policies are a pro-corporate stand, and neglecting the plight of the people, the state is withdrawing from its constitutional responsibility of creating an egalitarian society and providing social and economic justice. It has to be remembered that people are not just meant to achieve higher economic growth, but they are ends in themselves; every policy of government must put the people at the center of it as beneficiaries.

Welfare State and Goal of Inclusive Development:

The welfare state also usually includes the facilitation of basic public needs -education, health services, and housing etc. Inclusiveness is the indicator of human development and progress, that's indeed very necessary to be achieved by the nation in the 21st century. The concept of inclusiveness has many dimensions and phases as far as human development is a concern the inclusiveness give preferences to access to quality education, primary public health care, and other essential services to provide a good life. In order to make sure the minimum degree of security and steadiness for a society via a variety of institutions and policies broadly speaking at the state level, but additionally at the local level, a welfare state is needed. Inclusive development is core objective of a welfare state.

What is inclusive development?

Before knowing the meaning of inclusive development it is necessary to know the meaning of Inclusive, in the context of social science inclusion means attention on the distribution of well-being in a society like the equal opportunity of employment, education, healthcare, and security. Inclusive development is an instrument that benefits reach all those that make up the poor in the region, children, minorities groups and the extremely poor in the rural areas. The inclusive development process is depending upon theory, concepts and practice of welfare state adopt by the democratic countries.

Then if development, beyond growth, is to do with improvements in average levels of attainment along dimensions other than income, inclusive development is to do with the distribution of these improvements. Inclusive development occurs when average achievements improve and inequalities in these achievements fall. By analogy with the income case, we can define pro-poor development as occurring when improvements in average attainments are accompanied by improvements of achievements below a critical threshold. Thus when development is inclusive it is also pro-poor. But development can be pro-poor even though it is not inclusive, inequality in this non-income dimension increases, provided that this increase in inequality is not large enough to offset the impact on "non-income poverty" of the average improvement along this dimension.

Thus a move from just growth to inclusive development involves two steps— a move to evaluate the distribution as well as the average level of well-being along any dimension considered, and a move to include dimensions other than income in the assessment of performance.

Growth is a unidimensional measure of performance. As discussed above, pro-poor growth or inclusive growth, while still focused on income, face issues of aggregation across individuals— poverty indices are one way of effecting this aggregation, and more general social welfare functions are essentially methods of aggregating the myriad changes in income across individuals into a single national level index for evaluation. The concept of development introduces dimensions of wellbeing beyond income, but this raises the question of aggregating across these dimensions to arrive at a single measure of performance. What if income rises but health or education worsens? Even if all dimensions move in the same direction, if changes are at different rates in different countries for different dimensions, the evaluation question remains. The HDI resolves this in a particular way—it takes an equal-weighted average of the indicators along the three dimensions of income, education, and health. But it is not clear on what basis these weights, or indeed any other set of weights can be chosen. The extensive debate on the question has not resolved the issue.

Given the state of the literature, and accepting that growth by itself is not an adequate indicator of performance, I would argue that we should consider four things in assessment and evaluation:

i. Economic growth,
ii. Measures of income distribution, including income poverty,
iii. Measures of average performance along dimensions other than income, in particular education and health,
iv. Measures of distribution along non-income dimensions of wellbeing, including distribution not only across individuals but across salient groups such as gender or ethnicity.

In many ways, the MDG approach does this. There is an inevitable untidiness about the MDG approach since it has many dimensions and many indicators, but this is inevitable.

Amartya Sen Perspective of Development and Welfare;

Freedom has a thousand charms to show, that slaves however contented, never know. Sen explains how in a world of unprecedented increase in overall opulence, millions of people living in rich and poor countries are still unfree. Even if they are not technically slaves, they are denied elementary freedom and remain imprisoned in one way or another by economic poverty, social deprivation, political tyranny or cultural authoritarianism. The main purpose of development is to protect freedom and its 'thousand charms' to the unfree citizens (Sen & Draze , Development as Freedom, 2000).

Sen persuasively argues that at once the ultimate goal of social, economic arrangements and the most efficient means of realizing general welfare social and political institutions like markets, political parties, legislatures, the judiciary, and the media contribute to development by enhancing individual freedom and are in turn sustained by social values. Values, institutions, development, and freedom are all closely interrelated, and Sen links them together in an elegant analytical framework. There are many new problems as well as old ones, including persistence of poverty and unfulfilled elementary needs, occurrence of famines and widespread hunger, violation of elementary political freedoms as well as of basic liberties, extensive neglect of the interests and agency of women and worsening threats to our environment and to the sustainability of our economic and social lives.

There are both breadths in the scope of subjects considered and depth in the treatment of empirical data that he amasses as evidence for his conclusions. He shows, for example, how high per capita income does not necessarily correlate with greater life expectancy - poor Afro-Americans have a lower life expectancy than the poor in the Indian state of Kerela where public services have long been accessible to the poor. And further, the "Solution of the problem of population growth (like the solution of so many other social and economic problems) can lie in expanding the freedom of the people whose interest are most directly affected by over-frequent child-bearing and child-rearing. The solution to the population problem calls for more freedom, not less. Famines, he argues, are not a product of absolute shortages of food; rather, "Inequality has an important role in the development of famines and other severe crises the latter thrive on the basis of severe and sometimes suddenly increased inequality."

Sen's positive notion of freedom can be applied to men and women alike and is potentially sensitive to gender inequalities in social structures, in norms, and in economic institutions. On the basis of Sen's approach, it is possible to more clearly assess how women's freedom to live the lives that they value is generally less than men's freedom to do so, women have lower levels of education, women suffer reproductive health risks, women's behavior in the public domain is often restricted by gender norms, and they suffer from labor market discrimination, just to mention a few gendered 'unfreedoms'. He has vividly analyzed women's economic position in various publications.

Nothing, he believes, is as important today in the political economy of development as an adequate recognition of political, economic and social participation and leadership of women. This is indeed a crucial aspect of 'development as freedom'. His concern is about human potential, and how it can be liberated both as a means for improved economic performance and as the very purpose of economic and social activities.

Sen presents a treatise that integrates ethics, values and economic theory. "The formation of values, emergence and evolution of social ethics are also part of the process of development." He argues that a variety of social institutions including those involved in the operation of markets, administrations, legislatures, political parties, NGOs, the judiciary, the media and the 'community', all contribute to the process of development.

However, if increasing income in a country is not accompanied by the other factors that define a high standard of living then the country is only getting richer. It is not "developing" in the truest sense. The real meaning of development gets right to education, right to nutritious food, right to well live and the right to social equality etc. According to Sen, these above rights are necessary for the overall well-being of the citizens.

The MDM Scheme has been quietly feeding more than 10 crore children every day for more than 10 years. Unfortunately, this popular and relatively successful programme makes it to the headlines only when things go wrong - this time following the tragic death of 23 children in Bihar after eating at school on 16 July 2013. Recent economic research clearly documents the positive impact of the scheme on enrolment, attendance, retention, and nutrition. The MDM Scheme is meant to boost children's participation and learning at the primary stage. So it helps realize freedom and hence development. The existence of local power structures and social prejudices impose constraints on effective participation and responsive leadership that further impedes the successful implementation of welfare schemes like MDM. This further interrogates the failures of implementation that arise out of curtailment of freedom.

In an Uncertain Glory: India and Its Contradictions, two of India's leading economists argue that the country's essential issues lie elsewhere, specifically in the lack of attention paid to the indispensable wishes of the people, mainly the poor. The deep inequalities in Indian society have a tendency to constrict public dialogue in India's vibrant media to the lives and worries of the incredibly affluent. One of the biggest problems has been insufficient use of the public assets generated via economic increase to make bigger India's lagging bodily and social infrastructure (in sharp contrast, for example, to what China has done): “there is an endured inadequacy both social services such as schooling, medical care and immunization, and of physical offerings such as the provision of safe water, electrical energy, drainage, and sanitation. (Sen & Draze , An Uncertain Glory:India and Its Contradictions, 2013).

Dreze and Sen argue that growth and development underpinned by health and education are integrated. Growth provides the resources necessary to build capabilities, which, in turn, enhance growth via a more productive labor force. They go on to identify what they consider the apotheosis of the integration of growth with development, namely the "Asian Development Model". They trace its historical origins to Japan in the middle of the 19th century following the Meiji Restoration. Significant are both the zeal with which education was spread and the fact that this was mostly state-led. They suggest that in East Asia growth was combined with its distribution. This does not mean that the income distribution was equitable, but fairly equal.

Dreze and Sen (2002) state that "South Asian countries have had much in common particularly those relating to the expansion of basic education and healthcare, and India contrasts with all of them in this fundamental respect", the Government of India has thus far failed to establish and provide universal social policies with respect to social security, education, and health.

In the modern world, education is the necessary tool to get the welfarism and to end the superstitious conservative thinking. The importance of education has increased in the globalization era. The authors suggest that education is central to the process of integrating growth and development and thus to the progress of the people. The authors flag the very low standards of education in India, revealed both by student performance in international tests such as the programme for International student assessment but also form independent audits of learning in our schools. They identify the neglect of education by international standards in India both in term of coverage and quality. They emphasize that is not just unjust but also inefficient for a dynamic economy. So what is needed is universalization of education with quality.

There is an aspect of the working of Indian democracy that is of even greater relevance to the proposals of Dreze and Sen. They advocate a "rights-based" approach which includes welfare and the public provision of health and education. It is possible to be on the same page with the authors on this while at the same time remaining skeptical of the capacity, or even the intent, of the Indian state to deliver these outcomes without administrative reforms. The authors next move on to demonstrate that growth does not necessarily lead to development. This is done by comparing India with its neighbors in South Asia over the recent period of high growth. India's ranking in terms of social indicators, mostly with respect to health, has fallen behind many of them. Of particular interest is the case of Bangladesh, India has by now moved ahead with per capita income twice that of Bangladesh, but Bangladesh has moved ahead of India in terms of social indicators. Interestingly, the authors suggest that this may be related to the fact that Bangladesh has managed to involve its women in social programmes and thus the development process much more than India has.

The authors of this book provide a theoretical framework to understand problem-related with the governance of welfare programmes. They analyse, "the hierarchy chain of the government system of India and discuss the problem of less accountability and corruption. In the absence of good systems of accountability, there may not only be serious neglects of duties, but much temptation for officials to deliver at high 'prices' what they are actually supposed to deliver freely, as part of their job." Corruption is fostered and nurtured by the absence of systems of accountability. So there is a problem related to the governance of welfare programmes like the MDM scheme, Serva Shiksha Abhiyan, and other healthcare schemes. The authors of this book rightly analyze and evaluate the problem of Indian common people particularly socially and economically poor society, because the root problem of Indian democracy is social exclusion.

Goals of inclusive development in 11th Five Years Plan (2007-2012) :

The National Development Council in December 2006 accepted the Approach to the 11th Five 12 months Plan record titled "Towards faster and more Inclusive growth" and directed the Planning Commission to prepare a specified sketch to check the assets required to meet the large goal set forth in the Approach Paper. The designated model of the Eleventh Five Year Plan (2007-12) used to be accredited with the aid of the National Development Council in December 2007 (Eleventh Five year Plan, 2007).**The vision for the Eleventh Plan**

The National Development Council in December 2006 accepted the Approach to the 11th Five 12 months Plan record titled "Towards faster and more Inclusive growth" and directed the Planning Commission to prepare a specified sketch to check the assets required to meet the large goal set forth in the Approach Paper. The designated model of the Eleventh Five Year Plan (2007-12) got accredited with the aid of the National Development Council in December 2007.

Objectives of 11th Five Year Plan (2007-2012):

The Plan envisages an excessive increase of GDP of the order of 9 % for the country as a whole. This implies that per capita GDP would develop roughly at about 7.5% per 12 months to double in 10 years. However, the Plan document hurries up to add that the target is now not simply faster boom but also inclusive growth which ensures broad-based improvement in the satisfactory of the existence of the people, particularly the poor SCs/STs, OBCs, and the minorities.

An overview of the objectives of the diagram are the average GDP increase of 9% per year, agricultural GDP boom of 4% per year, generation of 58 million employment opportunities, reduction unemployment amongst the educated too much less than 5%, 20% make bigger in the real wage of unskilled people and Reduction in headcount ratio of poverty by 10 % factors.

Objectives for education are reduction in drop-out price amongst youth at the fundamental stage from 52.2% in 2003-04 to 20% by using 2011-12, creating minimum standards of attainment in fundamental schools, to make certain exceptional of education, increasing literacy rate for individuals 0-7 years or more to 85% by way of 2011-12, lowering gap in literacy to 10 % factors by 2011-12 and increasing of individuals going for higher education from 10% to 15% through 2011-12.

In the health zone cover infant mortality rate (IMR) is to be decreased to 28 and maternal mortality rate (MMR) to 1 per 1,000 by 2011-12, whole fertility rate to be reduced to 2.1 through 2011-12, clean ingesting water to be made available to all by using 2009, malnutrition among teens of age 0-3 to be decreased to half its existing level and anemia among female and girls to be decreased to half its existing level.

Objectives toward girls and kids are sex ratio for age team 0-6 to be raised to 935 by means of 2011-12 and to 950 via 2016-17, making sure that at least 33% of beneficiaries of all authorities' schemes are women and girl adolescents and making sure that all children experience a safe childhood, besides any compulsion to work.

Objectives for infrastructure to make certain electrical energy connection to all villages and BPL (Below Poverty Line) Households through 2009 and dependable power by means of the end of the Eleventh Five Year Plan, to make certain all, weather road connection to all habitations with population 1000 and above (500 and above for hilly areas) through 2009, to join each and every village by way of cell phone and furnish broadband connectivity to all village by way of 2012 and to supply homestead websites to all by 2012 and step up the tempo of housing development for the poor to cover all the poor by 2016-17.

Objectives toward surroundings to extend forest and tree cover with the aid of 5 % points, to attain WTO standards of air high-quality in all most important cities by 2011-12 and to treat all city waste water through 2011-12 to clean river waters.

Education and skill development is received high priority in the Eleventh Plan, both to meet the needs of a growing economy and to promote social equality by empowering those currently excluded because of unequal access to education and skills to participate fully in the growth process. Public expenditure (Centre and States) on education is only around 3.6% of GDP. The National Common Minimum Programme (NCMP) had set a target of raising it to 6%.

The action plan proposed in the Eleventh Plan for secondary education includes the following points:-

- Rapid upgradation of 15000 Upper Primary Schools to Secondary Schools, and the expansion of intake capacity in 44000 existing Secondary Schools;
- Establishment of 6000 high-quality model schools at the block level to serve as benchmarks for excellence in secondary schooling. About 3500 of these will be public-funded schools while 2500 would be through PPP;
- Provision for laboratories/libraries and also strengthening the existing facilities available;
- Continuous teacher training;
- Provision for hostels and residential schools for girls; and
- A more liberal approach on the part of State Governments on allowing private schools to be set up to meet the large unmet demand for quality education.

Good health is both an end in itself and also contributes to economic growth. Meeting the health needs of the population requires a comprehensive and sustained approach. Our health services should be affordable. The 11th Plan is tried to focus on the healthcare system-preventive, curative, palliative and rehabilitative. This is accompanied by an emphasis on access to clean drinking water, sanitation, diet, hygiene and feeding practices, which will significantly affect the health status of the people. Public health spending will be raised to at least 2% of GDP during the Eleventh Plan period.

The following targets were set during the Eleventh Plan to ensure an efficient public health delivery system under the National Rural Health Mission (NRHM), which was launched in 2005.

- Over 5 lakh Accredited Social Health Activists (ASHAs), one for every 1000 population in 18 Special Focus States and in tribal pockets of all States by 2008.
- All sub-centers (nearly 1.75 lakh) functional with two Auxiliary Nurse Midwives by 2010.
- Primary Health Centres (PHCs) (nearly 30000) with three staff nurses to provide round the clock services by 2010.
- 6500 Community Health Centres (CHCs) strengthened or established with seven specialists and nine staff nurses by 2012.
- 1800 Taluka or Sub-Divisional Hospitals (SDHs) and 600 District Hospitals (DHs) to be strengthened to provide quality health services by 2012.
- Mobile Medical Units for each District by 2009.
- Functional Hospital Development Committees in all CHCs, SDHs, and District Hospitals by 2009.
- Untied grants and annual maintenance grants to every Sub-centre, PHC, and CHC released regularly and utilized for local health action by 2008.
- All District Health Action Plans completed by 2008.

Planning initiatives in health, nutrition, care of children, care of the aged, education, skill development and expansion of social security services will create a large potential for employment for delivery of these services. Quantum jumps in the requirement of personnel, their skill and in their composition—by gender, by social group and by location in favor of the backward regions—will arise from:

- A massive increase in central funding of education which is a four-fold increase over the Tenth Plan in constant price;
- Emphasis on the next phase of quality of education;
- Reaching these services to the districts having a concentration of SC, ST, and minorities;
- Rapid expansion in the MDM scheme to cover 60 million additional children at the upper primary level by 2008-09; and
- Enrolling one crore children in vocational education- skill development streams.

Inclusive Development in Theory and Practice

The study will be taken up in the next section, focusing in particular on infrastructure interventions. But it is as well to address a tendency in some parts of the literature, that one set of outcomes are essentially all that we need to focus on, because the other dimensions track these outcomes very closely, statistically, and casually. This argument is indeed made for income traditionally for economic growth, but more recently for income poverty.

Thus, it used to be argued and is still argued, that education and health, for example, track income fairly closely, so we might as well focus policy on the income dimension. There are two problems with this argument. First, there is the straightforward statistical argument that education and health do not, in fact, track income perfectly. Even when there is a significant statistical relationship on average, there is considerable variation around the average, and countries at the same level of per capita income can have widely different achievements in non-income dimensions. This holds also at the relationship across individuals. Second, and more importantly, even the significant statistical relationship does not establish causality, at least not uni-directional causality from income to the other dimensions. There is significant evidence that education and health feedback positively on income. There is thus no substitute for careful analysis of each intervention and its impact on multidimensional outcomes taking into account feedback effects from each dimension on to the others. And, as a practical matter, the MDGs provide a useful way of structuring the outcomes to focus on.

Along with changing the time, the content of social welfare policies would change, and the state must conform to these changing needs, and provide services as per these changing needs. The Education and health both are requisite for sustainable inclusive development (SID) of people. "Education" plays a key role in livelihood vice versa livelihood play a key role in education. So Good education and nutrition are indeed necessary for the well-being and also these are the basic right for all citizen of the state.

Article 25 Everyone has the right to a standard of dwelling ample for the fitness and well-being of himself and of his family, inclusive of food, clothing, housing and scientific care and imperative social services, and the right to protection in the event of unemployment, sickness, disability, widowhood, historical age or other lack of livelihood in instances past his control. Motherhood and childhood are entitled to special care and help. All children, whether born in or out of wedlock, shall enjoy the same social protection (2015). Article 26 everyone has the right to education. Education shall be free, at least in the elementary and fundamental stages. Elementary education shall be compulsory.

1. Technical and professional education shall be made generally available and higher education shall be equally accessible to all on the basis of merit.
2. Education shall be directed to the full development of the human personality and to the strengthening of respect for human rights and fundamental freedoms. It shall promote understanding, tolerance, and friendship among all nations, racial or religious groups, and shall further the activities of the United Nations for the maintenance of peace.
3. Parents have a prior right to choose the kind of education that shall be given to their children.

Several National and International state have enactments and policies which guarantee or suggest to warranty the "Right to Food', which implies that food stands first amongst all. Food crisis additionally creates difficulties in reaching other social benefits. Therefore it seems like one of the primary potentials for capacity building. Food is a means to obtain other ends in life.

The MDMS as the inclusive policy was launched by Govt. of India with the objective of giving a boost to the universalization of education by increasing enrollment, attendance and retention and simultaneously improving the nutritional status of students in primary/upper primary classes.

Overall, enrolment numbers remain very high. Over 96% of all children in the age group 6 to 14 years are enrolled in school. This is the fourth consecutive year that enrolment levels have been 96% or more. Nationally, the proportion of children (age 6 to 14) who are not enrolled in school has gone up slightly, from 3.3% in 2011 to 3.5% in 2012. A slight increase is seen for all age groups and for both boys and girls. Girls in the age group of 11 to 14 years are often the hardest to bring to school and continue in school. In 2006, in eight major states, more than 11% of girls in this age group were not enrolled in school. By 2011, this figure had dropped to less than 6.5% in 3 of these states (Jharkhand, Gujarat, and Odisha) and less than 5% in 3 others (Bihar, Chhattisgarh and West Bengal). The situation in these states remained more or less unchanged in 2012.

However, in Rajasthan and Uttar Pradesh, the proportion of out of school girls (age 11-14) has increased from 8.9% and 9.7% respectively in 2011 to more than 11% in 2012. private school enrolment continues to rise in almost all States. At the All India level private school enrolment has been rising steadily since 2006. The percentage of 6 to 14-year-olds enrolled in private schools rose from 18.7% in 2006 to 25.6% in 2011. This year this number has further increased to 28.3%. The increase is almost equal in primary (Std. I-V) and upper primary (Std. VIVIII) classes. In 2012, among all private school children (age 6-14), 57.9% were boys. In 2012, more than 40% of children (age 6-14 years) in Jammu & Kashmir, Punjab, Haryana, Rajasthan, Uttar Pradesh, and Meghalaya are enrolled in private schools. This figure is 60% or more in Kerala and Manipur. Increase in private school enrolment is seen in almost all states, with the exception of Kerala, Nagaland, Manipur, and Meghalaya and Tripura (where private school enrolment was over 40% even last year). Since 2009, private school enrolment in rural areas has been rising at an annual rate of about 10%. If this trend continues, by 2018 India will have 50% of children in rural areas enrolled in private schools.

Conclusion

The MDM works as a decentralized programme, funded jointly with the aid of the Central and state governments. While the meals grain comes from Food Corporation of India through the state meals corporations, it is the School Management Committee (SMC) with the headmaster, Panchayati Raj Institutions (PRI) or different community representatives, and three fourths representation of mother and father of youngsters studying in that school, that is given the duty to buy pulses, vegetables, oil, spices, firewood, and so on as conversion cost.

Parents are seen as the biggest stakeholder and that is why the programmed shape furnished for the SMCs/Mothers' Committees to have a lead role in the administration and the accountability framework of the programme. Cooks paid Rs 1,000 a month and utensils furnished as a section of the scheme come via programme funds. Non-governmental organizations (NGOs) are assigned the accountability to run the programme in a few schools.

Akshay Patra-like NGOs have also been assigned the responsibility in many states. Despite the reference to unsatisfactory implementation reported, studies have mounted the role of the MDM in growing school attendance rates. Government schools have the largest segment of poor kids coming from underprivileged households where food safety at home is an issue. The hot cooked meal, with all its limitations, does keep again kids in schools in large numbers. Studies have additionally indicated how many children, particularly in states with a very excessive proportion of poor families, come hungry to school. MDM does make a distinction in the lives of these children and fulfil an inclusive agenda of public welfare.

Chapter III
Right to Education and Meal Scheme: Global and National Initiative

Right To Education Mechenisim Under The Right Of Children To Free And Compulsory Education Act Or Right To Education Act

---

Genesis of Right to quality Education

The scenarios of malnutrition and hunger phenomenon of the children those belong to the unprivileged and weak socio-economic background have been getting serious attention of government and non-government organizations across the world. The children those belong to these poor families face the problems of malnutrition due to extreme poverty in Indian society. In fact, malnutrition in the children is directly connected to the underdevelopment of their physical and educational growth.

According to the UNICEF report about 30% of the world's malnourished children live in India (UNICEF 2014 Report). As the result, every year 2.1 million Indian children die before reaching the age of five. Moreover, the fight against hunger and poverty increases the drop-out rate as well as increases the child labor. The drops out children have to participate in labor at various levels to earn their livelihood and this condition undermines the fundamental rights both national and international which are authorized to them as a child. A child cannot grow his/her physical and mental proficiencies properly without proper food and education even cannot live a life of self-esteem as well. Under Article 21 of the Constitution, all Indian children have the essential right to lifestyles and under Article 21A of the Constitution, the teens are entitled to free and obligatory schooling from the age of 6 to 14. And as the Supreme Court has made clear via its countless decisions, the right to existence is proper to live with dignity. The proper to schooling is now not ample to strengthen an infant until or unless his/her right to meals is fulfilled.

The safety of a baby and his rights from starvation has to be a serious subject of the state intervention. The right to food to alleviate hunger and malnourishment is an pressing issue in the contemporary world. Children have been the biggest victims of bad monetary prerequisites of a family when it is not possible to develop physical and intellectual competencies in the condition of hunger and malnutrition. International groups along with civil society agencies have raised countless relevant questions to supply meals protection to all the poor families. The meals protection for all adolescents coming from the poor monetary historical past ought to be the duty of the state. In 1989, the United Nations has focussed on social improvement of the youth and India is one of them.

Furthermore, in the Universal Declaration of Human Rights, it has been proclaimed by the United Nations that childhood is entitled to special care and assistance. The UNO has also recognized that the child should grow up in a family environment, in an atmosphere of love, happiness, and understanding for the full and harmonious development of his or her personality. The provisions intended in the Convention on the Rights of the Child and UN's declarations of human rights have enough ground to force the authorities of the state to adopt such policies and programs through which could provide the healthy environment could be provided to a child.

However, historically, school Meal arrived in 1906 when the Liberal reforms began with an attack on the health problems, which had been so frankly shown up by the Boer War[18]. There was a common belief at the turn of the century that the people of Britain were suffering a physical decline. Only a rigorous campaign of "national efficiency" could restore the strength of the nation and this had to start in the schools. The first social reform to be undertaken by the Liberals was concerned with children. This rigorous campaign included its demands for the provision of school meals for the children who were malnourished, disadvantaged and underprivileged.

In the first decade of Independent India, the number of illiterates and children out of school continued to grow despite higher enrolments, while drop-out rates of those enrolled also remained high. From the late 1980s, there was a new interest among state functionaries in primary education. A number of new and varied programmes were started in every planning period. The stated aims were to increase literacy levels in different age groups and sections, stimulate parents to send children to school, and involve the community in primary and non-formal education.

National Initiatives:

In India, social policies can be divided into procedures and measures which all citizens and citizen-workers can avail of. The responsibility of childcare primarily on women and though less than seven % of employed women are in the structured formal sector which is related to the first summary of the regulations. Then we find those appliances which are directed at workers in the unstructured sector and finally to procedures which are not secured to the work position of citizens. It is important to note at the beginning that despite concerns being expressed over the rights of women and women workers, childcare

[18] Boer War (two wars: the first when the Boers fought England in order to regain the independence they had given up to obtain British help against the Zulus (1880-1881); the second when the Orange Free State and Transvaal declared war on Britain (1899-1902).

has been accepted as a legitimate concern of the state not in terms of the labor of care or as women's rights but as a matter of child welfare and concerns regarding the nutrition, persistence, and well-being of children. Similarly, pre-schools which tie in with care practices have been planned in terms of child development and success in elementary education. In both, the poor quality of care provided by mothers often seems a theme but the issue of care time and the care burden is mostly absent.

This MDM programme has also been helpful in creating employment among women of the unprivileged classes. The ideology of this programme has also been an initiation for the better provision of primary education to the unprivileged children and has also been an executed weapon for promoting gender equality. This scheme has helped in improving attendance of youth to schools and performed a key function in imparting education.

The World Health Organization has estimated that in the year 2012, out of the 6.5 million deaths reported worldwide in the under-five year age group, around 2.4 million were from India alone. All these nutrition-related indices clearly reflect that the nutritional status of under-five children is still bad and needs concerted efforts from the policymakers and the healthcare professionals in the country.

The IVRS (Interactive Voice Response System) to reveal the everyday execution of the MDMS used to be showcased this year during the National Conference on ICT in School Education. There are two current interventions viz Tithi Bhojan and Social Audit designed to entice community participation and channelize it for the improvement of the MDMS. The Central Government has requested the States to reflect on consideration on the concept of Tithi Bhojan for mid-day foods in a suitable manner, to encourage local community participation in the programme. Social Audit, some other intervention below this Scheme capability is a system in which people collectively screen and consider the planning and implementation of the Scheme. It is considered as an on-going process of public vigilance. Bihar,

Karnataka, Maharashtra, Odisha, and Punjab have achieved Social Audit. Social Audit is under progress in Madhya Pradesh, Rajasthan, and Uttar Pradesh and Tamil Nadu.

The Central Government notified 'MDM Rules, 2015' on September 30th, 2015. The Rules inter alia provide for temporary utilization of other funds available with the school for MDM in case school exhausts MDM funds for any reason; food security allowance to be paid to beneficiaries in case of non-supply of meals for specified reasons; and monthly testing of meals on a random basis by accredited Labs to check its quality. These rules and their effective compliance by implementing agencies in the States will ensure better regularity in serving MDMs in schools. In the year 2015-16 children covered under the scheme are 9.60 crores; foodgrain allocated is 27.74 lakh MTs; projected demand is 11067.18 crores; budget estimates are 9236.40 crores and up to the first quarter of 2015-16 budget released is 6301.41 crores. Today, with more than 100 million children covered, India's MDM programme is by far the largest nutrition programme in the world. Above 200 million suffer from hunger, the 2008 Global Hunger Index ranks India 66 out of 88 countries.

Global Initiatives For Child Right (Health):

Initiatives of the United Nations Children's Emergency Fund (UNICEF)[19]:

UNICEF's overarching goal is to engage all relevant actors in the community, nationally and around the world – to unite to deliver the best possible results for children and women. From the household to the government head, many decisions are made each day that impact health. Among the most powerful strategies

[19] http://www.un-ngls.org/orf/documents/publications.en/ngls.handbook/a20unicef.html, visited on 18.03.2016, time: 11:05 pm.

available to influence public health and guide action is measuring health status. All health decision makers require reliable 'information for action.' UNICEF has committed to investing more in-depth country analysis with a particular focus on the health-related MDGs. UNICEF has also committed to supporting Multiple Indicator Cluster surveys every 3 years and to coordinating closely with DHS surveys so that the majority of the developing world continues to have access to nationally representative data every 3 years.

With its headquarters in New York, UNICEF works through eight regional offices and 125 country offices worldwide. It also has a research center in Florence (Italy), a supply operation based in Copenhagen (Denmark) and offices in Tokyo (Japan) and Brussels (Belgium). In 1998, it had nearly 6,000 personnel posts worldwide, 86% of them in the field. Country offices headed by UNICEF representatives are the key operational points for programming, support, and advocacy. They help relevant ministries and institutions conduct situation analyses on the well-being of children and women and pinpoint areas where their rights are not being realized. The offices then work with the government to implement and evaluate programmes of cooperation, often in collaboration with other UN agencies, civil society organizations, and communities.

The organization's work is further assisted by 37 National Committees for UNICEF, which raises awareness of children's rights issues to assist UNICEF in fundraising. UNICEF also benefits from its partnership with 179 Goodwill Ambassadors and celebrity supporters, who lend their time and talent to raise the organization's profile and influence global policy on behalf of children and women. UNICEF-assisted programmes combine interventions for children's health and nutrition, early education, healthful and sanitary environments and overall psychological and social well-being at the global level.

Article 71 of the United Nations Charter grants international non-governmental organizations Consultative Status to the United Nations and its specialized agencies. Currently, 191 international NGOs have Consultative Status with UNICEF. In addition to interacting with the UNICEF secretariat, Consultative Status enables CSOs to present their views to the UNICEF Executive Board

Initiatives of the World Health Organization (WHO)[20]:

Since 1948 many things have changed in the world of global health, in particular, a large number of new initiatives and institutions created that challenge WHO's role as a directing and coordinating authority. Examples include the entry of the World Bank into health sector lending on a large scale in the 1980s, the creation of new organizations such as UNAIDS, the GAVI Alliance (formerly the Global Alliance for Vaccines and Immunization), the Global Fund to Fight AIDS, Tuberculosis, and Malaria (The Global Fund) and UNITAID, developed to tackle specific disease problems; and new public-private partnerships for product development such as the Medicines for Malaria Venture or Drugs for Neglected Diseases initiative (2016). Yet, WHO's role in public health remains significant.

The constitution of WHO is notable for the scope and breadth of the agenda it lays out for the organization. Health is described as 'a state of complete physical, mental and social well-being and not merely the absence of disease or infirmity' and the enjoyment of the highest attainable standard of health as a fundamental human right. Governments have a responsibility to provide 'adequate health and social measures'. The constitution sets out 22 functions

[20] http://www.who.int/library/collections/historical/en/, visited on 18.03.2016, time: 11:05 pm.

for WHO, which cover almost every conceivable activity linked to the promotion of health.

WHO proposed new guidance and promoted cooperation between developed and developing countries on emerging health issues of global importance. The IHR (International Health Regulations) (2005) required countries to develop appropriate surveillance and response capacities to address these health concerns. All of these issues will require enhanced U.S. collaboration with other countries to protect and promote better health for all.

Universal health coverage is a new strategic priority for WHO. This combines two fundamental components: access to the services (promotion, prevention, treatment, and rehabilitation) needed to achieve good health; with financial protection that prevents ill-health from leading to poverty. Universal health coverage is important from a health governance perspective in two ways. At the country level, it represents a goal that is relevant to all countries as they seek to strengthen or reform their health systems. Also, in the debate about how to position health in the post-2015 agenda, it offers the potential to be a unifying goal, combining concerns about finishing the work on the current Millennium Development Goals, while at the same time accommodating the need to address non-communicable diseases and other causes of ill health.

At a global scale, the work WHO conducts is different from that of national and regional public health bodies. One of the best purposes of WHO is to monitor diseases throughout the world. This is essential not only as part of its mandate but also for the measurement of performance with regard to how well the MDGs are being met. The work WHO conducts is multidimensional, and while concentrating on mapping global health trends and disease eradication, it is probably the best-placed organization to ensure that the poorest countries receive the support they need. Another key role of WHO is to provide a body of technical expertise through the production, dissemination, and implementation of evidence-based guidelines. This is especially important because, in a globalizing world, it is becoming increasingly clear that national health policy measures may not be as effective as they once were.

History of School Lunch/School Meal/MDM in Global Perspective:

Every day more than 66 million children go to school hungry and, in many countries, fewer girls attend school than boys. Research shows that providing in-school meals, mid-morning snacks, and take-home rations through school feeding programs can alleviate short-term hunger, increase children's abilities to concentrate, learn, perform specific tasks, and has been linked to an increase in the enrolment of girls. These effects seem to be greater among children who are also chronically undernourished, usually the poorest children.

Low-income countries are expanding school feeding, because these programs help push them closer to reaching the Millennium Development Goals (MDGs) by drawing more children, especially young girls, into the classroom. To counter the challenges due to the changing scenarios such as demographic and epidemiological transition, urbanization, climate change, food insecurity, financial crisis, etc. health promotion has emerged as an important tool; nevertheless, the need for newer, innovative approaches cannot be understated. The child health scenario was still bad at the turm of the nineteenth-century. At that time, statisticians pointed out that during the horrors of the Industrial Revolution, the health of some people and particularly children was no healthier.

School feeding programs are increasingly being viewed as a potential safety net and as a social support measure that helps keep children in school. Challenges for school feeding programs can range from their high operational costs to the need to build the capacity to procure food locally. In order for a country to have an effective school feeding program that focuses their resources on the neediest children, countries must determine if school feeding is the most effective social safety net option. They should set program objectives and predicted outcomes, and determine administrative costs. They need to establish a system of effective targeting and select the type of food to be provided in school, explore opportunities for local procurement and the feasibility of offering take-home rations through the program. They must plan for school-level management, implementation, and monitoring of the ongoing school feeding activities and determine if complementary health and nutrition activities such as de-worming, supplementation, or fortification can be incorporated into the program to achieve additional benefits.

Comparative Analysis of School Meal Scheme:

i. United Kingdom Europe:

The First School meals were provided from the mid-nineteenth century and expanded after the 1870 Education Act, during rising concerns about undernourished children. (Gillard , 2003) (2016).[21] In 1904, a Parliamentary committee reported that poor physique of volunteers in the Boer War was a result of underfed children and by 1920 one million children were taking school meals across Britain. However, it was not until 1941 that a National School Meals policy was introduced and the first nutritional standards

---

[21] Gillard D (2003) "*Food for Thought: child nutrition, the school dinner and the food industry*" www.educationengland.org.uk/articles/22food.html, visited on 18.03.2016, Time: 10:58 pm.

for school meals were set. These laid down levels of protein, fat, and calories which should be provided by a school meal. Shortly after, the Education Act (1944) made it a duty of all Local Education Authorities (LEAs) to provide school meals for those who wanted them, and from 1947, the full net cost of school meals was met by the Government. Although the principle of a standard charge for the school meal was introduced in 1950, full financial responsibility for the school meal service was passed to LEAs in 1967. The cost of a school meal continued to rise and was 12 pence in 1971. (Evans & Harpert, 2009)[22]

The standards for school meals were updated several times. In 1955, a circular stated that school dinners must take into account the possibility of deficiencies in a child's home diet (Ministry of Education Northern Ireland, 1955). In 1966, the standards set out by the Department of Education stated that the average meal should contain 29 g of protein, 880 kcal and 32 g of fat (Department of Education and Science, 1966). These nutrient levels were the standards set for children of 12 years of age and were reduced accordingly for primary school children. The last update to these original standards was made in 1975 when some food-based (e.g. fresh meat should be served 3 days a week) standards were introduced.

In 1986, the Social Security Act limited the right to free school meals to those children whose parents received supplementary benefit. Two years later, the Local Government Act (1988) introduced Compulsory Competitive Tendering, obliging all LEAs to put school meals services out to tender. The guiding principle was the 'lowest bid wins', and this put economy above quality in the provision of the service. Local Authority providers

---

[22] C. E. L. Evans* & C. E. Harpert (2009), "A history and review of school meal standards in the UK", Journal of Human Nutrition and Dietetics, Hum Nutr Diet, 22, pp. 89–99.

who won contracts were defined as Direct Service Organizations and private sector companies entered the market. In effect, an unregulated school meals market had been created (School Meals Review Panel, 2005). In 1998, the principle of 'best value' replaced Compulsory Competitive Tendering for public service procurement and, as a result, decisions about school meal provisions were increasingly driven by finance (School Meals Review Panel, 2005). Concern about the nature of school meal provisions grew..

The model was replicated in many in European Counties. The lunch pack include at least one portion of fruit and one portion of vegetables (a handful, raw or cooked), a portion of starchy food (e.g. bread roll, pitta bread, tortilla wrap, pasta, rice), whole grain varieties when possible, a portion of dairy food (e.g. semi-skimmed milk, cheese, yoghurt), a portion of protein food like meat, fish, eggs, or pulses, a drink of water, fruit juice, or semi-skimmed milk, some snack unsalted nuts, fresh or dried fruit, or chopped vegetables with cheese or a small packet of crisps or fruit-based cakes and bars can be included from time to time for variety and appeal.

Many countries in Europe have programmes to help schools provide nutritionally balanced meals which also reflect the general eating culture of each nation. Often, lunch is eaten in a cafeteria-like setting where children receive food from a central service point (e.g. Scandinavian Countries). In Finland and Sweden, where all school meals are fully funded by the government, lunches follow national dietary guidelines including the 'plate model'. An example meal is presented to guide children's self-service.

School meal standards introduced again in each part of the UK (England, Scotland, Wales and Northern Ireland) has developed nutrient-based standards or guidelines for school meals independently (see Table 1 for nutrient-based standards). A description of the process taken for each country is described below. (Fifth Review Mission Uttar Pradesh , 2013-2014)

Country	England	Scotland	Wales	
Proposed or final nutrient-based standards	Final	Final	Proposed	
Introduction date*	September 2008	September 2009	August 2008	August 2008

Nutrient	Max or Min	Primary	Secondary	Primary	Secondary	Primary	Secondary
Energy kJ (Kcal)		**2220 (530) ± 5% (26.5)**	**2770 (646) ± 5% (32.3)**	**2330 (557)**	**2780 (664)**	**2220 (530)**	**2700 (646)**
Carbohydrate (g)	Min	70.6	86.1	74.3	88.5	70.6	86.1
NMEs (g)	Max	15.5	18.9	16.3	19.5	15.5	18.9
Fat (g)	Max	20.6	25.1	21.7	25.8	20.6	25.1
Saturated fat (g)	Max	6.5	7.9	6.8	8.1	6.5	7.9
Protein (g)	Min	7.5	13.3	8.5	13.6	7.5	13.3
Fibre (g)	Min	4.2	5.2	4.5	5.3	4.2	5.2
Sodium (mg)	Max	499	714	745 (686)	894 (824)	499	714
Vitamin A (lg)	Min	175	245	150	187	175	245
Vitamin C (mg)	Min	10.5	14.0	9	11	10.5	14.0
Folate (lg)	Min	53	70	45	60	53	70
Calcium (mg)	Min	193	350	165	300	193	350
Iron (mg)	Min	3.0	5.2	3	4.4	3.0	5.2
Zinc (mg)	Min	2.5	3.3	2.1	2.8	2.5	3.3

*Nutrient-based standards may be introduced prior to this date.

Nutrient-based standards are different for single-sex secondary schools.

Not more than 38% of the Scientific Advisory Committee Nutrition (SACN) recommendation, and (by 2010) not more than 35% of the SACN recommendation.

Source: C. E. L. Evans & C. E. Harper (2009), "A history and review of school meal standards in the UK", Journal of Human Nutrition and Dietetics. The British Dietetic Association Ltd 2009 J Hum Nutr Diet, 22, pp. 89–99

In France, each school lunch has to include a main dish (based on meat, fish, eggs, offal or cheese), a side dish, a dairy product and either a starter or dessert. The nutritional standards regulate how frequently dishes are served in a 20 meal cycle. Portion sizes are set by dish and age group. Some European Countries like Norway, Denmark, the Netherlands, and Belgium do not have a compulsory system of school meals.

ii. United States (Poppendieck, 2010):[23]

School meals began in the U. S. during the Progressive Era, roughly the period from 1890 until World War I. In 1990, these early programs were purely local efforts, usually initiated by women's organizations or charitable groups outside the school system. Private charities and local school boards provide funding for school lunches in some locations in response to concern over the learning abilities of malnourished students. As compulsory school attendance laws brought large numbers of very poor children into the elementary schools, educators and social reformers became convinced that they were too hungry to concentrate on their lessons. At the same time, the activists of the school hygiene movement became concerned about the nutritional quality and safety of foods sold to children by street vendors, concessionaires, and school janitors. They urged the

[23] Poppendieck, Janet (2010), "*Free for all: Fixing School Food in America*", University of Cal ifornia Press, Berkeley os Angeles London, isbn 978-0-520-24370-5

establishment of lunchrooms under the direction of home economics teachers or dietitians that would provide safe, healthy meals and teach students the basics of the emerging science of nutrition.

Together, the two groups of reformers were able to start school lunch programs in most of the nation's largest cities; often they succeeded in persuading the school board or municipal government to take over their operations. There was no movement for federal participation in such efforts, however. Schools were a local matter; federal involvement in school food would have to await the Great Depression of the 1930s. (Poppendieck 2010: 47)Since 1930s locally organized school lunch programs receive Federal loans and agricultural surpluses. In 1935, The Works Progress Administration (WPA) provides labor to schools for cooking and serving lunches. Emergency relief was supplanted by work relief, and the creation of the Works Progress Administration (WPA) added a new actor to the school food mix. School lunch projects provided an ideal solution. There were schools in every community, the projects required very little capital investment, and women were assumed to have cooking skills. School lunch work projects were established in every state and gave useful work to more than sixty-four thousand persons; soon they were serving more than two million school lunches a day. In 1936, USDA becomes authorized to purchase surplus farm commodities and distribute them to local school lunch programs.

National School Lunch Act (NSLA) was enacted in 1946. This Act established the National School Lunch Programme (NSLP) which includes the special requirements like meals must meet minimum nutritional standards, lunches must be available to low-income students at no cost or reduced price without discrimination, Program must be nonprofit, School lunch must use surplus commodities to the extent practical, Schools must report expenditures and receipts to State educational agencies.

The Child Nutrition Act (CNA) was enacted in 1966. The Act stated that combine school food service programs from other agencies into one program under USDA, funding a 2-year pilot project of a school breakfast program, funding a foodservice equipment assistance program, providing additional funds for schools serving low-income students, including equipment and administrative costs. Concern over hunger in America increased political support for school meal programs. CNA was amended to create the Summer Food Service Program and the Child and Adult Care Food Program, to fund State administrative expenses, and to extend program authority for the School Breakfast Program to 1971.

During the decade of 1980, Omnibus Budget Reconciliation Acts of 1980 and 1981 were enacted. The Acts had important articles to improve transparency in school lunch program that reduce reimbursement rates for reduced-price and paid lunch, introduce verification procedures, reduce the cash value for commodities, provide for a revision of income-eligibility guidelines, raise income limit for free lunches from 125 to 130 % of poverty and lower limit for reduced price from 195 to 185 % of poverty, terminate assistance for foodservice equipment and reduce the appropriations for nutrition education and training grants.

In 1993, School Nutrition Dietary Assessment (SNDA) was done to see how work school meals generally meet the nutritional needs of children and found that school lunches do not meet the dietary guidelines for fat and saturated fat as a percentage of calories. Healthy Meals for Healthy Americans Act requires school lunches to conform to the *Dietary Guidelines* by 1996 and requires that commodities account for at least 12% of total assistance. USDA launched the School Meals initiative for Healthy Children to implement changes in meal requirement regulations and support improvements in the nutritional content of school lunches through technical assistance, nutritional improvement in commodity donations, and an alternative nutrient-based meal planning system. The Healthy Meals for Children Act added a menu-planning option that allowed for more fruits, vegetables, and grains and provides schools with more flexibility in meeting nutrition standards with regard to the use of commodity provisions.

In 2001, Results from the 1998-99 SNDA II found that the average fat content of school lunches fell from 39 to 35% of calories but still did not meet the 1995 Dietary Guidelines 2002 Nutrition Title of 2002 Farm Act provided $6 million for the Fruit and Vegetable Pilot Program to provide free fresh and dried fruits and fresh vegetables to designated schools in four states. Fifty million dollars is allocated for fresh produce for school meals through the Department of Defence.

The Child Nutrition & WIC Reauthorization Act was enacted in 2004. The Act provided some provisions that expanded the certification period to one year, aligning law with common practice, requiring direct certification to be phased in as a required part of certification process, requiring schools to conduct hazard analysis and Critical Control Point plans for food safety in meal production, and increases food safety inspections from once to twice annually, Authorizing Fresh Fruit and Vegetable Pilot as a permanent program and expands to new States and Indian Tribal Organizations, requiring school food authorities to develop wellness plans specifying nutritional standards for all foods in schools and goals for physical fitness of students.

In 2005, Release of Dietary Guidelines for Americans had implications for school meal requirements. New guidelines recommended different calorie limits for different levels of activity and recommended fat intake between 25% and 35 % of calories, rather than below 30 %. Agriculture, Rural Development, Food, and Drug Administration and Related Agencies Appropriations Act of 2006 further expanded the Fresh Fruit and Vegetable Program to a total of 375 schools in 14 States and 3 Indian

Tribal Organizations. 2007 Results from the 2004-05 SNDA III found that less than one-third of schools served lunches containing at most 30 % of calories from fat and less than 10 % of calories from saturated fat.

In Africa[24]

In 2003, the New Partnership for Africa's Development (NEPAD), together with the United Nations World Food Programme (WFP) and the Millennium Hunger Task Force, launched a pilot Home Grown School Feeding and Health Programme (HGSFHP) in twelve countries. So far, Côte d'Ivoire, Ghana, Kenya, Mali, and Nigeria are already implementing the programmes. HGSF (Home Grown School Feeding) is truly demand-driven from Africa, with many international locations repeatedly asking for support from development partners. To assist the transition from externally-driven college feeding to HGSF, the Partnership for Child Development (PCD) has launched a new programme, "PCD HGSF programme" that Government aid to deliver sustainable, nationally-owned faculty feeding programmes sourced from nearby farmers in sub-Saharan Africa. The PCD HGSF programme, supported in phase by the Bill and Melinda Gates Foundation, is offering direct, evidence-based and context-specific support, and expertise for the format and administration of school feeding programmes linked to nearby agricultural production.

The State of Osun School Feeding Programme (O'Meals) was once initiated as a pilot programme by the Federal Government in 2006. O'Meals had step by step grown to serve 1,382 public schools with over 190,000 students in all the 31 LGAs in the state of Osun. As an approach to banish hunger by using growing meals production, family incomes and food protection in disadvantaged

---

[24] Report (2012), "*Elementary School Feedingand Health Programme Transition strategy*", hgsf-global.org/.../252-elementary-school-feeding-and-health-programm... visited on 18.03.2016, Time: 11:35 pm

communities, the O'Meals programme emerged as famous. The O'Meals is carried out in all the 31 LGAs in the kingdom of Osun except any National monetary support. Coordination and implementation are undertaken with the aid of the O'Meals Secretariat, with programme oversight provided through the Ministry of Education (MOE). Technical help is furnished through the Programme Steering Committee, although a variety of Non-Governmental Organisations (NGOs) and bilateral organizations are also involved with technical support. The O'Meals programme had loved a range of achievements in education, health, and institutional capacity building, however, except superb monitoring and impact assessment the extent of these achievements has now not been quantified.

In April 2012, the Government of the State of Osun in Nigeria pioneered a statewide college ingredients programme for all elementary school students in public schools. The meals programme recognized as the O'Meals programme (an acronym for the Osun Elementary School Feeding and Health Programme), gives lunch to 254,000 adolescents in a whole of 1,375 Elementary Schools across the State of Osun. In addition to staples such as rice, beans, yam served with stews, soups, and vegetables, the programme contained every day fruits on the menu.

The programme is presently being applied to the use of a whole variety of 3,007 educated meals vendors/cooks. All meals objects are sourced domestically from farmers and others in the grant chain, bettering the employment degree inside the State. Addressing youth malnutrition has raised their academic performance and has increased the school enrollment making Osun the best possible model for school meals. It enforced student's enrolment in Nigeria to 80%.

In East Asia:

There are two developed countries China and Japan where school lunch program play a key role in the development of these countries. In China, health, education and nutrition support and enhance each other. For instance, healthy nutritional status improves educational potential by positively affecting attention span, learning capacity and ability to engage fully in educational experiences. Undernourishment in early childhood can negatively influence school aptitudes, time of school enrolment, school attendance and concentration (WHO, 1996). Schools are ideal settings for nutrition programmes and services, because nutrition and education are closely linked, and because dietary, hygienic and exercise habits that affect nutritional status are formed during the school-age years (WHO/FAO, 1998). The World Health Organization (WHO) and Food and Agriculture Organization (FAO) are collaborating in promoting and strengthening school-based nutrition interventions in developing countries. A project in China illustrates the approach the two organizations are advocating. (P. Glasauer, C. Aldinger, Yusen - Hai, Xia Shi-Chang and Tang Shu-Ming, 2003: 27)

The Government of China and WHO had collaborated to establish health promoting schools (HPS) in 1995. This called for collaboration among health and education officials, teachers, students, parents and community leaders to foster health and learning through improvements in school environments, policies and practices (WHO/FAO, 1998). In 1999, the Chinese Ministries of Health and Education requested assistance in the development of HPS with a focus on nutrition. WHO entrusted the Education Development Center (EDC) with the task of providing technical assistance in the field of health promotion in schools. FAO joined the initiative, providing technical expertise in the field of school-based nutrition education and, alongside EDC, advice on project planning, implementation and evaluation.

In Japan, The earliest Japanese school lunch program was initiated in a school in Yamagata prefecture in 1889. The monks who built the local school began offering rice balls, grilled fish, and pickles to children from poor families. This idea spread across the country, though it was temporarily suspended during the food shortages of World War II (WWII). It was reinstated in December of 1947 with the aid by Licensed Agency for Relief in Asia (LARA), United Nation's International Children Energy Fund (UNICEF), and other organizations. Through their activities, approximately 2.9 million children benefited from school lunch programs in 1947. The School Lunch Act was enacted in 1954, officially making school lunch as a part of education system in Japan with the aim to enrich school life and promoting a spirit of cooperation by instilling proper dietary habits and its knowledge. Later, this system expanded to all the Compulsory Education Schools in 1956. Following the World War II, bread was the staple food of school lunch over two decades. After which, they officially introduced rice in school lunch in 1976.

They aimed to foster ideal dietary habits among school children by introducing rice in school lunch, as rice is basic traditional food in Japan. Besides, there was increasing effort to incorporate locally produced ingredients into school lunch. The use of local ingredients would ensure freshness and also play a vital role in food education fostering the sense of links with the local community and appreciation for foods. Under this movement, they came to recognize the importance of rice, rather than bread from western diets. Nowadays, rice is served around three times a week in school lunch. (Nobuko Tanaka RD, Miki Miyoshi RD MPhil 2011: 155)

Japanese school lunch program aimed to promote healthy mental and physical development of school children, and to contribute to the improvement of their dietary habits by providing balanced meals. Not only serving nutritional food, but school lunch program also serves as an important educational method for school children to acquire proper dietary habits and its knowledge, and a sense of gratitude in children. School children are responsible for arranging and cleaning the tables and serving meals in their classrooms. They could also learn proper mealtime greetings and manners, by having meals together with classmates. Furthermore, understanding of balanced nutrition, food culture, and history was to be enhanced through learning the menu of each meal. (Nobuko Tanaka RD, Miki Miyoshi RD MPhil 2011: 155)

On May 2009, over 10 million school children in 32,400 schools (94.3% of all elementary schools, junior high schools, special needs schools, and evening high schools in Japan) participated in the school lunch program, according to the Ministry of Education, Culture, Sports, Science and Technology (MEXT)[25]. (Nobuko Tanaka RD, Miki Miyoshi RD MPhil 2011: 155)

India: National And State Level Initiatives

India is one of the South Asian countries where MDM/School Meal is implemented. It is the cooperative mission of the central government and the state governments of India and they are running schools to provide free education and MDM. Still many children do not attend primary and secondary schools, particularly from the deprived sections of society. School meal programmes facilitates wealthy nutrition to children and has been incentive to families belonging to deprived and poor section of society to send children to school. It is the socio-economic relief to those families by the Government.

In the Indian context, the constitution made special Acts for the care, protection, and prevention of the exploitation of children.

[25] Nobuko Tanaka RD, Miki Miyoshi RD MPhil (2011), "School lunch program for health promotion among children in Japan", Asia Pac J Clin Nutr 2012;21 (1):155-158

Article 24 described infant labor that prohibits employment of children below the age of 14 years in any factory or mine or in any different hazardous employment. The Directive Principles of state policy in the constitution, Article 39 said that the tender age of the children is not abused and the citizen is no longer pressured by way of economic necessity to enter avocations unsuited to their age and strength that youth are given possibilities and services. Article 45 ensured that the state shall endeavor to grant free and compulsory schooling for youngsters up to the age of 14 years.

Regarding the improvement of adolescents, MDMS is being applied in some states of the country including Uttar Pradesh considering that August 1995. It is at first began in 2408 blocks in the country and in 1997-98 the NP-NSPE used to be delivered in all blocks of the country (2014)[26]". NP-NSPE states that it aims to tackle "classroom hunger" and to attend school usually and assist them to pay attention to school room activities.

The Supreme Court of India handed an order on 28 November 2001 and directing all state governments to put into effect the MDM Very few states, however, brought cooked ingredients in primary schools earlier than the Supreme Court's initial deadline of February 28, 2002. The primary schools are taking initiative with reference to this order, several states of the Union have provided for MDMs at different tiers of education, protecting a large populace of children.

The thought of School meal is no longer new at the National level as its roots can be traced again to a pre-independence generation when British administration initiated a School Meal Programme for deprived teenagers in Madras Municipal Corporation in 1925. During the British rule in India, the School Meal was introduced for disadvantaged and underprivileged youngsters (children of poor socio-economic status) in Madras Municipal Corporation.

---

[26] Accessed 24 Jan. 2014, 8:17 pm URL :http//:mdm.nic.in/aboutus.html

Tamil Nadu had launched a cooked MDMS in the Nineteen Fifties and multiplied it significantly in 1982. MDM programme used to be at the beginning brought in rural areas for pre-school teens in the ageing group of 2-5 years and for foremost school adolescents in the age group of 5-9 years. Consequently, this scheme was extended to city areas in September of 1982. Old age pensioners had been included under the scheme from January 1983. From September 1984, the scheme included school students of 10-15 years of age. With impact from December 1995, pregnant female has been introduced under the scheme.

Gujarat was the second state in the country where have MDMS got introduced in 1980. This Scheme was added in the state of Kerala in 1984 in the Primary Schools functioning in 222 Villages, having fishermen as the majority. During 1985, the scheme used to be prolonged to all Primary schools (Std. I to IV). The scheme was extended to all Primary Schools (std. V to VII) at some point of 87-88. Besides this, the state of Kerala, and some pockets of Madhya Pradesh and Orissa, commenced offering cooked ingredients in 1995. In the mid-1980s, three States viz. Gujarat, Kerala and Tamil Nadu and the UT of Pondicherry had universalized a cooked MDM Programme with their own sources for adolescents analyzing at the predominant stage and in 1990-91 the variety of States enforcing the MDM programme with their very own assets on a well-known or a giant scale had expanded to twelve states (SWNMP Department, Secretariat, Chennai, 2012)[27]

---

[27] SWNMP Department, Secretariat, Chennai, Letter No19869/ NMP.1/2012-4 Dated : 18.04.2012

The Parliamentary Debate for implementation of MDMS (1995):[28]

Parliament bring laws of legislation has a fundamental role to play in promoting policies, programmes, and good governance. As the democratically elected representatives of the people, parliaments have greater accountabilities for people's welfare. In the overall performance of their key features of the legislation, representation and oversight parliaments can actively engage in the development of laws, policies, and practices that promote democracy and good governance.

Nowadays, the function of Parliaments around the world has transformed drastically over the years. It is not great confined to enacting laws. Parliaments are now multi-functional institutions. The Indian Parliament is an expression of the trust that the people of India have in democracy. Any hassle or problem is solved through the participation by way of human beings in the decision-making manner who is the consultant of public and authorities by consent. The features of Parliament performe the roles of emerging executive accountability, lawmaking, and managing over the Budget, representational role, academic role, informational functions, training and recruitment of leadership etc.

Mid-Day Meal scheme is also a logical outcome of the long crucial debates in parliament over child right, health and education. Kumari Selja guaranteed that under this new scheme are going to supply in the subsequent three years no longer cooked meal or pre-cooked meal to all the adolescents in the important schools all over the country. She said that in 1995-96, about 2,368 Employment Assurance Schemes under the revamped PDS blocks and forty low female literacy blocks in the State of Punjab and primary schools in notified city slums in Goa were covered. In

---

[28] Lok Sabha Debate 1995.

1996-97, Delhi, Pondicherry, and Chandigarh will be included with all the different nearby illiteracy blocks which come to the fig. of 2,005. By 1997-98, all the other primary schools in the country which numbered 828 blocks and 3000 odd Nagar Palika will be blanketed under the subsequent three years.

It was also expected to have an impact on the nutrition of the students. The purpose of these tactics was the smooth functioning of this scheme. Panchayats, women groups, village education committees, ward committees or Gram Sabhas on the local level were involved in this scheme so that no complaints are received. That is why community participation was needed in the programme to make it successful.

The authorities of Tamil Nadu has not been implementing the MDMS for last 20 years. The question was raised whether or not the funds will be furnished to the State government or the Centre will at once enforce the scheme. The Tamil Nadu government is implementing this scheme efficaciously with the aid of no longer only providing noon meal however additionally nutritious meal via offering egg and nutrition content foods. According to the populace ratio, at least 10% of the funds have to be supplied to the Tamil Nadu Government.

During that session, it was proposed that F.C.I. Food Corporation of India will be paid immediately to furnish meals at the price of one hundred grams per day per child. The Central Government will also furnish assistance for lifting these grains from the nearest FCI store to the school and that will be at the rate of Rs. 25 per quintal which is the standard. Labor charges for cooking the food will also pay and this will be done under rural development schemes like the Jawahar Rozgar Yojna and Urban Area programmes etc. This was the way it was proposed to be implemented it from the Centre. If the State Government wants to provide anything additional they had to do it on their own and this was going to be the uniform pattern all over the country which we are going to provide.

It was the further stated that the Scheme named as Anganwadi, under I.C.D.S provided meals items like gram, porridge etc. In this regard, complaints were received that the children were not given their share and if they were given at all it was in a very less quantity. Therefore this problem was addressed in that session and the concerned authority was required to go through the I.C.D. scheme under which children are given some help and to remove all the drawbacks in it.

The data was presentd that showed World Bank was providing a credit of approximately Rs. 800 crores spread over years for implementing the District Primary Education Programme in 23 districts of six states namely Assam, Haryana, Maharashtra, Tamil Nadu, Karnataka, and Kerala. A similar credit of approximately Rs. 728 crores were provided for implementation of Uttar Pradesh Basic Education Project covering 10 districts in Uttar Pradesh. World Bank funds are made available on a reimbursement basis. Implementation of the District Primary Education Programme commenced only in December 1994. Under the Uttar Pradesh Basic Education Project Rs. 3839 crores were reimbursed by the World Bank against 1994-95 expenditures. The District Primary Education Programmes was launched in December 1994. All arrangements were in place to monitor the programme. The programme has commenced well Detailed financial and administrative guidelines for the programme were drawn up and circulated to all the states periodic reviews of the Uttar Pradesh Basic Education Project have said nice development in implementation.

The names of the Regions of Uttar Pradesh where primary schools were proposed to be opened with the World Bank assistance indicating the number of such schools are:

S. No.	District	No. of Primary Schools
1.	Gorakhpur	262
2.	Varanasi	163
3.	Allahabad	327
4.	Banda	152
5.	Sitapur	386
6.	Etawah	251
7.	Aligarh	171
8.	Saharanpur	102
9.	Pauri Garhwal	113
10.	Nainital	125
	Total	**2052**

Source: Lok Sabha Debate 1995.

This scheme was applied in 171 blocks of Maharashtra all through 1995-96. At present, only 2368 blocks were protected under this scheme during 1995-96 in the whole country, in the same way, 2008 blocks covered underneath the scheme during 1996-97 and in the year 1997-98, all blocks of us of a will be blanketed under this scheme.

The State as properly as Union Government's share in the expenditure probable to be incurred on the recently launched scheme for providing MDM to children. It has been published that this programme has been implemented in all the States however it has not been implemented in any of the 18 districts of Jharkhand location in Bihar.

The authorities of India give trucks for transportation of food grains. The Rural Development Department of Central Government has issued guidelines in the matter of putting up the kitchen. Utensils and Kitchen maids are provided below JRY. Pulses, Oil, nutrients and other things are furnished via the State Government.

There is a provision in the pointers at the district stage it should be headed with the aid of collector, at the State degree by means of Chief Secretary or Additional Secretary or Development

Commissioner and at municipality degree through chairman and for community participation at Panchayat level, vital human beings of each and every village are protected to run this programme in every school under the chairmanship of Sarpanch of the village. It has just been launched and it will take at least two years' time in implementing it in the whole, country. It is doing well in states where it is institutionalized but will take time to pick up in once where it has just been introdued.

In the State of Andhra Pradesh, instead of cooked food, they are presenting rice to the mother and father of the children. The query again raised that when they are going to begin giving cooked meals to the adolescents of the school by way of supplying a prepared dinner and the utensils to the schools. It is for the State Governments to see whether or not the cooked food is being supplied or not. It is under their domain. They can enforce the scheme to supply cooked food.

The Indian Government is giving more than 350 energy of cereal to every boy and girl of the country. So, per month, 3 kilograms of rice or wheat is given. So, it is however natural that the State Government would additionally come ahead with a budget which neccesary allocated to them via the Department of Rural Development. The tips have also been issued in this regard to unique State Governments.

Stale/Union Territory	No of Blocks	Enrolment in classes (IV)	Allocated Qty. o` Foodgrains (In Quintals) (For the period 15.8.95 to 31.10.95	
			Wheat	Rice
1. Andhra Pradesh	155	3017302	-	226297.65
2. Arunachal Pradesh	56	94519	-	7089.02
3. Assam	142	1960708	-	147053.10
4. Bihar	266	2377648	82446.94	95877.19

5. Goa	4	1810	-	135.75
6. Gujarat	131	2330792	65728.33	43818.85
7. Haryana	44	580898	15103.35	15103.35
8. Himachal Pradesh	18	145617	-	10921.28
9. Jammu & Kashmir	44	218675	-	16400.63
10. Karnataka	119	2989893	224241.98	
11. Kerala	21	314576	-	15414.22
12. Madhya Pradesh	297	4061937	146711.32	157933.95
13. Maharashtra	171	3754603	-	281595.65
14. Manipur	22	104969	-	872.68
15. Meghalaya	32	218581	-	16393.58
16. Mizoram	20	77293	-	5797.03
17. Nagaland	28	97335	-	7300.22
18. Orissa	175	1502489	-	-
19. Punjab	37	495599	37169.94	-
20. Rajasthan	172	28118007	210885.53	-
21. Sikkim	8	62122	-	4659.15
22. Tamil Nadu	89	1150745	-	5753.22
23. Tripura	17	359375	-	26953.13
24. Uttar Pradesh	248	2541295	79048.65	111548.90
25. West Bengal	128	1693435	3561.68	123443.33
26. A & N Islands	2	5305	-	397.88
27. Chandigarh	1	64770	485.77	-
28. D & N Havell	1	15694	-	1177.05
29. Daman & Diu	2	7232	-	542.46
30. Delhi		600000	45000.00	-
31. Lakshadweep	4	4744	-	355.80
32. Pondicherry	4	105037	-	5251.33
Total	2458	33766805	910383.52	146951.38

Source: Lok Sabha Debate 1995.

The MDM programme envisages that excluding rice and wheat, the State Government is responsible for other things like pulses, oil etc. The cooked food meal scheme is being implemented in seven States. Pulses and other proteins part is coming, from the States and the States are monitoring this programme. The Central Monitoring Cell gets only' information. Nutritional education is there in the nook and corner of the country, because under the 'Health for All' scheme, all primary health centers and sub-centers are inspecting different schools' to monitor this program.

Judiciary Action:

On 28 November 2001, the Supreme Court of India passed an order directing all state governments to enforce the MDM with a minimum content material of 300 calories and 8- 12 grams of protein, each day of school for a minimum of 200 days ". Very few states, however, introduced cooked meals in primary schools before the Supreme Court's initial deadline of February 28, 2002. The primary schools are taking initiative with reference to this order, several states of the Union have provided for MDMs at different levels of education, covering a large population of children. Along with this, several NGOs and different other organizations also aid this scheme, throughout the nation.

In compliance with the Hon'ble Supreme Court's order dated 28 November 2001 cooked meal is being served to the recipients of MDM from 1st September 2004 in Uttar Pradesh. The food being served has been enriched by raising its protein contents and calorific value from 15th August 2006 and now it must have 450 calories of energy and 12 grams of protein in primary schools. In upper primary schools, it should provide 700 calories and 20 grams of protein. The scheme became applicable in upper primary schools from 17 October 2007 in 695 educationally backward blocks and forest areas of 66 districts. Now, this programme is running in upper primary schools for all blocks of the state. The improved weekly menu has been circulated. The menu provides for such a diet so as to meet the enhanced energy level and protein contents.

Report of Comptroller & Auditor General (CAG) of India on MDM (2015)[29]

The performance audit of the MDMS from 2009-10 to 2013-14 i.e. report no. 36 of 2015, it was found that the actual implementation of this scheme still suffers from various shortcomings and lapses across the board. As a result, the enrolment of children was increased by 38% in private schools but unfortunately, this percentage declined by 5.58% in MDM covered, government and government-aided schools. Audit observed discrepancy in the data relating to the number of children availing MDM as reported in relation to the number of children actually availing MDM during the day of a visit to sampled schools by the monitoring institutions. Through this report, it was also found that in most states adequate numbers of health check-ups of children were not conducted, in the absence of which the impact of MDM Scheme on the nutritional status and required micronutrient supplements of the children could not be ascertained. Cases of financial indiscipline such as the furnishing of incorrect Utilization Certificates, misappropriation of funds, fudging of data to claim the higher cost of food grains were widespread. The monitoring by both the Ministry and States was inadequate.

After releasing the report, it was recommended by auditor that the Ministry should establish a system to capture reliable data on the actual number of children availing MDM to implement the

[29] Report no. 36 (2015), "Performance Audit of MDM Scheme", Comptroller and Auditor General of India, cag.gov.in/sites/default/files/press_release/36of2015.pdf, visited on 21.12.2015, Time: 05:32 pm.

scheme economically and efficiently, rates of cooking cost may be revised in proportion with inflation, to provide meal with nutritional norms and calorific value prescribed under MDM Scheme. The system of inspections must be strengthened to ensure that food grains at fairly average quality, the convergence activities and most importantly the monitoring and inspection mechanisms should be strengthened at all levels to prevent leakages and misappropriations.

Conclusion

In the Indian federal system, when the central government formulates development policies at the central level, it is the state governments or the local bodies that implement as being units of local administration. The state governments are expected to adopt certain development policies that are aimed at ensuring equality of opportunity for all regarding access to the basic necessities, education, health services, food, housing, employment, fair distribution of income and so on. On the other hand, they are also expected to create conditions by undertaking appropriate economic and social policies to correct the social injustices. In this context, the public sector and private sectors organizations coordinate, not only among themselves but also with other national and international Institutions as well as with the civil society to implement the scheme.

Chapter IV
Quality Education and Meal Scheme in Uttar Pradesh: Issues and Challenges

The Right to quality Education in India: Emergence, Prospects and Challenges

---

Every Nation recognizes the importance of their children with regard to the future stability and prosperity of the national. The founder of 'The international children's Centre, Paris', Prof. R. Debre[30] had said, "The Child is a modern invention". He observed the child as an invention who will be a necessary part of the development process of the nation. The value of children as a potential human resource, for the future of the nation, is being released (Rajendran, 1981).

The MDMS was introduced on 15 August 1995 in Uttar Pradesh. Under the scheme, 3 kg of wheat or rice was to be supplied to each student based on 80% of monthly attendance tested via the teachers. This pattern has persevered till August 31, 2004. In compliance with the Hon'ble Supreme Court's order dated 28 November 2001 cooked meal is being served to the beneficiaries of MDM from 1st September 2004 in Uttar Pradesh.In Uttar Pradesh September 2004, the scheme was revised and set the standard of cooked MDMS with 300 calories and 8-12 grams of

---

[30]Rajendran M. M. (1981), *"Profile of the Child in India: Policies and Programmes "*, Ministry of Social Welfare, Government of India, New Delhi. pp 57

protein to all children from class I–V in Government and aided faculties and EGS/ AIE centers. In addition, (two to free provision of food two grains) this revised scheme also supplied Central Assistance for cooking fee @ Re 1 per toddler per college day, transport subsidy was once raised from the formerly maximum of Rs 50 per quintal to Rs.100 per quintal for unique category states, and Rs seventy five per quintal for other states, management, monitoring and contrast expenses @ 2% of the price of meals grains, transport subsidy and cooking help etc. and provision was made to furnish MDM at some point of summertime vacation in drought-affected areas.

MDM Scheme (MDMS) and Its Implementation in Uttar Pradesh

Uttar Pradesh, the most populous state of India is lying in north-central India. It is bordered with the Uttarakhand, Nepal, Bihar, Jharkhand & Chhattisgarh, the state of Madhya Pradesh to the south, and the states of Rajasthan and Haryana and the countrywide capital territory of Delhi to the west. On January 26, 1950, when India became a republic, the nation used to be given its current name, Uttar Pradesh. This state is literally known as the Northern state.

Uttar Pradesh is India's second biggest state and the fifth biggest in area. Lucknow is the capital of Uttar Pradesh and Kanpur is the financial and industrial capital of the state. The density of population in the state is 173 people per square kilometer as in opposition to 274 of the country. 80 % of the population in the state consists of the rural poor making it one of the most deprived economies.

Uttar Pradesh has 75 districts which have 18 divisions. Each district is governed via a District Collector or a District Magistrate, appointed by the Indian Administrative Service or the Uttar Pradesh Public Service Commission. Each district of the state is divided into Sub-Divisions, ruled through a Sub-divisional magistrate. Sub-divisions are further divided into blocks, which include panchayats and town municipalities.

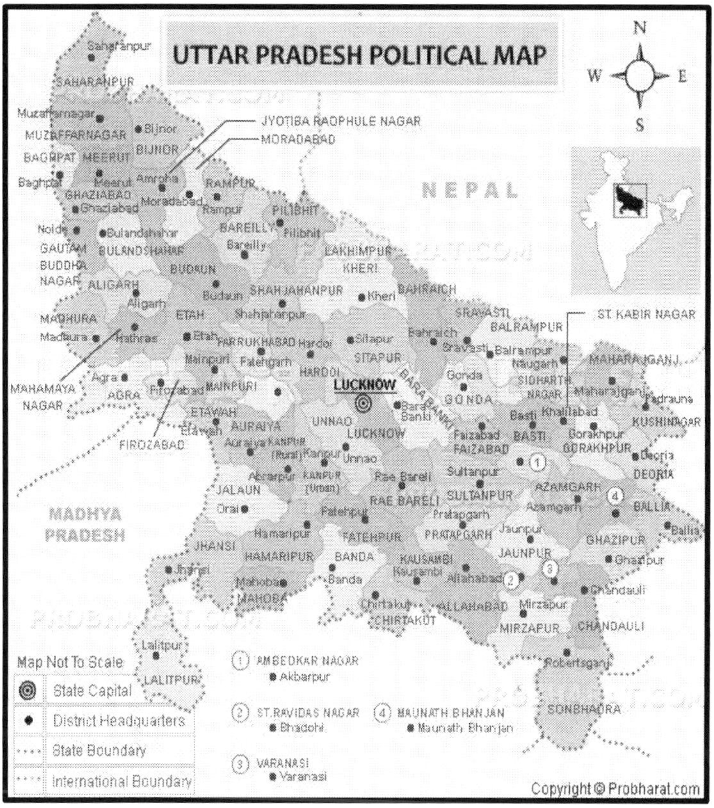

More than 60% of the populace depends on agriculture for their livelihood which makes the Uttar Pradesh an agrarian economy. The state is the largest producer of meals grain in India and presents a numerous agro-climatic condition which is conducive for agricultural production. Uttar Pradesh is recognized for its very best production of sugarcane through which this state has the superb contribution to the nation. However, the state gives incredible investment possibilities for industrial development.

Institutional Structure for Supervision of MDMS in U.P.:

The MDMS has been managed via the institutional mechanism at the national, state, district, block and gram panchayat levels. In rural areas, gram panchayats are accountable for presenting cooked meals to the students and the provision of presenting cooked food in urban areas of Uttar Pradesh has been given to the ward and municipalities. These are management arrangements for MDMS at the national, state, district, block and gram panchayat levels.

The National Level

At the national level, a National Level Steering Cum Monitoring Committee (NSMC)[31] to look after the implementation of the programme. Its duties are to guide a variety of implementing agencies, screen programme implementation and check the effect on of the scheme.

National Level Steering Cum Monitoring Committee is constituted to guide the number of measures for the success of the scheme. (National Guidelines of NP-NSPE, 2006)[32].

The State level (Uttar Pradesh)

A State level is also a Steering cum Monitoring Committee and is similar to the function of the National Level committee. Each state government designates one of its departments as the nodal department.

---

[31]NSMC is set up by the Department of School Education and Literacy, the Government of India.

[32]National Guidelines of NP-NSPE, Government of India, 2006, pp-12.

The composition of State Level Steering cum Monitoring Committee in Uttar Pradesh[33] (Sikligar, 2011)

Sl.No.	Designation of the Officers	Status
1.	Principal Secretary Education/Principal Secretary Basic Education	President
2.	Principal Secretary/Secretary Panchayati Raj	Member
3.	Principal Secretary/Secretary Employment	Member
4.	Principal Secretary/Secretary Finance	Member
5.	Principal Secretary/Secretary Urban Development	Member
6.	Principal Secretary/Secretary Food and Supply Department	Member
7.	Managing Director, Uttar Pradesh State Food and Essential Commodities	Member
8.	Director, Basic Education Department	Member Secretary
9.	Director, Panchayati Raj Department	Member
10.	Finance Controller, Uttar Pradesh Basic Education Council	Member

Source: Sikligar, P.C. (2011)

As there is a Nodal Department in each and every state to put in force the scheme, it mediates between the Central and the state governments and conveys the district smart allocations of food grains and the finance. The nodal departments carry the district clever allocation for meals grains, cooking costs, the building of cooking cum kitchen units to the district nodal departments. It co-ordinates amongst the districts nodal businesses and maintains

---

[33] Sikligar, P.C. (2011), "MDM Scheme and School Education: Planning Implementation and Effectiveness", Publisher :Concept Publishing Company Pvt .Ltd., New Delhi-110059 (India), ISBN No .9788180697876, pp 78.

files for attendance, drops out and retention of kids in primary schools.

The District level (Uttar Pradesh)

The duty for implementation and supervision of the programme in the district is assigned to the gram panchayat in rural areas and municipality in the city areas. There is also a District Nodal Agency in every district. The state nodal organization conveys district-wise allocation for the financial year to all district nodal agencies. The national nodal agency ensures that the district nodal groups have sub-allocated month-to-month district allocation to the sub-district level, which would further allocate to each school.

The composition of the District Level Steering cum Monitoring Committee in Uttar Pradesh (Sikligar, 2011)[34]

Sl.No.	Designation of the Officers	Status
1.	District Collector	President
2.	Chief Development Officer	Member
3.	District Education Inspector	Member Secretary
4.	District Programme Officer	Member
5.	District Supply Officer	Member
6.	Chief Medical Officer	Member
7.	Deputy Chief Medical Officer	Member
8.	District Development Officer	Member
9.	Project Director DRDO	Member

---

[34]Sikligar, P.C. (2011), "MDM Scheme and School Education: Planning Implementation and Effectiveness", Publisher: Concept Publishing Company Pvt. Ltd., New Delhi-110059 (India), ISBN No. 9788180697876. pp 79.

10.	District Social Welfare Officer	Member
11.	District Panchayati Raj Officer	Member
12.	District Basic Officer	Member
13.	Commissioner/Executive Officer Municipality	Member
14.	District Officer Food and Essential Commodities	Member

Source: Sikligar, P.C. (2011)

The Block Level (Uttar Pradesh)

At the block level, implementation of MDMS lies with Urban Local Bodies/Municipality in urban areas and the Sub-Divisional Magistrate, Assistant Basic Education Officer, Deputy Tehsildar and Deputy Block Development Officer, Panchayat or members of municipalities are involved for the implementation of the scheme.

The composition of the Block Level Steering cum Monitoring Committee in Uttar Pradesh (Sikligar, 2011)[35]

Sl.No.	Designation of the Officers	Status
1.	Sub-Divisional Magistrate	President
2.	Assistant Basic Education Officer	Member-convener
3.	Block Development Officer	Member
4.	Medical Officer at Block Level	Member
5.	Deputy Block Development Officer	Member
6.	Deputy Tehsildar	Member
7.	Officer (one) Nominated by Deputy Collector	Member

[35]Sikligar, P.C. (2011), "Mid Day Meal Scheme and School Education: Planning Implementation and Effectiveness", Publisher: Concept Publishing Company Pvt. Ltd., New Delhi-110059 (India), ISBN No. 9788180697876. pp 79.

8.	Supply Inspector	Member

Source: Sikligar, P.C. (2011)

The Gram Panchayat Level

At the gram panchayat level, a steering cum monitoring Committee is created for the implementation of the scheme. The committee consists of the Gram Pradhan/Sarpanch, two women (guardians) nominated by gram pradhan, Head Master/Mistress and two men (guardians) nominated by gram pradhan. The pradhan of gram panchayat make an arrangement of providing cooked food to the students.

The composition of Gram Panchayat Level Steering cum Monitoring Committee in Uttar Pradesh (Sikligar, 2011)[36]

Sl.No.	Designation of the Officers	Status
1.	Gram Pradhan/Sarpanch	President
2.	Head Master/Mistress	Member-convener
3.	Two women (guardians) nominated by gram pradhan	Member
4.	Two men (guardians) nominated by gram pradhan	Member

Source:Sikligar, P.C. (2011)

[36]Sikligar, P.C. (2011), "Mid Day Meal Scheme and School Education: Planning Implementation and Effectiveness", Publisher: Concept Publishing Company Pvt. Ltd., New Delhi-110059 (India), ISBN No. 9788180697876. pp79.

Administrative Structure for Execution of MDMS in Uttar Pradesh:

The edifice of the MDMS of Uttar Pradesh can be divided into 5 broad hierarchical degree viz. state level, district level, tehsil level, block level, and school level. The hierarchy of state-level starts from Principal Secretary, basic education department followed by two horizontal officers Director and Finance Controller (MDMA). Further Director is followed by Additional Director (MDMA), Additional Director followed by the Joint director, Joint director followed by two Deputy Director (MDMA). District level structure starts with three horizontal officers Assistant Deputy Director, Nutritional Expert and Training co-ordinator under the authority of deputy director (MDMA). With assistant deputy director, there are seventeen regional assistant directors and regional assistant directors and a district basic education officer. At tehsil level, there is a deputy basic education officer under the authority of district basic education officer. At the block level there is assistant basic education officer under the authority of deputy basic education officer and at the school level, there are school headmaster and village education committee under the assistant basic education officer.

Administrative Flow Chart of MDMA

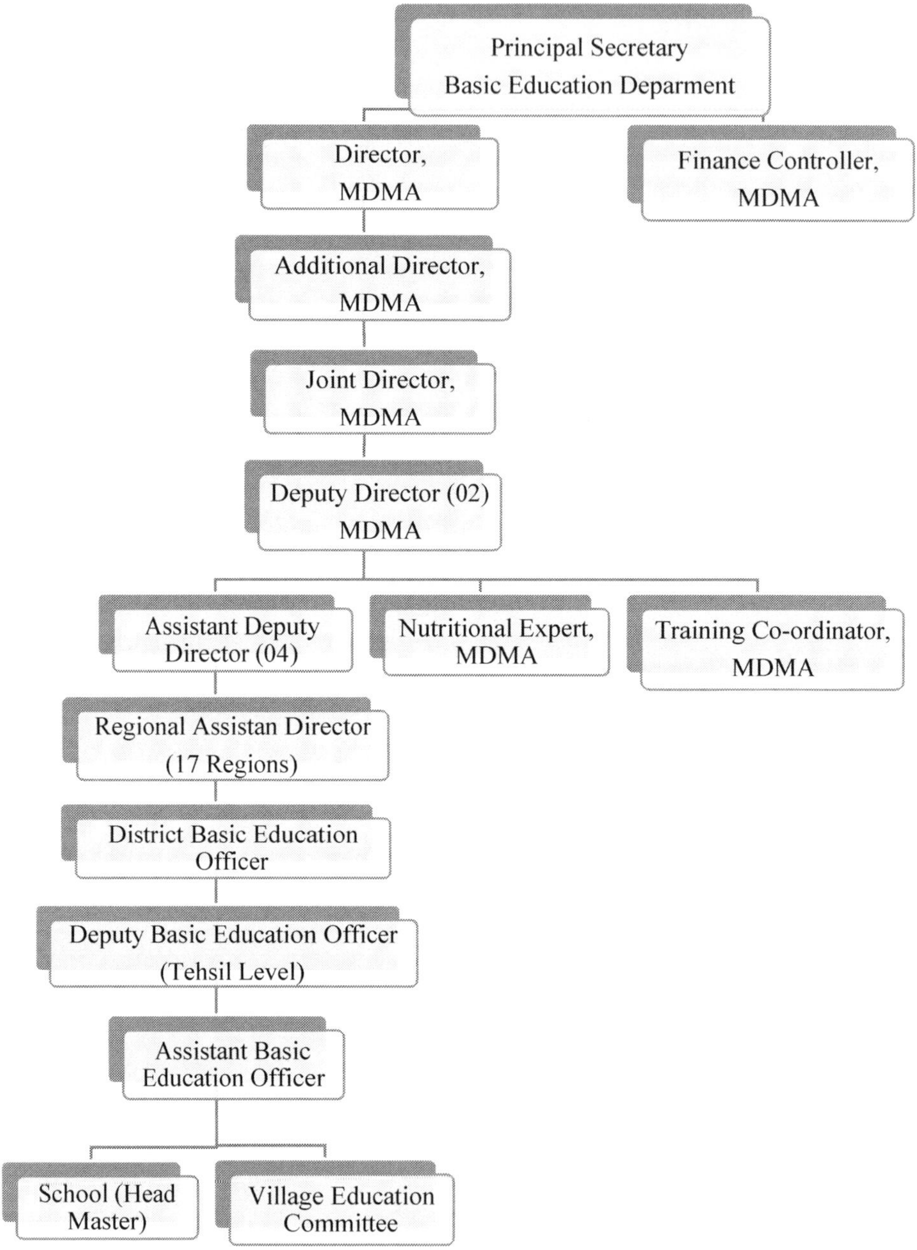

Source :http//:upmdm.org

The coverage of MDMS is given in the following desk

Year	Primary schools (I -V)		Upper Primary with Primary schools (I - VIII)		Upper Primary without Primary schools (VI-VIII)		Total No. of Existing Institut-ions	Total No. of Institut-ions serving MDM
	No. of Existing Institut-ions	No. of Institut-ions serving serving MDM	No. of Existing Institut-ions	No. of Institut-ions serving MDM	No. of Existing Instituti-ons	No. of Institut-ions serving MDM		
2009-2010	105815	105026	21175	20647	25511	24512	152501	150185
2010-2011	107546	106345	21362	20244	31168	26938	160076	153527
*2011-2012	116107	105775	912	659	52587	51071	169606	157505
2012-2013	115683	109312	1142	931	52796	51690	169621	161933
2013-2014	115451	112226	1120	951	52899	52302	169470	165479
2014-2015	114323	114283	1152	964	53003	52429	168478	167676

Source :http//:upmdm.org

* *Maximum upper primary with primary schools (I-VIII) have been merged in upper primary (VI-VIII) in 2011 .*

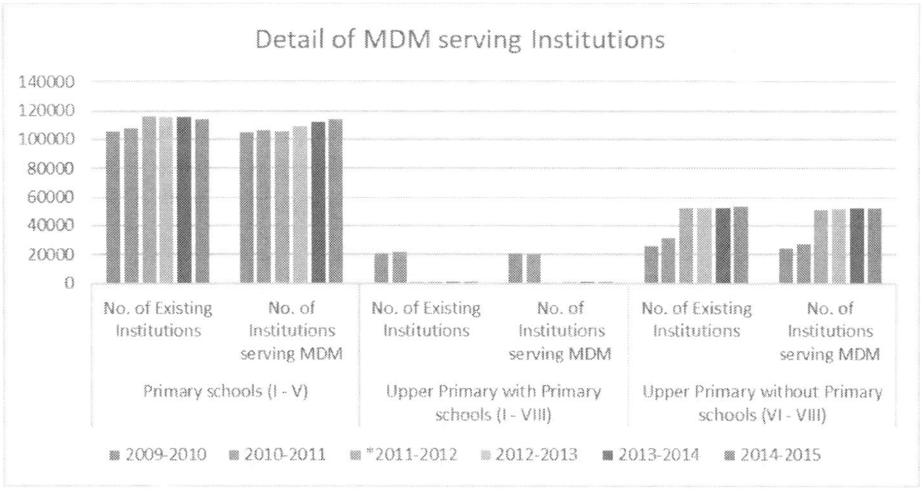

MDM scheme plays an important position to empower female by means of supplying employment such as cooks and helpers, etc. The total members of personnel employed in cooking was 188699 (49333 male and 139366 female) in various institutions (primary and upper primary), in which maximum employees were women. Subsequently, the no. of employees continued to increase and in 2015 the total no. of employees occurred 400383 (31230 male and 369153 female) giving a huge benefit to the female employees.

Year	Male/ Female	SC	ST	OBC	Minority	other	Total
2009-2010	Male	11700	663	26317	2007	8646	49333
	Female	29461	1825	79135	5414	23531	139366
	Total	41161	2488	105452	7421	32177	**188699**
2010-2011	Male	6939	105	13974	1825	5845	28688
	Female	97659	3823	149313	9437	62340	322572
	Total	104598	3928	163287	11262	68185	**351260**
2011-2012	Male	6626	152	14828	2093	7279	30978
	Female	104586	4153	171164	13056	56684	349643
	Total	111212	4305	185992	15149	63963	**380621**
2012-2013	Male	7243	156	14127	2283	6929	30738
	Female	105623	4662	180233	14943	52707	358168
	Total	112866	4848	194360	17226	59363	**388906**
2013-2014	Male	6959	256	13707	2069	7234	30225
	Female	107314	4450	192354	14903	51332	370353
	Total	114273	4706	206061	16972	58566	**400578**
2014-2015	Male	7874	318	13863	2309	6866	31230
	Female	106796	6213	190455	16328	49361	369153

	Total	114670	6531	204318	18637	56227	**400838**

Source :Data has been taken by http//:upmdm.org/awpb.html

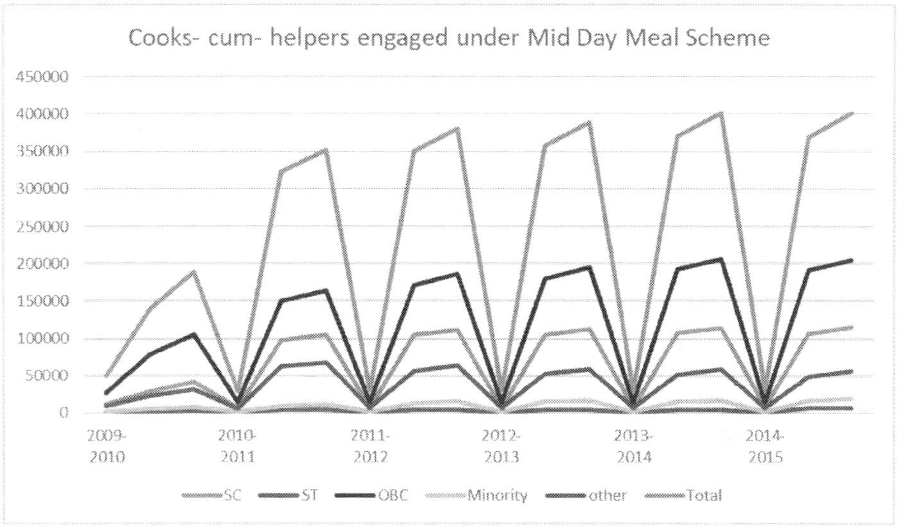

The total number of students enrolled in 2009-10 was 20345456 and all the students availed the MDM. The enrollment and number of students availed MDM used to be extra or less same till 2012-13 however astonishingly in final two academic year (2013-14 and 2014-15) the complete number of enrollment as nicely as the complete, the number of students availed the MDM has drastically come down to 19824273 and 10378444 respectively in 2013-14 and 19161620 and 10419875 respectively in 2014-15. The primary reason for the scheme was to enlarge the enrollment of the students but the facts show that enrollment and the number of students availing the MDM have decreased opposite to the goal of the scheme. The facts additionally indicate that even all the enrolled students are not availing the MDM.

Year	Enrollment vis-a-vis MDM Primary Classes (I-V)	Enrollment vis-a-vis MDM Upper Primary Classes (VI-VIII)	Total Enrollment	Total No. of children

	Enrollment	No. of children availed MDM	Enrollment	No.of children availed MDM		availed MDM
2009-10	15865317	15865317	4480139	4480139	20345456	20345456
2010-11	15170833	15170833	5832249	5832249	21003082	21003082
2011-12	14318772	14318772	6024330	6024330	20343102	20343102
2012-13	14097256	14097256	5999945	5999945	20097201	20097201
2013-14	13810510	7413602	6013763	2964842	19824273	10378444
2014-15	13372102	7358391	5789518	3061484	19161620	10419875

Source :Data has been taken by http//:upmdm.org/awpb.html

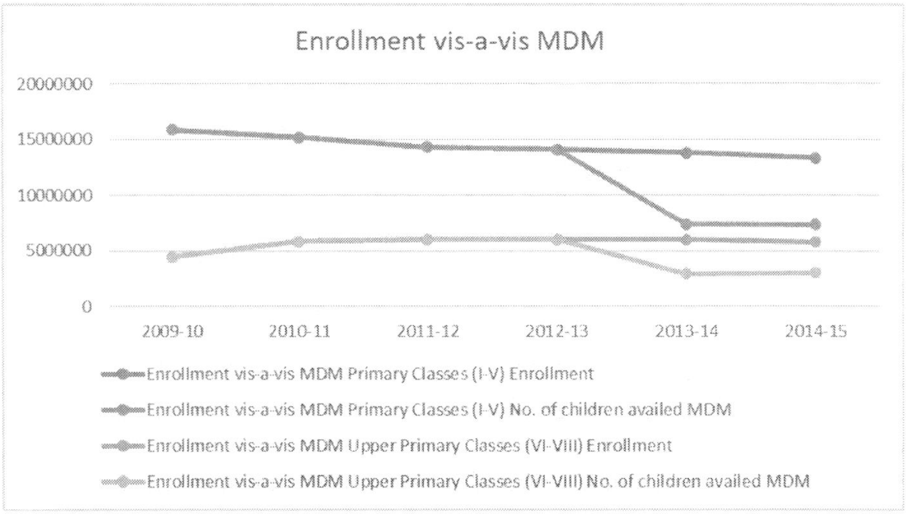

Financial Composition of MDMS in Uttar Pradesh

The Indian Government releases money in three installments and the first installment of 25% is released after acquiring the unutilized balance from the States and UTs. The scondinstalment of 40% is launched after taking into consideration the expenditure function of the first two installments. The State Government after looking for credit score confirmation from State Finance Department releases third instalment to Basic Education of Uttar Pradesh.

Fund Flow for MDM (PAISA District Surveys: MDM Scheme, 2012) (2013)[37]

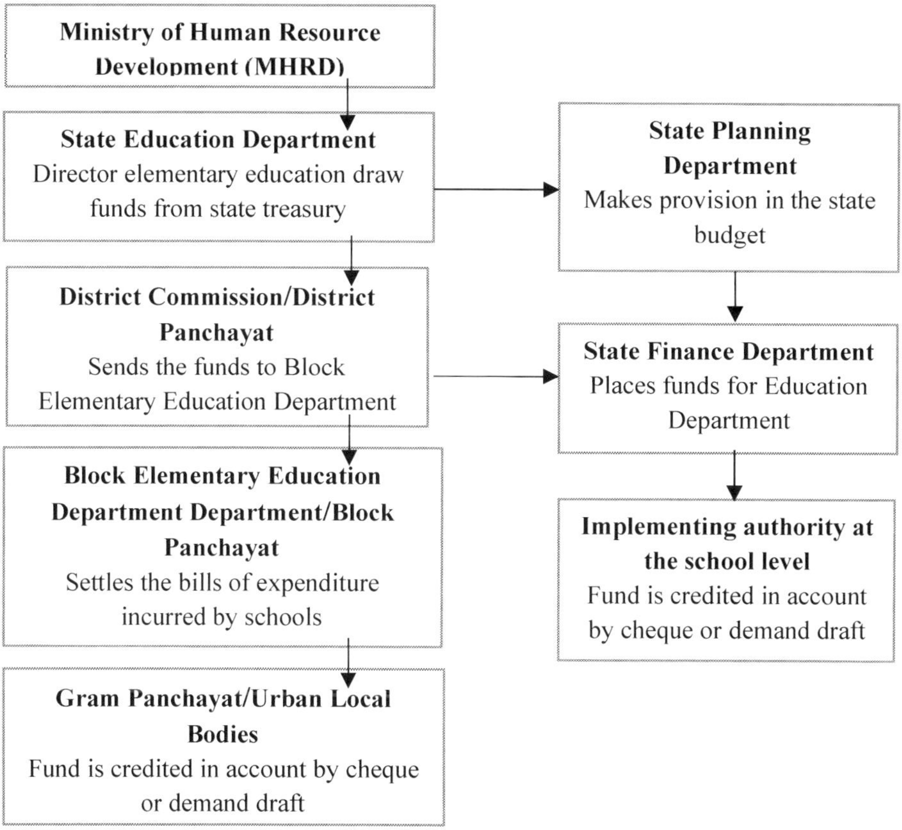

---

[37]Report (2012), http://mdm.nic.in/Files/OrderCirculars/Final_PAISA_MDM_Report_18july_2013.pdf, visited on 18.03.2016 time: 06:15 pm.

Food grain Management[38] for MDMS in U.P. (Fifth Review Mission Uttar Pradesh , 2013-2014):

The base of the MDMS is meals grain. The requirement of meals grain is discovered by the state authorities. The Government of India through HRD distributes meals grains on the basis of an average attendance of young people in the course of the foregoing 12 months in concurrence of the branch of food and public distribution.

The Food Corporation of Indiainforms state devices and sends grains to regional go-downs through district nodal authority. District nodal authorities, in turn, allot food grain to blocks and inform State Food and finally, it reaches to rashan dealerstores. Then state meals firms lift disbursed food grains from FCI go down and provide them to blocks. From there the kotedars elevate the food grains and provide it to respective schools. PDS Dealers lifts meals grains from State Food Corporation godowns and they are supposed to take that to schools. The rashan dealerstores owners acquire the grains from block go-downs and they, in turn, make it accessible to Gram Pradhan/Ward members/NGO. Food grain used in a cooking meal is under CMDM in charge.

---

[38]Report (2013-14), http://mdm.nic.in/Files/Review/Fifth_Review/UP/Final_Report_JRM_UP.pdf, visited on 18.03.2016 time: 06:15 pm.

Food Grain Management

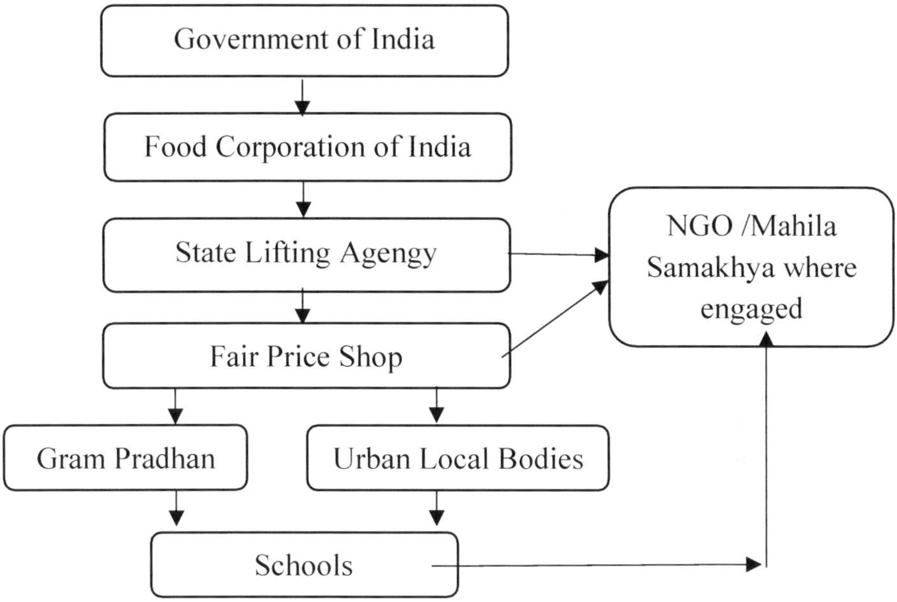

Source: Fifth Review Mission-Uttar Pradesh 2013-14.

Concerns relating to the MDMS:

1. Corruption

The scenario of adolescents in India has been described as "critical urgency". India has some of the worst signs of child well-being in the world. NP-NSPE which is popularly recognized as the MDMS was launched by the Indian Government in 1995, NP-NSPE states that it targets to tackle "classroom hunger" and inspire poor children, belonging to deprived sections, to attend faculty often and assist them to pay attention to classroom activities. The MDM programme is a multi-faceted programme of the Indian Government that, among different things, also seeks to address the troubles of meals security, lack of vitamin and get education on a nationwide scale. The Scheme is the world's largest child feeding programme attending about 12 crore teens in over 12.65 lakh schools/EGS centers throughout the country.

When the MDMS was launched in 1995, state governments were given the duty and two years to put this quintessential scheme in place so as to be in a position to furnish a cooked meal to predominant school children. But the CAG reviews and other information suggests the inefficiency of state governments in the applicable implementation of this scheme.

MDM scheme in India is estimated to be costing the exchequer a whopping Rs 13,000 crore per annum. This fee is generally borne by way of the Government of India and also shared through the respective state governments. While the food grain for cooking is supposed to reach schools each month at a subsidized price from the FCI warehouses, the conversion cost per scholar per day is paid to the school. This levels from Rs 3.34 per infant per day per school for major kids to Rs 5 upper primary, shared in the ratio of 75% and 25% between the Central authorities and the state governments.

Anyone can locate these details on NIC and MHRD websites, along with several well-articulated reports which outline structure to monitor, support and control this scheme. It appears that adequate manpower has also been sanctioned right from the state level to the school monitoring committee. Different states have created variants of this scheme for its execution roping in the NGOs, and cooking the meal centrally or making the teachers responsible to cook in schools. The scheme execution is supposed to be tracked through MDM-MIS portal, and have routine inspection and exchange of reports between the MHRD and the state governments.

Since the implementation, this scheme has been suffering from many drawbacks. "Huge corruption" at all levels was destroying the scheme. Children are getting low quality and insufficient food;

hence there is a lack of nutrition. Corruption is involved in the delivery system. Fake enrolments are being done to embezzle money. These rackets are killing this very important scheme, and the main reason is the lack of guidelines and institutionalization.

Lack of monitoring and massive corruption and misuse of funds has been destroying the scheme. Some of the troubles most often mentioned in a range of studies related to the MDM programme in distinctive components as the poor infrastructure facilities (e.g. cooking shed, water grant and utensils); repetition of the identical menu every day; disruption of study room processes due to the fact instructors had to oversee the operation; poor variety of food; poor hygiene (including reports of sickness after meals); inadequate price of salaries to cooks; insufficient budgetary allocation toward conversion fees which reportedly resulted in the constant menu; caste bias amongst some parents in some places; restrained possibilities for parental participation in the programme; lack of sufficient plates in some cases, ensuing in teenagers ingesting off leaves or paper; irregular and delayed shipping of meals grains and funding in some cases; the volume and first-rate of meals were probably to be less than the minimal stipulated by way of the court; low-quality rice was once supplied by using FCI, which required suppliers to change it for better pleasant rice from the market etc.

Besides these drawbacks, corruption has made the situation and scheme worse position. In 2014, Ananth Kumar, Union Minister for Chemicals and Fertilizer, expressed his displeasure MDMS in the country. While distributing plates and glasses for 5,000 young people studying in the government and aided schools, blanketed via the Adanya Chetana Programme run through the Smt. Girija Shastri Memorial Trust, for the midday meal scheme in Gulbarga, the minister expressed his resentment over the corruption-infested scheme and the irregularities in enforcing the same nationwide. He said the noon meal scheme had failed to benefit even 50% of 12 crore students enrolled in government schools in India. He added that the scheme had even failed to grant mid-day meals typically to 1.15 crore youngsters in colleges in the State.

Recently in March 2016, the 5-year old girl reportedly died and two others had been discovered serious after consuming MDM at an aanganwadi center in Katni district of Madhya Pradesh. All of these teenagers fed on food at an aanganwandi center in Majhgawan village in Bahoriband tehsil of the district.

This MDMS, like different schemes of government, has been a victim of corruption leakage. Various scams involving the MDMS have been unearthed ones, it was started. In December 2005, the police had seized eight truckloads (2,760 sacks) of rice supposed for primary school kids being carried from Food Corporation of India (FCI) godowns in Bulandshahar district of Uttar Pradesh to North Delhi. When the police detained the trucks, the drivers claimed that the rice used to be being delivered all the way to Delhi to be cleaned at a factory. However, according to the guidelines, the rice has to be taken at once from FCI godown to the school or village concerned. Later it was once located that the rice used to be being siphoned off via an UP-based NGO, Bharatiya Manav Kalyan Parishad (BMKP), in connivance with the government officials.

In January 2006, Delhi police unearthed a rip-off in the MDMS. In November 2006, the residents of Pembong village at the Mim tea property (around 30 km from Darjeeling), accused a crew of teachers of embezzling MDMs. In a written complaint, the residents claimed that students at the primary school had no longer got MDM for the previous 18 months.

In December 2006, The Times of India reported a scam involving authorities schools that siphon off meals grains under the MDMS by faking attendance. The attendance register would exaggerate the number of students enrolled in the class. The additional students would not exist -they were "enrolled" to get additional food grains which were pocketed by the school staff. The scam was exposed, when P. Asha Kumari, an assistant teacher at the government model primary school, Jakkur, in Yelahanka acted as a whistle blower. She informed the Lokayukta, who conducted a probe and indicted four persons for misappropriation. The whistle blower was harassed by the school staff and requested a transfer. She was transferred to a government primary school at Cholanayakahalli, where she again found the same modus operandi being used to siphon off the food grains. She again complained to the Lokayukta, who issued a notice to the school.

Cases of financial indiscipline such as the furnishing of incorrect utilisation certificates, misappropriation of funds, fudging of data to claim the higher cost of foodgrains were widespread. The monitoring by both the Ministry and States was inadequate. CAG found most disturbing is the total disregard for the quality of the meal being given to children. The system of involving mothers in the process of cooking has not worked. In Andhra Pradesh, 86 out of 120 schools test checked found no involvement of mothers; in Odisha in 103 schools mothers were not involved to supervise preparation of meals. To add to this, CAG said sanctioned calorific value was not being maintained in meals. In Chhattisgarh, Meghalaya, Sikkim, Tripura, and Andaman no record was maintained to ensure minimum calorie and protein content. CAG also discovered excess payment has been made to few a non-governmental organizations.

In Delhi, Sri Ram Institute for Industrial Research tested samples of cooked food of 37 service providers and 80% of them failed to meet the prescribed standards. In nine states, the shortfall in the supply of food grains in the meals served to children against prescribed quantity was noticed in selected districts.

Monitoring of hot cooked meal to children of primary and upper primary classes in over 1,265,000 schools across India is a colossal task, which needs manpower, infrastructure, and training. This is clearly not possible as the scheme is already marred by corruption top to bottom and again kickback of money from the bottom to top. But for agencies supporting Midday Meal scheme, this is a trivial task and can be achieved by spending more money, this is exactly what the problem is when people try to fix symptoms rather than stopping the scheme.

2. Management Hazzards

There are many hindrances in the management of this scheme which makes its implementation complicated. In most places, it is a matter for the institution to manage. In some places, NGOs or private contractors do the job. The scheme is better managed in south Indian states, but in the northern part of the country, the situation is pathetic.

The CMDM guidelines envisage the constitution of Steering-cum-Monitoring Committees at State/District/Block/Village levels to advise, monitor, coordinate and take remedial measures for improving the implementation of the scheme. However, it has been observed by our field teams that though SMCs have been constituted at all the levels.

The most important component of CMDM i.e. supply chain management has some flaws due to which food grain allotment gets delayed. Such delay hampers the supply chain of funds/food grain and adversely affects the provision/quantity of meal to children. District nodal authority should get utilization certificates from the implementing authority at school level regularly so that further funds/food grain is allotted /delivered timely (Mathur, 2005).[39]

---

[39]Mathur, B.(2005), "Situation Analysis of MDM Programme in Rajasthan," University of Rajasthan and UNICEF, pp 62.

The implementing agency at school level shall be responsible to Gram Panchayats. As per central government norms, kitchen-cum-store; adequate water supply for drinking, cooking and washing utensils; cooking devices/utensils; and containers for storage of food grains and other ingredients are to be provided to schools for serving a cooked meal to the students.

3. Infrastructure

Adequate and appropriate infrastructure is crucial to ensure hygiene. Most of the sample schools in all the surveyed states reported inadequate infrastructures like lack of kitchen sheds, the absence of separate space for cooking and serving meals, no storage facilities and no clean source of water. Even where kitchens were available, they were not in good condition and had poor ventilation. In many sample schools, cooking was done in open space or under the shade of trees.

4. Availability of manpower

Under CMDM, teachers have the responsibility to monitor and supervise at the school level. Cooking and serving is entrusted to women's SHGs/NGOs etc. However, teachers are also found to be involved in arranging provisions and serving meals. In the case of EGS (Employment Guarantee Scheme) centers, the problem is more acute, because, no provision for cook has been made. At the state level, the average wage for cooking, per child, per school day comes in the range of Rs. 0.40 to Rs. 0.50 only. It has been observed that in schools where student strength is less than 50, it becomes difficult to hire a cook at such a small honorarium. Also, in schools where student strength is more than 100, it becomes difficult for one cook to cook the meal in time. Hence there is a need to enhance the amount of honorarium to cooks/helpers.

5. Maintenance of Records/Cashbooks

It has been observed that the maintenance of records needs improvement at all levels. At the school level, maintenance of records is very poor. It has been observed that cash books are written once/twice a month. There is no common format for maintenance of cash accounts and stock of food grain. In most states, teachers are found to be responsible for maintaining accounts while they do not have any training for such type of jobs. The situation is worse in EGS centers. Their estimates are erratic without proper maintenance of records. In the absence of item-wise utilization of various ingredients used in the preparation of cooked MDM, it was difficult for the field team to estimate the nutritious content of the food supplied to children. Also in the absence of proper records, a lot of scope is left for manipulation of actual expenditure and utilization of the food grain/funds provided under the programme.

Public-Private Partnership (PPP) can be the way in which the Cooked MDM can be provided in schools. PPP involves a contract between the Government agencies and a private institution where the onus of providing a public service is on the private institution. Under the PPP mode, the quality of service being provided is expected to improve which can result in an improved performance of the cooked MDMS.

Social and Political issues (Jain & Shah, 2005)[40]

Besides Institutional weakness, there are social and political drawbacks which makes the scheme weak. Children's poor parents were getting the support of at least one meal for their children and were sending them to school in the bargain. But if

---

[40]Jain, J. and Shah.M. (2005), "MDM in 70 most backward villages of Madhya Pradesh," Samaj Pragati Sahyog, Madhya Pradesh pp 32.

their children will be served bad quality food then their parents will now be reluctant to allow them to consume MDM, and eventually, the dropout rate might increase once these children become little older. The rotten wheat or contaminated dal, although may be filling the stomach, does not help in building the children's health, much less their brain. A clean and healthy meal, which is the right of every child, is being taken away by the greedy middlemen. No parents, howsoever poor, would ever feed their child in the oil laced with insecticide. Here is a yet another case of poor execution of a good scheme, leading to larger damage in the long run.

Instead of fixing these issues, the leaders of various political parties were neglecting it. The Bihar authorities are pointing towards a conspiracy by sympathizers of the opposition party. There is lack of political will. The time has come to provide adequate planning for the implementation of such a welfare scheme, and not squander away taxpayer's money. This is ultimately harming the very cause it is expected to address. All those who are found guilty in serving poor and contaminated food should be charged not just for negligence.

The media's attention and awareness have brought to light several incidents from across states during the last few weeks, including Delhi, where these meals are being served after cooking in unhygienic conditions. Similar complaints have also come after children falling sick after taking iron tablets across several states. This shows that all good-schemes are falling prey to bad execution, poor monitoring and greedy middlemen who take their cut.

Already students have started to shun the MDM, and teachers all across Bihar have protested to not get involved in the meal distribution scheme. Rightly so, as their job is to teach and not get involved in preparation and serving of meals. There was a time when the children were considered as the future of our nation. But with these incidents, it seems that their own future and survival is threatened.

Politicians are always busy in blame game politics; no matter what the issue is, they have to criticize the government and in that politicians will go to any extent. They make living on dead bodies by shouting, hauling and protesting by forcefully getting the shops closed in some regions; showing their worth as a party member to their high command. None actually wanted to help the victims or alleviate the pain of family members but politicians start blaming each other to get the political mileage in the coming. Like Chief Minister of Bihar did not even visit the place to get a feel on ground reality and to check what action police has taken. Almost all politicians were busy making a statement in the news channel and media that state government did not do its job properly and even after the incident the cover-up stories were given in the media and newspapers. Some politicians went ahead and started spreading the rumors in other places where the midday meal scheme is running that food is horrible and children in other schools too are getting the getting sick. These acts need to be condemned by the society but more importantly, the mental degradation of politicians to needs to look upon a side effect of the bogus scheme.[41]

In most of the schools it has been seen especially in the outer areas of Delhi, the school authorities treat children like a burden. The manner of distributing the meal is not dignified. The MDM programme was introduced to mitigate social inequalities inherited through the hierarchical division of society. This structural discrimination directly impedes equal access to the benefits of development by excluding the poor and marginalized.

---

[41]www.yojana.gov.in/mid-day-meal-scheme, visited on 18.03.2016 time :06:20 pm.

Enrolments of children belonging to SCs and STs have increased since 2005 when the new cooked MDM was implemented in all the eight sample schools. Before 2005, many of the children from these disadvantaged sections did not participate in primary schooling. After 2005, the provision of the hot cooked meal, which included a staple diet of roti, vegetable, and pulse, improved the situation. Parents appreciate this initiative and consider it as a subsidy for schooling costs. Most of the children relish this hot cooked food, which is much similar to their home food. All the eight schools serve different food items on a daily basis. (n.d.).[42]

Enrolment in school is the foremost criterion for school participation. Low enrolments for disadvantaged groups result in their dismal representation at all levels of education. The enrolment of children belonging to marginalized sections has increased under MDM between 2005 and 2009, during the same period, enrolment of children belonging to general category declined steadily. Most of the parents send their younger children of pre-school age for getting a free meal under MDM. One positive fallout of this practice is that this has brought down the enrolment age to five-six years from the previous average of 8-10 years. This also contributed to retention rate.

A well-organized MDM can be used as an opportunity to impart good habits to teens and to teach them about the significance of smooth water, suitable hygiene and different associated matters. MDM can assist spread egalitarian values, as kids from a variety of social backgrounds analyze to sit together and share a common meal. In particular, the MDM can assist to ruin the limitations of caste in school. Appointing cooks from Dalit communities is some other way of instructing adolescents to overcome caste prejudices.

The gender hole in school participation has also tended to narrow, as the MDMS helps erode the barriers that prevent girls from

---

[42]http//:timesofindia.indiatimes.com/, visited on 18.03.2016 time :06:15 pm.

going to school. MDMS also gives a beneficial source of employment for female and helps liberate working women from the burden of cooking at home in the course of the day. In these and different ways, girls and girl children have a unique stake in MDM Scheme. This scheme has given some psychological advantages additionally through emotional support. Physiological deprivation leads to low self-esteem, consequent insecurity, anxiety. The MDM scheme helps address this and facilitate cognitive, emotional and social development.

Conclusion

A key problem in implementation has to do with both the quantum of funds required and the flow of funds in the scheme. Until the revised norms of 2006 came into effect, the States, on their part, pleaded serious financial constraints in mobilizing the resources for cooking costs. Subsequent experience has shown that even the revised norms do not solve the resource problem completely. Even without ensuring legal minimum wages for cooks and helpers, the cooking costs have been going up.

It is the duty of the nodal ministry to evaluation the infrastructure development given for MDM scheme in the meetings of SMC and representatives of other nodal ministries which run the infrastructure improvement schemes have to be invited to these meetings. Steering-cum-monitoring committees ought to be made useful and active at district/block levels for high-quality implementation, convergence, and monitoring of the scheme.

Utilization certificates of meals grains/funds from the school should be taken by the block level officer on priority groundwork and be dispatched to the district authority so that the release of cash is expedited. All authorities or non-government or civil society must get together to implement the scheme successfully. There need to be higher monitoring, higher accountability and better administration by using the same government organization which has a weak record in implementing any policy. Monitoring of warm cooked meal to adolescents of major and higher essential classes in over 1,265,000 schools throughout India is a massive task, which desires manpower, infrastructure, and training.

Chapter V
Education and Quality food: Local Governance and their functioning

Introduction

The idea of institution varies from extra limited to more elaborated meanings along several dimensions. One dimension is the degree of formalization of an institution. At the most casual perspective, it is common to communicate of 'habits', 'customs' or 'conventions'. The idea of Institutionalism has concerned the find out about the origins, effects, and possible for reform of institutions. Institutional theory in political science has made first-rate advances in recent years this addresses the static nature of institutional principle with the aid of inspecting the notion of institutionalization. This includes institutional explanations for other social and political phenomena.

The institutionalism involves a formal and informal element of institutions. Institutions encompass the totality of social types and social structures and can also be set up by way of law or custom. Consequently, three kinds of institutions are mainly vital in India: social institutions, such as family, religion, cast, marriage and inheritance; constitutions, which are the written or unwritten regulation governing the workout of public power and the processes for making legal guidelines themselves, and regimes, which refers to the manner of giving something the personality of an institution. Social establishments govern relationships amongst folks within societies and for this reason set up a social order. Constitutions alter the relationships among citizens, political representatives, and the country and therefore create a political order.

The evaluation of the state of an institution must, of course, be extra than a discovering call and we, therefore, want to develop some criteria to assess the extent of institutionalization. One set of criteria of institutionalization has been superior according to Samuel Huntington, who argues that there are 4 dimensions thru which we can choose the level of institutionalization of any structure that we observe: autonomy, adaptability, complexity, and coherence. These four have been utilized to quite a few sorts of institutional arrangements and they do provide one avenue for grasp the transformation that structures ought to make in order to live on and to be capable to influence their individuals and their environment.

1. **Autonomy**: represents a problem with the capacity of establishments to make and put into effect their personal decisions. Arguably, to the extent that they are no longer based upon some other employer or group they can be said to be institutionalized. This idea may be operationalized in phrases of budgets and autonomous sources of revenue;

2. **Adaptability**: the extent to which an organization is capable of adapting to changes in the environment, or more importantly capable of molding that environment.

3. **Complexity**: demonstrates the ability of the institution to construct inside buildings to fulfill its dreams and to cope with the environment. Again, this idea is analogous to thinking in systems idea and structural-functionalism that mentioned the importance of structural differentiation (see Almond and Powell, 1967);

4. **Coherence:** represents the potential of the organization to manage its personal workload and to develop tactics to procedure tasks in a well-timed a realistic manner. This additionally represents a capacity of the institution to make

decisions about its core duties and beliefs and to filter out diversions from those.

These four attributes may additionally assist in the tough undertaking of measuring the degree of institutionalization, and therefore of measuring establishments themselves. Institutionalization itself may additionally be higher represented via the complexity and coherence dimensions that point out the inner administration of the MDMS.

Local Level Institutions:

The governance system is decentralized and autonomy may be required by local institutions for adaptability. These attributes are mutually enforcing for MDMS. The role of the local level institution should reach new heights in the appliance of the MDMS from the district level to panchayat level. Yet, the primary focus in the decentralization is on the structures and functions of devolved formal authorities. Formal government systems are embedded in the local social-organizational context. Hence understanding how and when local governments become inclusive and function effectively in basic service provision relating to MDM and another interrelated mechanism formal as well as informal. The Local Level Institutions in Uttar Pradesh particular in Rampur provides an important context relative to MDM and its mechanism. The qualitative data explores the history, politics, and dynamics of local level institutions, municipalities and other local bodies of government in different blocks in Rampur.

In Rampur District, local level institutions are established at three levels which are as below:

1. District Level
2. Block Level
3. Village level

1. District Level:

For the Governance of the MDMS in the whole district of Rampur, the task force at the district level have been constructed in the chairmanship of District Magistrate and its other members are as under:

1.	District Magistrate	-	President
2.	Chief Development Officer	-	Member
3.	District Inspector of School	-	Member
4.	District Program Officer	-	Member
5.	Zila Basic Shiksha Adhikari	-	Member/Secretary
6.	District Supply Officer	-	Member
7.	Chief Medical Officer	-	Member
8.	All Deputy Chief Medical Officer	-	Member
9.	District Development officer	-	Member
10.	Project Director, D.R.D.A.	-	Member
11.	District Social Welfare Officer	-	Member
12.	Zila Panchayat Raj Adhikari	-	Member

Every member of this task force is authorized to inspect a minimum five schools every month. Under the chairmanship of District Magistrate, the meeting of this task force is held every month and necessary measures are taken in the interest of various MDM projects after studying the narrations acquired.

2. Block Level:

Second Local level institution is established at block level. For the Governance of the Mid-day meal scheme in the blocks of Rampur a task force at block level has been constructed in the chairmanship of Sub-Divisional Magistrate and its other members are as under:

1.	Sub-divisional Magistrate	-	President
2.	Sahayak Basic Shiksha Adhikari	-	Member/Secretary
3.	Block Development Officer	-	Member
4.	Incharge Medical Office (Primary Health Centre)	-	Member
5.	Assistant Development Officer Panchayat	-	Member
6.	Nayab Tehsildar	-	Member
7.	Other Officer nominated by SDM	-	Member
8.	Supply Inspector	-	Member

Every member of this task force is assigned to inspect minimum five schools every month in his/her concerned block and meeting of this task force is held every month in the chairmanship of Sub-Divisional Magistrate. Sub-Divisional Magistrate takes various majors in the interest of proper implementation of Mid-day meal scheme after studying narration acquired by the members of the task force. Task force send various proposals to the District Magistrate that can be taken at district level.

Check List :

- **General Inspection:** The officials inspect the execution, implementation and overall mechanism of MDM on the basis of points as name of School and name of Block and District in which it is situated. Other points are inspection time, date and duration, numbers of registered students, numbers of appointed teachers in the school, numbers of contractual Shikshamitra in the school, name of the cooks, the state of the honorarium paid to the cooks (how long paid and how much paid), whether the menu is a stick in the school or not, name and address of nodal officer at the block level and whether Gram Pradhan concern to the school has got training under MDM or not.

- **Inspection of Food and Food Grains:** Officials inspect the food and food grains on the basis of points as matching food grain with a standard sample, standard of cleanliness of food grains, place of keeping food grains and measures to prevent it's from rats and insects, the quantity of food grains utilized every day, how many times food grains are picked up from a warehouse in a month and an average how much food grain is utilized in a month.

- **Availability of Conversion Cost:** Officials inspect the availability of conversion cost on the basis as amount of conversion cost available to Gram Pradhan, average amount spent every day and the frequency of getting conversion cost (half monthly, monthly, quarterly, yearly)

- **The arrangement of other Foodstuff:** Officials inspect in arrangement of other food stuff as whether cooking oil is open oil, egg-mark oil, Branded Egg-mark oil or vegetable oil. Other inspections in whether salt is iodised, grind sealed packed or not, whether pulses are standard or not, whether vegetables are fresh or not, whether spices are standard or not, whether milk is fresh, open, packed or powder i.e. suitable for the children or not and whether sugar or Khandsari is standard or not.

- **The arrangement of Fuel:** Officials inspect in the arrangement of fuel on the basis as whether school uses traditional Stove or gas cylinder (Single Burner or Double Burner) or Kanda (dry dung) or coal or other fuels. Other inspection regarding are quantity of available fuel and how much fuel utilize every day.

- **Points related to Hygiene:** Officials inspect hygiene available in the school on the basis as state of cleanliness of cooking utensil, state of cleanliness of eating utensil, substances used for cleaning utensil (ash, clay or detergent), state of cleanliness of the place where utensils are cleaned, availability of water for cleaning (i.e. use of tap, hand pump, well or any other system), whether children wash their hand and mouth and gargle before and after taken meal or not, whether detergent is used for cleaning or not and state of cleanliness of the place where hands are washed.

- **Measures of Safety:** Officials inspect in the measures of safety taken by the school on the basis as prior accidental events and measures taken by the school to avoid the repetition, whether cooked food is checked before serving or not and who does check cooked food (i.e. teacher, guardian, cook or Gram Pradhan). Other points are state of cooked food at the time of serving (i.e. hot, less hot orcold), which persons can visit the cooking place (i.e. cook/teacher/Gram Pradhan/Children /outsider), utilization of left food (i.e. threw or given to children to take it to their homes or given to the Anganwadi's children or utilized next day, whether animals and birds come near to the place of food at the time of cooking and eating, standard of cleaning of school and its surroundings and whether dirty smoke, dust etc. are interim in the campus of school from the nearby mills or road or not.

- **Narration in regards to a self-service organization (whether self-service organizations are working):** In case of Self-service Organization working in school officials inspect on the basis as utensils used by the self-service organization for food serving (i.e. steel, aluminium or other), time it taken between cooking and serving, whether food is checked before serving to the children or not and who does check it . Other points are whether teachers acknowledge the person who brings the food or not, sufficiency and quality of acquired food and whether foods are being served as per the menu or not.

3. Gram Panchayat Level Institution:

The various committees are as under:

i. Village Management Committee
ii. Parents Management Committee
iii. School Management Committee.

i. **Village Management Committee (VMC):** It has 8 - 10 literate members belonging to the village.

Role of the Committee: The main role of this committee is to mediate between school and parents whose children are studying in the school. An other roles of the village management committee are as under:

1. It motivates the Guardian to send their children to the school
2. It aware the guardian of the various benefits provided by the government and government policies
3. It provides assistance to the guardian on how to maintain the attendance of the children at the school

4. Members of the committee are authorized to check food/food grains
5. It ensures the hygiene in food and cleanliness of school campus and its surrounding

ii. **Parent Management Committee (PMC):** It is an important committee and the president of this committee is the father of one student in the school who is literate and it has 8 - 10 members. The members are the guardian of the children of the school. The meeting of this committee is organized by the Head Master or teacher of the school.

Role of the Committee: The various role of this committee is as under:

1. To taste the cooked meal for the children
2. To inspect the quality of food grains and cooked meal
3. To inspect the sanitation condition of the kitchen, school, and its surrounding
4. To check the availability of utensils
5. To inspect whether every student has got a uniform and books or not
6. This committee checks whether toilets are available for the male and female children separately or not

iii. **School Management Committee (SMC):** This is a very important committee for the proper implementation and this committee is constituted for the period of two years. After two years the committee is dissolved and a new committee is again constituted. The committee has a joint bank account in the name of its president and secretary.

Constitution of the School Management Committee (SMC):

The Committee includes following members in which 50% must be female:

i. Parent of a student (President)

ii. Parent of another student (Vice President)

iii. Head Master (Secretary)

iv. 6 or 7 parents of students

Role of the Committee: The main role of this committee is given below:

1. The committee checks the enrolment procedure.
2. It gives suggestions to increase the number of enrollments.
3. The committee ensures the proper maintenance of the school.
4. The committee issues the fund and other expenses of the scheme of the school.
5. To ensure the availability of utensils for the eating of children.
6. It ensures the availability of toilets for the male and female students separately.

Monitoring of the MDMS:

Monitoring of the MDMS is very important for good governance and proper implementation of the scheme. The Monitoring of MDMS is being done using Web-based Information and Communication System (ICT), Training of various stakeholders, officials visit the schools, checking of school records, etc. Some important systems of monitoring of MDM Scheme are enlightened bellow:

1. Web-Based Management Information System
2. Monitoring through Interactive Voice Response System (IVRS)
3. Stakeholder Training and Capacity Building
4. The system of online budget allocation and e-payment to Madhya Bhojan Nidhis of the schools
5. Proactive efforts in Financial Management of Scheme
6. e-Communication
7. Social Audit (This does not exist in uttar Pradesh)

1. Web-Based Management Information System:

This is a web-based reporting system. This web-based reporting system, each and every district has to report on a monthly basis on the given prescribed structure of Quarterly Progress Reports (QPRs) by Government of India. The month-to-month reports despatched by all the districts are accrued spontaneously at State level and after analyzing the information furnished by using the all districts the gadget generates the reviews as wished by the MDM Authority (MDMA). State officers take a number decisions depending upon the records furnished by way of the device for the appropriate governance of the MDMS in the total state. Moreover, for the reporting of FCI Bills and payment module in the Management of Information System (MIS) for higher monitoring of payment to Food Corporation of India (FCI), in modern times a provision has also been incorporated on the web. For that, this reporting machine is very useful at the state level for the monitoring of the MDMS. At every and each and every district, FCI Officers will have to log in on this reporting system and enter their bills and add a reproduction of the bill, instantly those payments will be visible to the respective district's Basic Shiksha Adhikari (BSA) login portal. Making Payment to the Food

Corporation of India (FCI), BSA will log in and enter the fee made against the consignment raised with the aid of the FCI. This price popularity will be visible to the FCI officials. This web-based reporting device is also well supported with the aid of the coverage of e-Governance and e-payment of Government of India.

2. Monitoring through Interactive Voice Response System (IVRS):

Monitoring via Interactive Voice Response System is real-time monitoring of MDMS. I.V.R.S. is another essential Monitoring system of MDMS. It has been introduced to supervise the implementation of MDMS at school level on daily basis. Punctuality and regularity of every day MDM furnished to the teenagers in the school are being monitored correctly on a real-time foundation via IVRS. Interactive Voice Response System (IVRS) two calls the Head Master of the involved school and acquire data asking for the quantity of youth having MDM on the current day. System asks the Question "Aaj Aapke Vidyalay Me Kitne Bachchon Ne Khana Khaya, Kripaya Batan Daba Kar Bhariye". Head Master has to respond to calls following the guidelines of the Interactive Voice Response System via typing the wide variety of students having a meal that day. If Headmaster/teacher fails to select the name of the device then IVRS name them again at an extraordinary time to take their responsibilities. At end of the month facts brought with the aid of using Interactive Voice Response System (IVRS) is validated with the aid of matching the files of MDM register page maintained at the school level. SMSs are despatched to the teachers about the data of food grain, conversion cost and cooks-honorarium allotted to their schools. It is additionally being planned to affirm the payment of cooks via I.V.R. system. Configurable Exception reviews like MDM now not served schools, Information not received; Teachers now not responding to IVR call and BEO/NSA, not-logged-in is accessible on the website. Apart from these an SMS is also sent to the Director MDM, DM, BSA and BEO/NSA related to the number of schools with no MDM served on a daily basis. Similarly, the data of Schools where MDM is not serve for greater than three days is also sent by means of e-mail to the DM and BSAs on weekly basis.

3. Stakeholder Training and Capacity Building

Since the year 2010 officials of the Basic Education Department of the Government of Uttar Pradesh at Division, District, and Block level, as well as NGO partners, have undergone orientation on various aspects of implementing the MDMS. The training experience of UP has been shared by MHRD with other states as a best practice with a recommendation for replication.

4. The system of online budget allocation and e-payment to Madhya Bhojan Nidhis of the schools

In compliance of recommendations of the 1st JRM which visited the State in 2010 the State Govt. has released Madhyanh Bhojan Nidhi for all the schools in the nearest CBS branches. From FY 2013-14 the State Government has introduced a system of e-payment from the treasury to the bank accounts.

Since the schools already have their accounts in CBS branches, the system of e-payment has been implemented in a smooth manner. Along with that the State Government has also implemented online budget allocation. As a result, the budget is allocated by Finance Controller MDMA from a central point against the sanctions and the time delay which was experienced in manual budget allocation at the district level.

5. Proactive efforts in Financial Management of Scheme

It is remarkable to note that State Finance Department released Central and State share well in advance to districts in anticipation of the release of central assistance by the Government of India.

6. e-Communication

All communications including Government Order and Mid-Day Meal Authority circulars, fund and foodgrain releases are sent through emails to District Magistrates, AD Basic, BSAs and officials of the MDMA at Division and District level. Simultaneously system generated SMS alerts are also sent to these levels.

7. Social Audit:

Social audit as a term was used in the 1950s. There has been a flurry of activity and interest in the last seven to eight years in India and neighboring countries. Voluntary development organizations are also actively concerned. Social audit is based on the principle that democratic local governance should be carried out, as far as possible, with the consent and understanding of all concerned. It is thus a process and not an event.

A social audit is a concern with measuring, understanding, reporting and finally improving an organization's social performance. A social audit helps to narrow gaps between vision/goal and reality, between efficiency and effectiveness. It is a technique to understand, measure, verify, report on and to improve the social performance of the organization.

Social auditing creates an impact on governance. It values the voice of stakeholders, including marginalized/poor groups whose voices are rarely heard. Social auditing is taken up for the purpose of enhancing local governance, particularly for strengthening accountability and transparency in local bodies.

The key difference between development and social audit is that a social audit focuses on the neglected issue of social impacts, while a development audit has a broader focus including environmental and economic issues, such as the efficiency of a project or programme.

The followings are the major aspects which have been covered in the social audit of MDM.

- Regularity in MDM Supply
- Use of MDM
- Supply of food grains
- Regular payment of food grain cost
- Social equity in MDM
- MDM supply as per menu
- Satisfaction of students with quantity and quality of MDM
- Status on personal hygiene of cooks
- MDM infrastructure
- Safety and hygiene
- Community participation
- Inspection and supervision
- Impact of MDM

Although the thought of Social Audit is perceived to be very essential for the proper governance and execution of MDMS but in India, Andhra Pradesh was the first state to enforce the social Audit. Although Report of 5th Joint Review Mission on MDMS, Uttar Pradesh performed the social Audit in Uttar Pradesh it was limited to solely two districts viz. Sravasti and Sitapur. Consequently, in district Rampur, there is no provision of Social Audit. In the absence of incorporation of Social Audit in MDM

Scheme in Rampur district, it is discovered that there is a lake of genuine Monitoring of the Scheme which leads to poor governance and ideal implementation of the MDMS in the entire District.

Conclusion

The policy of the MDMS is very top for the primary education especially in rural and backward areas the place most of the population is residing in poverty. But it is determined that there is a large discrepancy in the applicable implementation and excellent governance of MDM Scheme.

Chapter VI
Social and Local aspects of Governance of Right to Education

This chapter, has focussed on the three fundamental dimensions Perception, Participation, and Accountability in MDM scheme in Uttar Pradesh. The Perception dimension has four components Institutional Efficiency, Food Delivery, Corruption and Mismanagement, and Implementation Failure, the Participation dimension has two components Public Participation and Public Inaccessibility and Accountability dimension has added two factors such as Management of Funds and Monitoring and supervision of MDMS.

We adopted the two analysis technique first stage analysis through frequency check and second stage analysis via descriptive and t-test for the three sorts of respondents that are Parents, Teachers, and Gram Pradhans but students and BSA are no longer included in the t-test analysis. For students and BSA, the researcher has utilized solely frequency test due to the fact there is only one BSA appointed in a district and students are not familier with the ranking scale questionnaire.

There are three kinds of t-test, one sample t-test, independent sample t-test and parried t-test but the researcher has utilized the independent t-test due to the fact in this study the researcher has to examine the two independent blocks such as Chamrauvaa and Shahabad with respect to a number of parameters of MDM such as Institutional Efficiency, Participation, Social Auditing, Role of State (Leadership), Poor Delivery, Public Inaccessibility, Corruption Mismanagement and Implementation Failure in Uttar Pradesh. In this study, there were 120 parents in which 60 parents from each Chamrauvaa and Shahabad block, 12 teachers in which

6 teachers and 6 Gram Pradhans in which 3 Gram Pradhans. The researcher has set the significance level at 5% that means there would be 5 % wrong in accepting or rejecting the null hypothesis or 95% correct in the decision making. Therefore the decision rule will be such as

If the sig value (p-value) is less than 0.05, then Reject Null Hypothesis (H0)

If the sig value (p-value) is higher than 0.05, then Accept the Null Hypothesis (H01)

First Stage Analysis: For Students (Frequency Test)

Do you have a daily meal at your school?

		Frequency	%	Valid %	Cumulative %
Valid	Yes	120	100.0	100.0	100.0

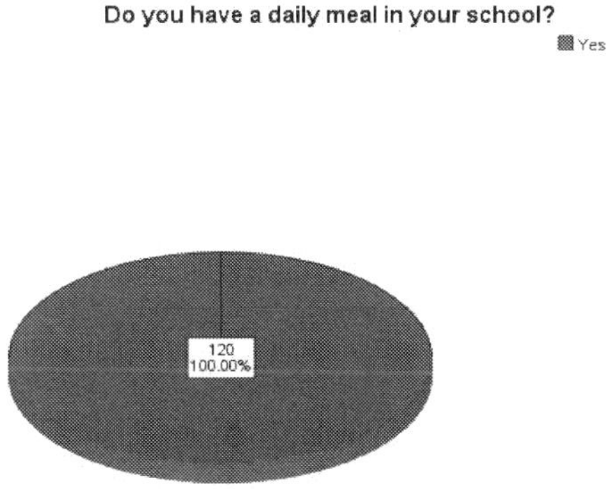

From the above table and pie chart, it is clear that all the students are taking MDM daily and the researcher can conclude that the mid-day scheme is attractive among the students Uttar Pradesh.

Do you get food according to the weekly menu in your school?

		Frequency	%	Valid %	Cumulative %
Valid	Yes	74	61.7	61.7	61.7
	No	46	38.3	38.3	100.0
	Total	120	100.0	100.0	

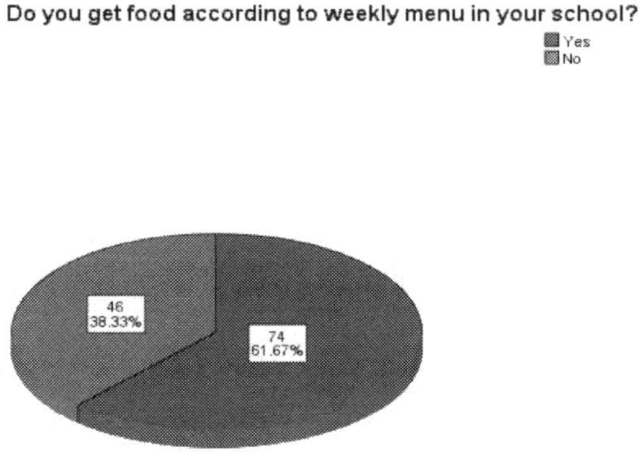

From the above table and pie chart it is clear that 61.67% students said that they get the MDM according to the weekly menu whereas 38.33% students said that they do not get the MDM according to the weekly menu, hence the researcher can conclude that most of the students are saying that they are getting the MDM according to the weekly menu in their school in Uttar Pradesh.

Do all children sit and eat together in your school?

		Frequency	%	Valid %	Cumulative %
Valid	Yes	64	53.3	53.3	53.3
	No	56	46.7	46.7	100.0
	Total	120	100.0	100.0	

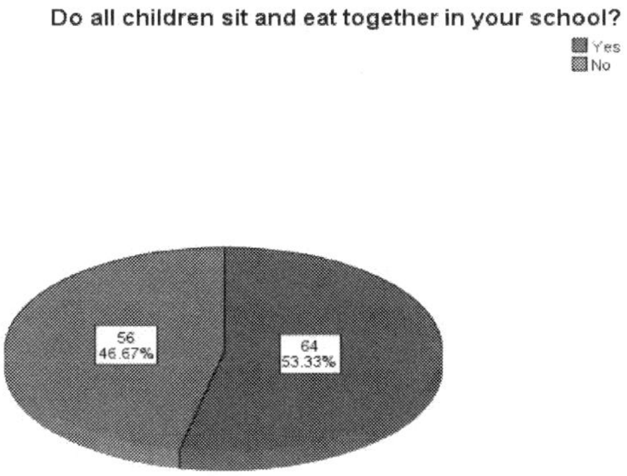

From the above table it is clear that 53.33% students said that they all are sitting together and also taking their MDM together whereas 46.67% students said that they do not sit together and do not eat together in the school, hence the researcher can conclude that in this case there is mixed response of the students at Rampur district in Uttar Pradesh.

Do you get milk and fruits every week at your school?

		Frequency	%	Valid %	Cumulative %
Valid	Yes	54	45.0	45.0	45.0
	No	66	55.0	55.0	100.0
	Total	120	100.0	100.0	

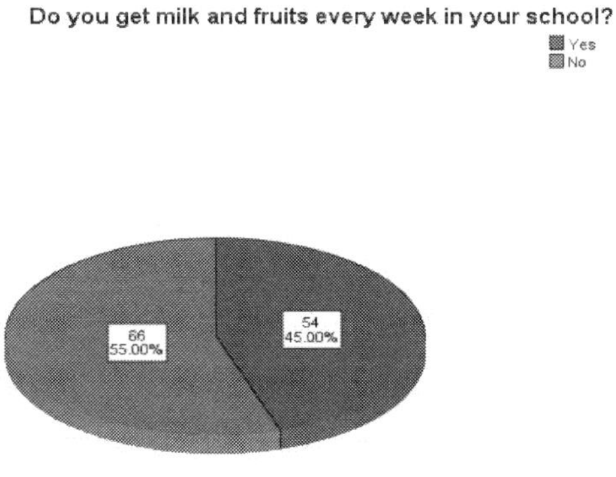

From the above table and pie chart it is clear that 55% students said that they do not get the milk and fruits every week in the MDM scheme whereas 45% students said that they get the milk and fruits every week and hence the researcher can conclude that most of the students do not get the milk or fruits, because most of the students are absent on that day in which there is a milk and fruit distribution day under this mid-day scheme for the school at Rampur district in Uttar Pradesh.

Do you bring the utensils from your home to eat food at school?

		Frequency	%	Valid %	Cumulative %
Valid	Yes	68	56.7	56.7	56.7
	No	52	43.3	43.3	100.0
	Total	120	100.0	100.0	

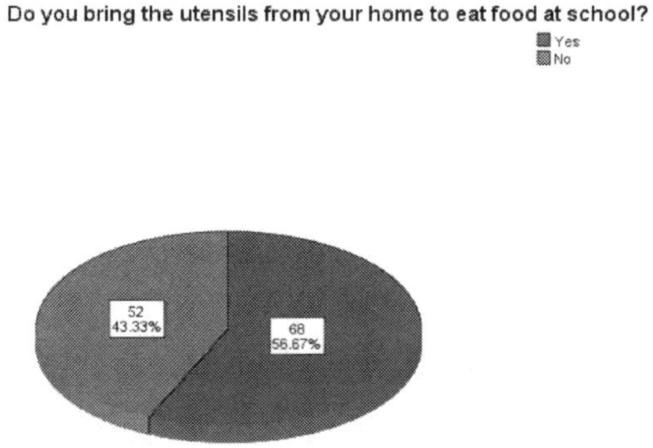

From the above table and pie chart it is clear that 56.67% students bring their utensils from the home to eat the MDM in the school whereas 43.33% students said that they do not bring the utensils from the home because the school administration is providing the utensils to the students, hence the researcher can conclude that more than 50% students bring their utensils from their home to eat the MDM in the school at Rampur district in Uttar Pradesh.

Do the teachers at your school first eat food?

		Frequency	%	Valid %	Cumulative %
Valid	Yes	22	18.3	18.3	18.3
	No	82	68.3	68.3	86.7
	Some Times	16	13.3	13.3	100.0
	Total	120	100.0	100.0	

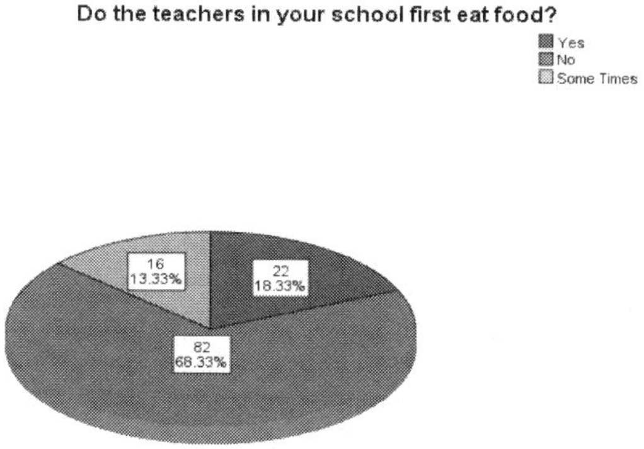

From the above table and pie chart it is clear that 18.33% students said that teachers first eat the food, 68.33% students said that teachers do not first eat the food under the MDMS in the school and 13.33 % students said that teacher sometimes first eat the food in the school, hence the researcher can conclude that teacher do not first eat the food provided in the school to the children under MDMS at Rampur district in Uttar Pradesh.

Do you eat the food you got at your school and bring it home?

		Frequency	%	Valid %	Cumulative %
Valid	No	120	100.0	100.0	100.0

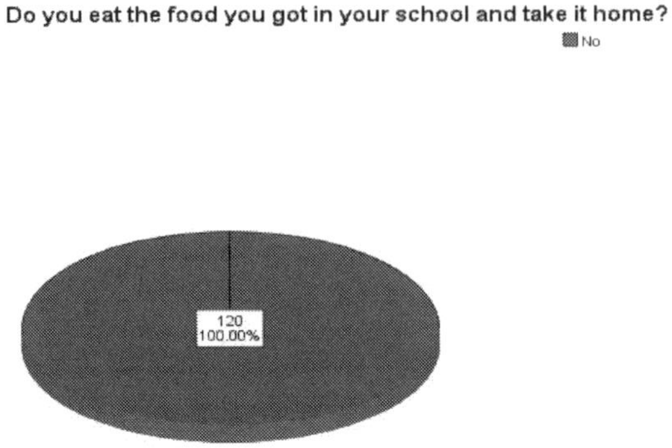

From the above table and pie chart, all the 100% students said that they do not bring the food to the home whereas they consumed their food in the school, hence the researcher can conclude that every student consumed the food in the school at Rampur district in Uttar Pradesh.

Does your school have a Gas Stove or a Wooden Stove?

		Frequency	%	Valid %	Cumulative %
Valid	Gas Stove	48	40.0	40.0	40.0
	Wooden Stove	72	60.0	60.0	100.0
	Total	120	100.0	100.0	

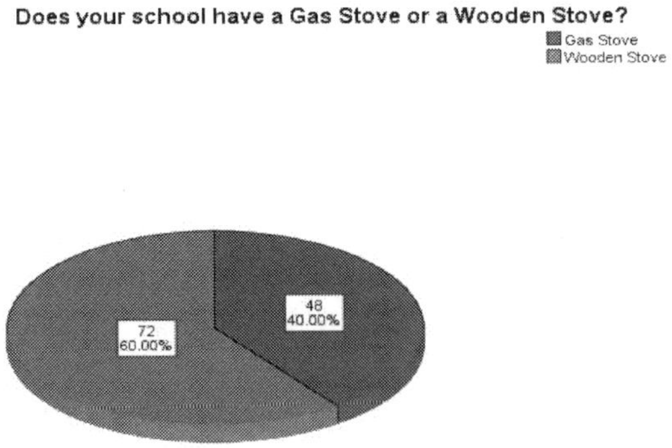

From the above table and pie chart, 60 % of students said that the food is prepared on the Wooden Stove whereas 40% students said that foods under MDM scheme are prepared on the Gas Stove, hence the researcher can conclude that most the school administration does not have the Gas Stove facility in their school and this is a serious issue because under PM Ujjala scheme every village is getting the Gas facility by the Government department and there may be one reason that Woods are easily available in the village, therefore, the school administration is using the Wooden Stove for the preparation of MDM for their school at Rampur district in Uttar Pradesh.

Are your parents inspecting the foods from time to time?

		Frequency	%	Valid %	Cumulative %
Valid	Yes	44	36.7	36.7	36.7
	No	76	63.3	63.3	100.0
	Total	120	100.0	100.0	

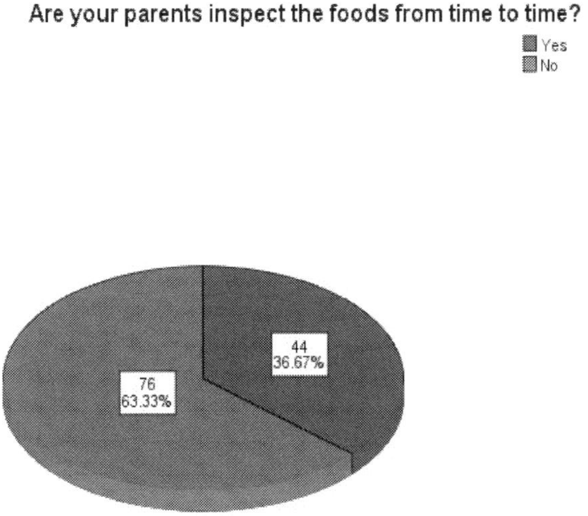

From the above table and pie chart, 63.33% students said that their parents do not inspect the meal time to time whereas 36.67%

students said that their parents inspect the food quality, hence the researcher can conclude that most of the parents do not care about the food superiority at Rampur district in Uttar Pradesh.

Is there a Hand pump at your school?

		Frequency	%	Valid %	Cumulative %
Valid	Yes	120	100.0	100.0	100.0

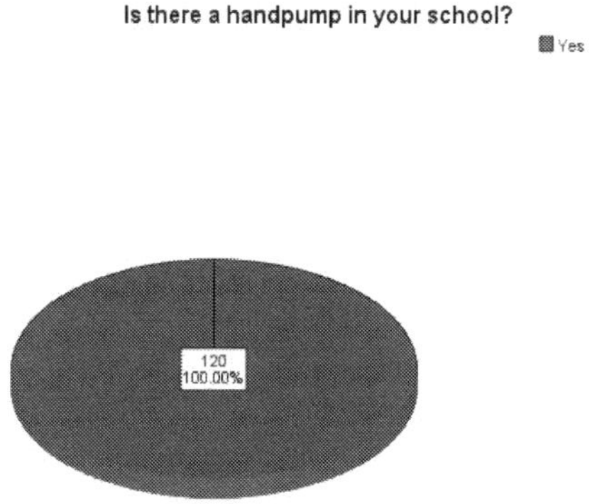

From the above table and pie chart it is clear that there is Hand pump facility in their school, hence the researcher can conclude that school administration is providing the Hand Pump facility for their students under MDM scheme at Rampur district in Uttar Pradesh.

First stage Analysis: For BSA (Frequency Test):

Since for every district there was only one BSA, therefore the Frequency test was analysed for one BSA who was appointed in the Rampur district in Uttar Pradesh and his expert views and response about the MDMS is given below:

Are you providing administrative support in the inspection of the MDMS?

		Frequency	%	Valid %	Cumulative %
Valid	Yes	1	100.0	100.0	100.0

Are you providing administration support in the inspection of the Mid-Day Meal Scheme in schools?

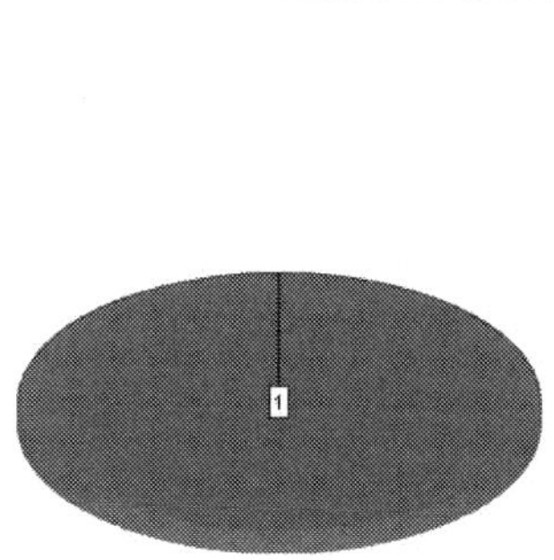

From the above table and pie chart, The BSA (Basic Shiksha Adhikari) was providing the administrative support in the inspection; hence the researcher can conclude the BSA appointed was monitoring the MDMS at Rampur District in Uttar Pradesh.

Are you getting full support at the government level in the MDMS?

		Frequency	%	Valid %	Cumulative %
Valid	Yes	1	100.0	100.0	100.0

Are you getting full support at the government level in the Mid Day Meal Scheme?

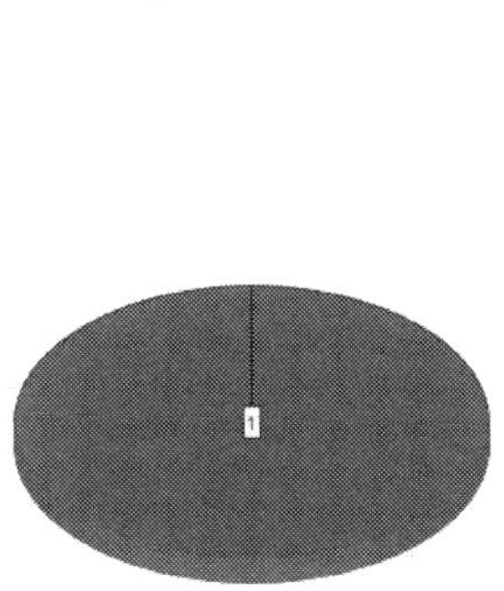

From the above table and pie chart, The BSA (Basic Shiksha Adhikari) said that he was getting the full support at the government level the scrutiny of the MDMS in the schools; hence the researcher can conclude the officer is getting administrative support from the government departments in the observing of the MDMS at Rampur District in Uttar Pradesh.

Do you have a heavy workload?

		Frequency	%	Valid %	Cumulative %
Valid	Yes	1	100.0	100.0	100.0

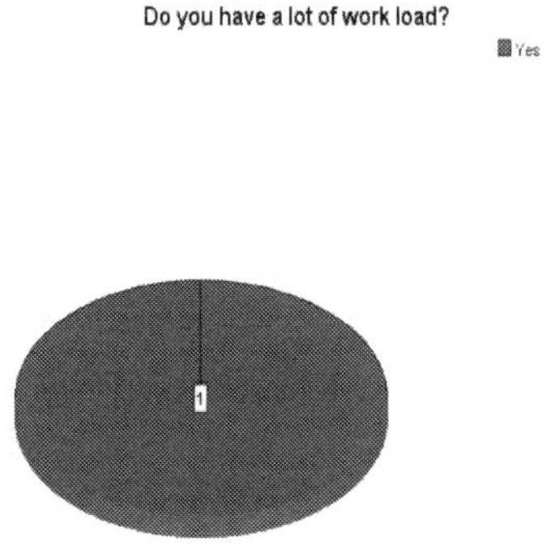

From the above table and pie chart, The BSA (Basic Shiksha Adhikari) said that he had the maximum workload in addition to the scrutiny of the MDMS in the schools; hence the researcher can conclude that the BSA officer was overloaded with the administrative work from the government departments.

Corruption at school level in the execution of the MDMS.

		Frequency	%	Valid %	Cumulative %
Valid	Yes	1	100.0	100.0	100.0

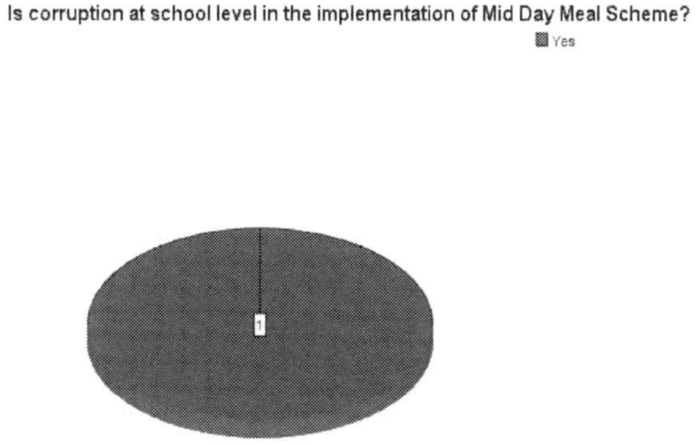

From the above table and pie chart, The BSA (Basic Shiksha Adhikari) said that there was corruption involve at the school level ,hence the researcher can conclude that the BSA officer accepted about the corruption at school level in the MDMS at Rampur District in Uttar Pradesh.

Is MDMS attractive for children?

		Frequency	%	Valid %	Cumulative %
Valid	Yes	1	100.0	100.0	100.0

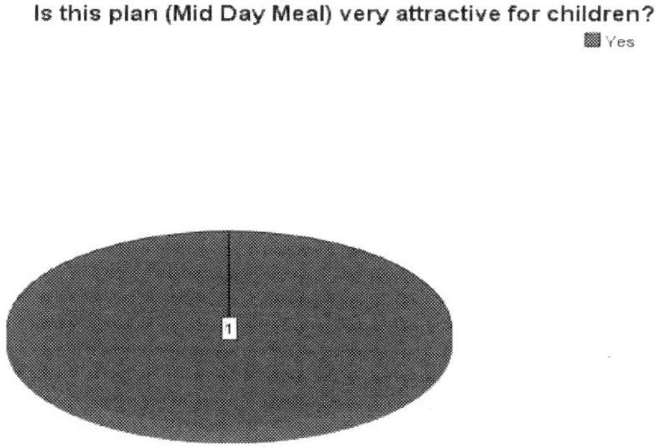

From the above table and pie chart, The BSA (Basic Shiksha Adhikari) said that this mid-day plan is very attractive scheme among the children in the schools, hence the researcher can conclude that the officer accepts that this mid-day scheme is very attractive in the school level at Rampur District in Uttar Pradesh.

Is education and health of the children improving through MDMS?

		Frequency	%	Valid %	Cumulative %
Valid	Yes	1	100.0	100.0	100.0

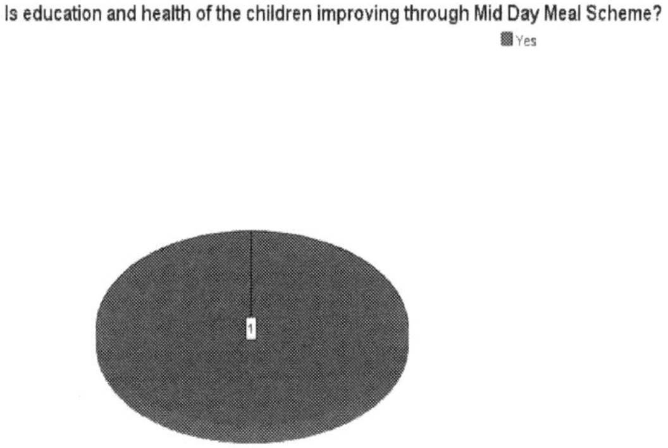

From the above table and pie chart, The BSA (Basic Shiksha Adhikari) said that the education and health of the children was enlightening through the MDMS at the school level , hence the researcher can conclude that the officer agree with the opinion of health and education was improving among the children at Rampur District in Uttar Pradesh.

Is there a local level politics between the Gram Pradhan & other people in implementing MDMS smoothly?

		Frequency	%	Valid %	Cumulative %
Valid	Yes	1	100.0	100.0	100.0

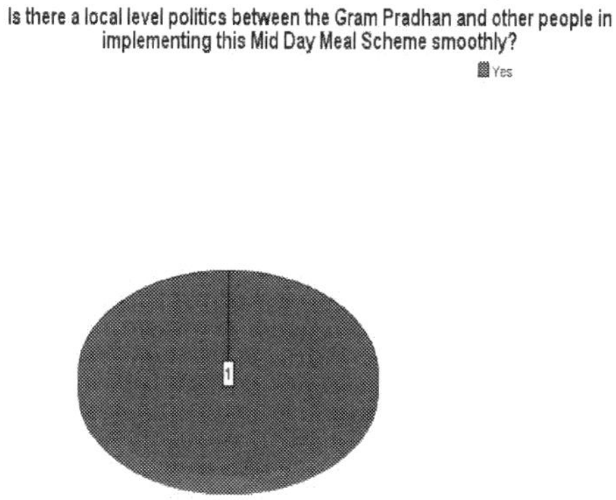

From the above table and pie chart, The BSA (Basic Shiksha Adhikari) said that there is a local village politics between the Gram Pradhan and village people under MDMS at school level at Rampur District in Uttar Pradesh.

Is there any online monitoring system should be for the MDMS?

		Frequency	%	Valid %	Cumulative %
Valid	Yes	1	100.0	100.0	100.0

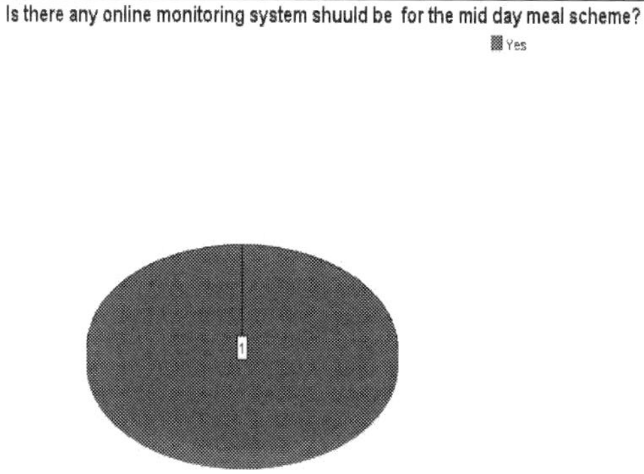

From the above table and pie chart, The BSA (Basic Shiksha Adhikari) said that there should be an online monitoring system in the smooth execution of the MDMS, hence the researcher can conclude that online monitoring system was required for the smooth execution of the MDMS at school level at Rampur District in Uttar Pradesh.

Is their heavy paper work involved in the reporting of MDMS?

		Frequency	%	Valid %	Cumulative %
Valid	Yes	1	100.0	100.0	100.0

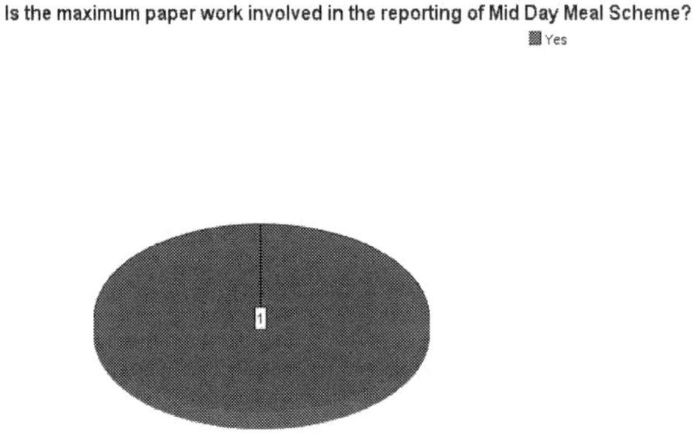

From the above table and pie chart, The BSA (Basic Shiksha Adhikari) said that there was maximum paperwork involved in the reporting of the MDMS at the school level , hence the researcher can conclude that the MDM reporting system was complex and involved the heavy paperwork for the smooth execution at school level at Rampur District in Uttar Pradesh.

Whether adequate financial assistance is provided by the government for implementation of MDMS?

		Frequency	%	Valid %	Cumulative %
Valid	Yes	1	100.0	100.0	100.0

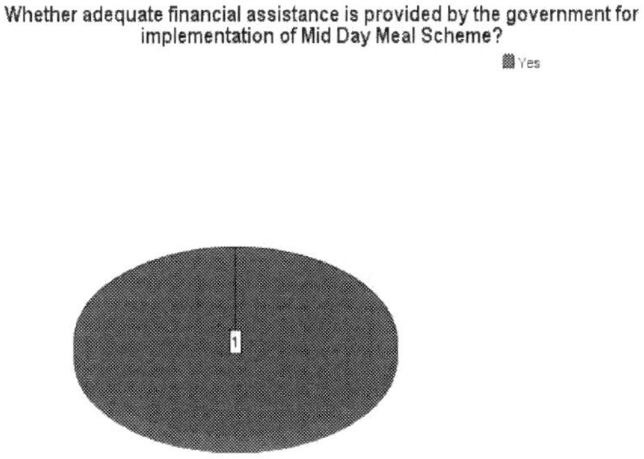

From the above table and pie chart, The BSA (Basic Shiksha Adhikari) said that the government was providing adequate financial assistance in the execution of the MDMS at school level at Rampur District in Uttar Pradesh.

Do teachers attend school regularly?

		Frequency	%	Valid %	Cumulative %
Valid	No	1	100.0	100.0	100.0

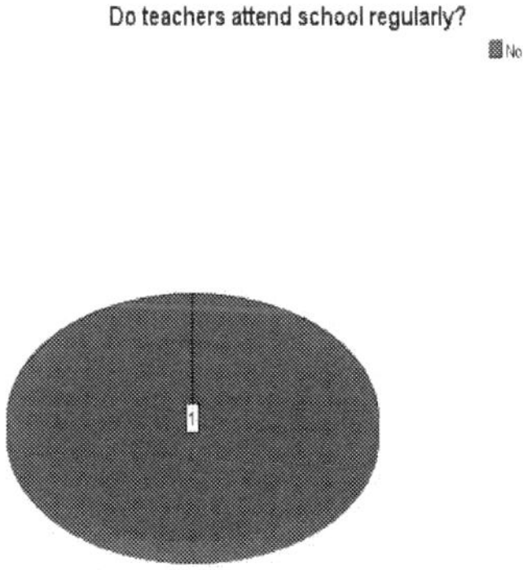

From the above table and pie chart, The BSA (Basic Shiksha Adhikari) said that teachers attendance was not regular at the school level, hence the researcher can conclude that teacher's attendance was not regular for the smooth execution of the MDMS at school level at Rampur District in Uttar Pradesh.

Is the presence of kitchen staff and associates regular?

		Frequency	%	Valid %	Cumulative %
Valid	No	1	100.0	100.0	100.0

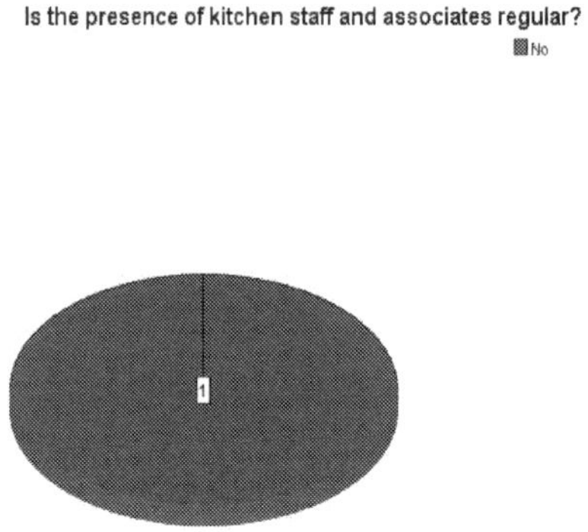

From the above table and pie chart, The BSA (Basic Shiksha Adhikari) said that kitchen staff and his assistant's attendance was not regular at the school level, hence the researcher can conclude that kitchen staff and his assistant's attendance was not regular for the smooth execution of the MDMS at school level at Rampur District in Uttar Pradesh.

Is the presence of students in the school regular?

		Frequency	%	Valid %	Cumulative %
Valid	No	1	100.0	100.0	100.0

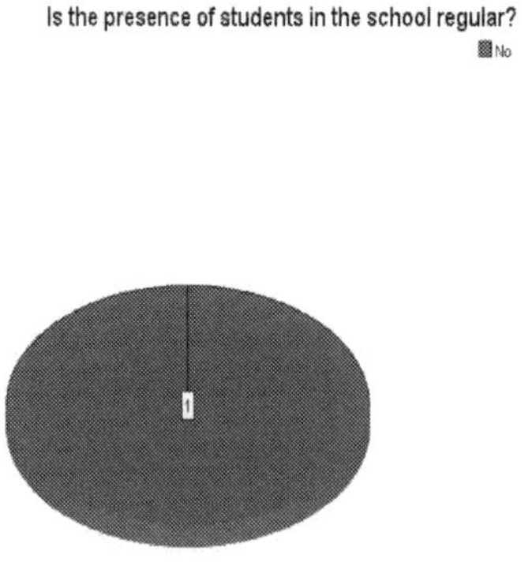

From the above table and pie chart, The BSA (Basic Shiksha Adhikari) said that student's attendance was not regular at the school level, hence the researcher can conclude that student's attendance was not regular for the smooth execution of the MDMS at school level at Rampur District in Uttar Pradesh.

Is there a proper arrangement for food hygiene ?

		Frequency	%	Valid %	Cumulative %
Valid	Yes	1	100.0	100.0	100.0

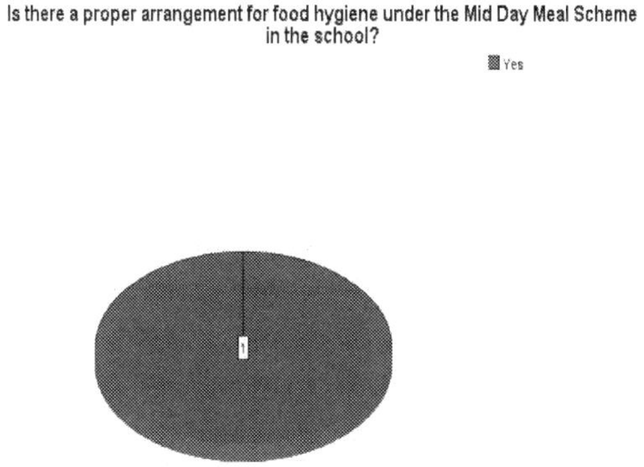

From the above table and pie chart, The BSA (Basic Shiksha Adhikari) said that there was a proper arrangement for the food hygiene, hence the researcher can conclude that proper hygiene was sustained at school level under MDMS at Rampur District in Uttar Pradesh.

Whether the quality of food is being checked regularly?

		Frequency	%	Valid %	Cumulative %
Valid	Yes	1	100.0	100.0	100.0

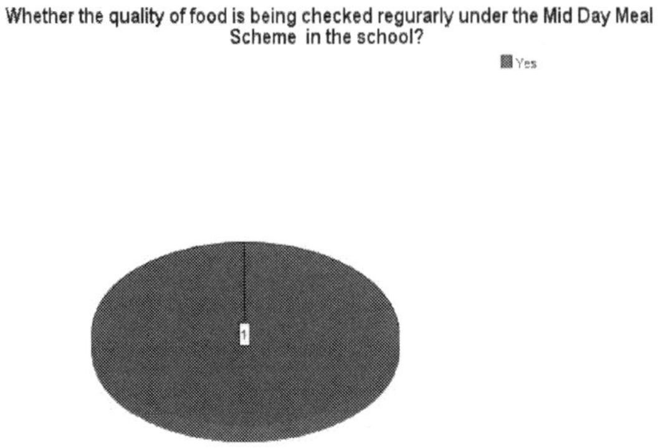

From the above table and pie chart, The BSA (Basic Shiksha Adhikari) said that food quality was regularly checked by the administration , hence the researcher can conclude that food grain quality was under monitoring and supervision of BSA at Rampur District in Uttar Pradesh.

Is there MDMS on a weekly menu basis?

		Frequency	%	Valid %	Cumulative %
Valid	Yes	1	100.0	100.0	100.0

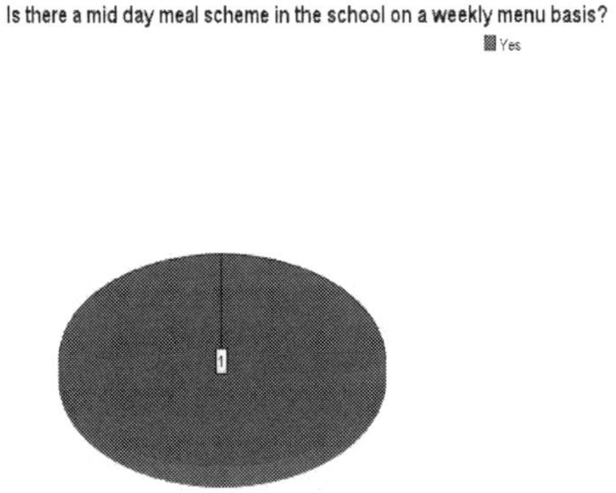

From the above table and pie chart, The BSA (Basic Shiksha Adhikari) said that food given to the children was according to the strict weekly menu basis , hence the researcher can conclude that proper weekly menu system was following by the school administration at Rampur District in Uttar Pradesh.

For Parents: Perception about MDMS:

First Stage Analysis: For Parents (Frequency Test)

Does your child go to school every day?

		Frequency	%	Valid %	Cumulative %
Valid	Yes	120	100.0	100.0	100.0

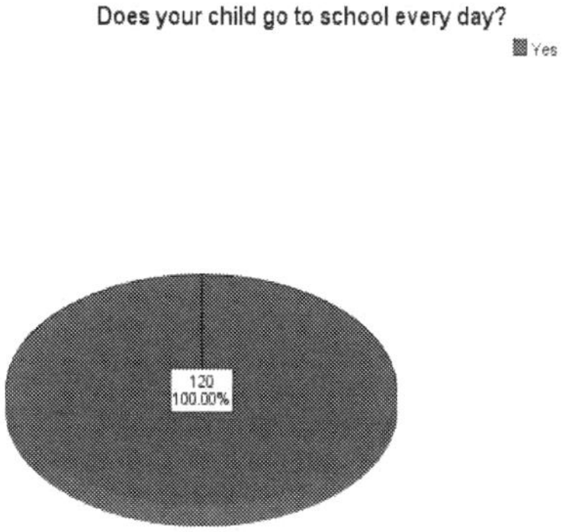

From the above table and pie chat, all the parents said that their children went to the school every day; hence the researcher can conclude that the parents know the importance of the education in their children's growth and development through the MDMS at Rampur district in Uttar Pradesh.

Does your child get daily food under the MDMS?

		Frequency	%	Valid %	Cumulative %
Valid	Yes	120	100.0	100.0	100.0

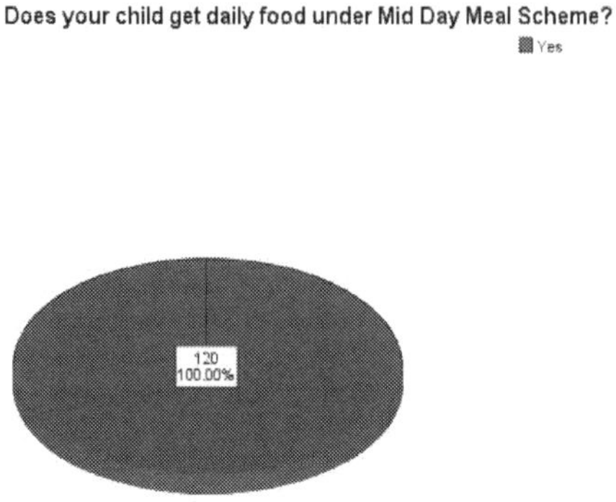

From the above table and pie chart, all the parents said that their children get MDM every day in the school; hence the researcher can conclude that this mid-day scheme is popular in the village among the students and parents at Rampur district in Uttar Pradesh.

Does your child do a midday meal at school or at home?

		Frequency	%	Valid %	Cumulative %
Valid	School	120	100.0	100.0	100.0

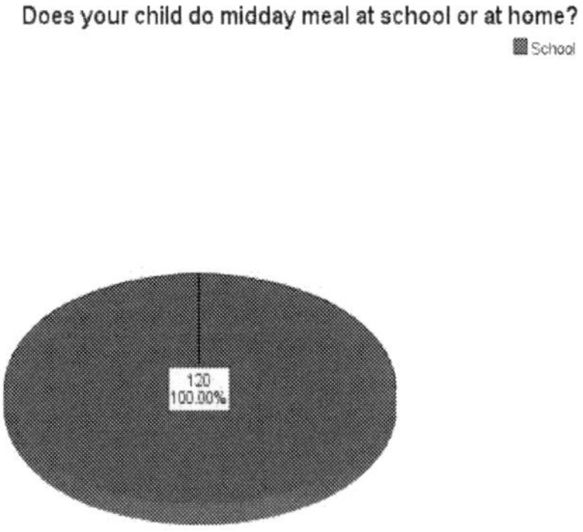

From the above table and pie chart, all the parents said that their children take the MDM in the school, not at home; hence the researcher can conclude that students get the MDM in the school at Rampur district in Uttar Pradesh.

Do you observe MDMs at a fixed interval?

		Frequency	%	Valid %	Cumulative %
Valid	Yes	32	26.7	26.7	26.7
	No	88	73.3	73.3	100.0
	Total	120	100.0	100.0	

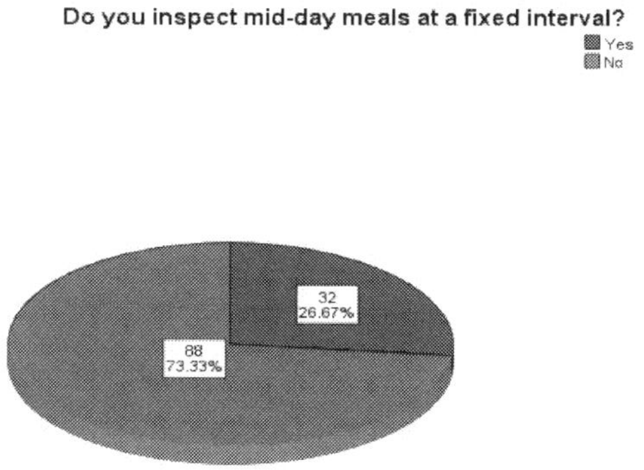

From the above table and pie chart, 73.33 % parents said that they do not inspect the food quality under MDM scheme whereas only 26.67% parents inspect the food quality, hence the researcher can conclude that most of the parents are not inspecting the food provided to their children under MDM scheme in the school in Rampur district in Uttar Pradesh.

Does your child get midday meal according to the weekly menu?

		Frequency	%	Valid %	Cumulative %
Valid	Yes	38	31.7	31.7	31.7
	No	82	68.3	68.3	100.0
	Total	120	100.0	100.0	

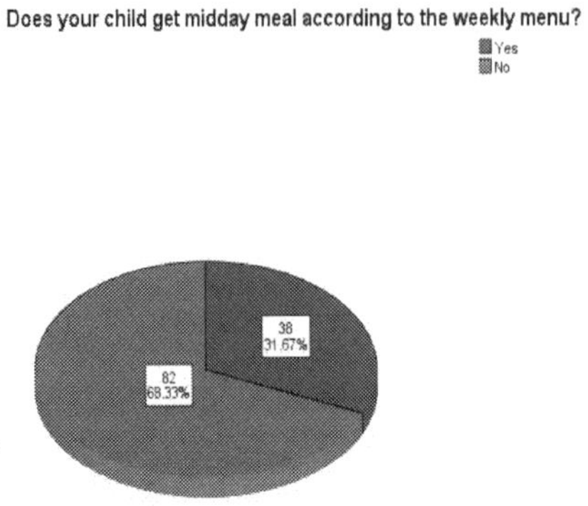

From the above table and pie chart, 68.33% parents said that school administration is not providing the food according to the weekly menu under MDM scheme whereas 31.67% parents said that the food providing to their children are according to the weekly menu, hence the researcher can conclude that school administration is not providing the food according to the weekly menu under mid-day scheme at Rampur district in Uttar Pradesh.

Do you participate in the meeting of the School Management Committee?

		Frequency	%	Valid %	Cumulative %
Valid	Yes	66	55.0	55.0	55.0
	No	54	45.0	45.0	100.0
	Total	120	100.0	100.0	

Do you participate in the meeting of the School Management Committee?

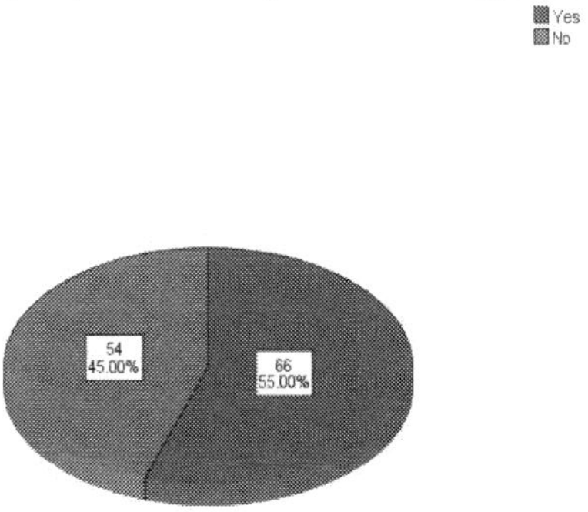

From the above table and pie chart, 55% parents were participating in the meeting of School Management Committee whereas 45 % parents did not participate in the meeting of school management committee under MDMS; hence the researcher can conclude that there were mixed response from the parents about the available and unavailability in the meeting of mid-day scheme at Rampur district in Uttar Pradesh.

Are the issues related to MDM resolved in the School Management Committee raised by you?

		Frequency	%	Valid %	Cumulative %
Valid	Yes	38	31.7	31.7	31.7
	No	82	68.3	68.3	100.0
	Total	120	100.0	100.0	

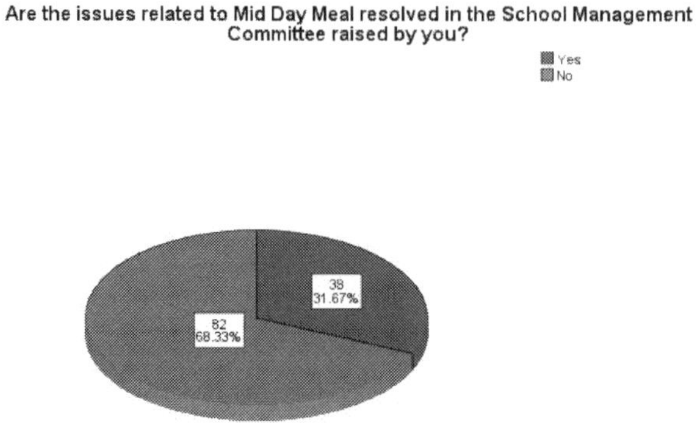

From the above table and pie chart, 68.33 % parents said that the issues raised by them related with the MDM are not resolved in the school management committee by the school administration whereas only 31.67% parents said the issues raised by them are resolved, hence the researcher can conclude that most of the parents are not satisfied by the working of the School Management Committee for the execution of the MDMS at Rampur district in Uttar Pradesh.

Does village level politics affect the MDMS?

		Frequency	%	Valid %	Cumulative %
Valid	Yes	40	33.3	33.3	33.3
	No	80	66.7	66.7	100.0
	Total	120	100.0	100.0	

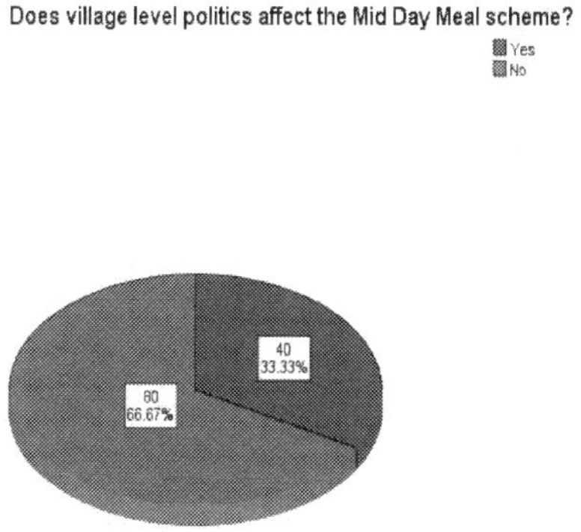

From the above table and pie chart, 66.67% parents said that village politics did not affect whereas 33.33% parents said that village-level politics affected due to the MDMS, hence the researcher can conclude that most of the parents said that village-level politics did not affect MDMS at Rampur district in Uttar Pradesh.

Do children in your village school be seated in different groups on caste basis during MDM distribution?

		Frequency	%	Valid %	Cumulative %
Valid	Yes	36	30.0	30.0	30.0
	No	84	70.0	70.0	100.0
	Total	120	100.0	100.0	

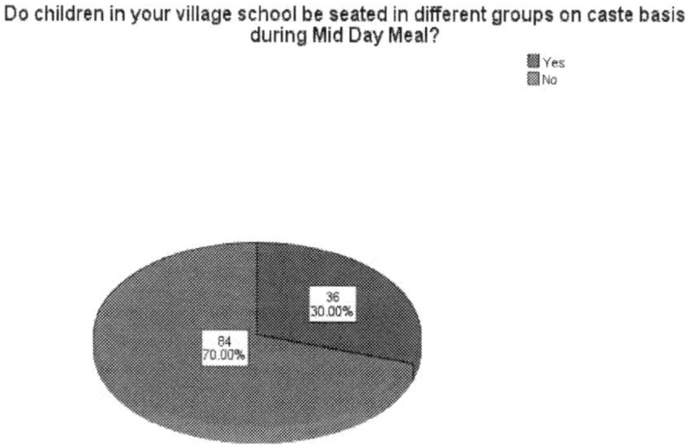

From the above table and pie chart, 70% parents said that their children are not sitting on the basis of caste groups in the school while taking the MDM whereas only 30% parents said that their children are sitting on the caste groups in the school, hence the researcher can conclude that most of the parents are satisfied with the sitting arrangement during MDM because there is no caste biases by the school administration at Rampur district in Uttar Pradesh.

Do your children get the utensil from the school during the MDM?

		Frequency	%	Valid %	Cumulative %
Valid	Yes	32	26.7	26.7	26.7
	No	88	73.3	73.3	100.0
	Total	120	100.0	100.0	

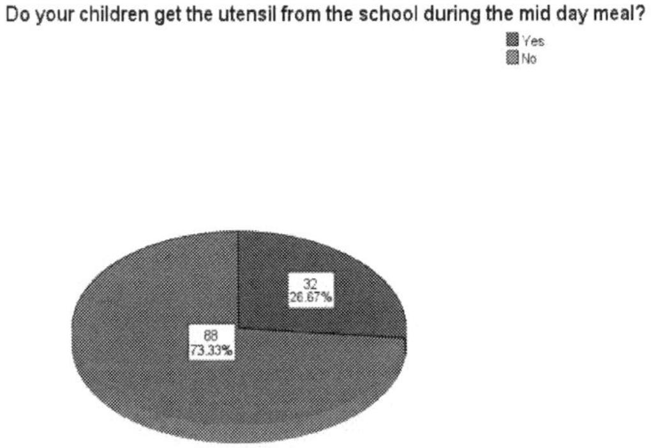

From the above table and pie chart, 73.33% parents said that their children did not bring the utensil from home for taking MDM in the school whereas only 26.67% parents said that their children brought the utensils, hence the researcher can conclude that most of the parents agreed that the utensils were provided by the school administration under the MDMS at Rampur district in Uttar Pradesh.

Do you inspect the grain quality under the MDMS?

		Frequency	%	Valid %	Cumulative %
Valid	Yes	24	20.0	20.0	20.0
	No	96	80.0	80.0	100.0
	Total	120	100.0	100.0	

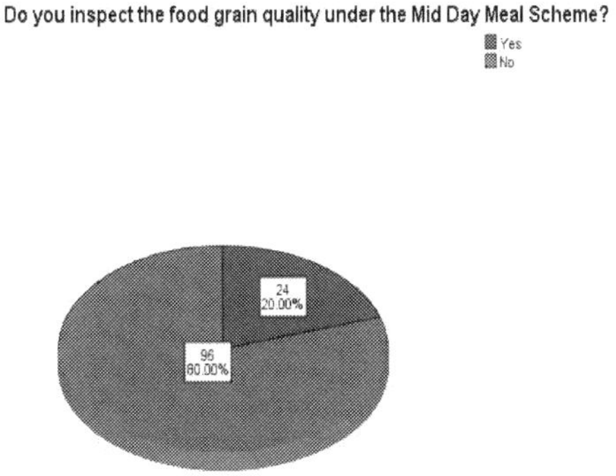

From the above table and pie chart, 80% parents did not inspect food grain superiority whereas 20% parents inspect the food grain quality, hence the researcher can conclude that most of the parents inspected the food grain superiority under the MDMS scheme at Rampur district in Uttar Pradesh.

Do you observe the taste of the baked food?

		Frequency	%	Valid %	Cumulative %
Valid	Yes	20	16.7	16.7	16.7
	No	100	83.3	83.3	100.0
	Total	120	100.0	100.0	

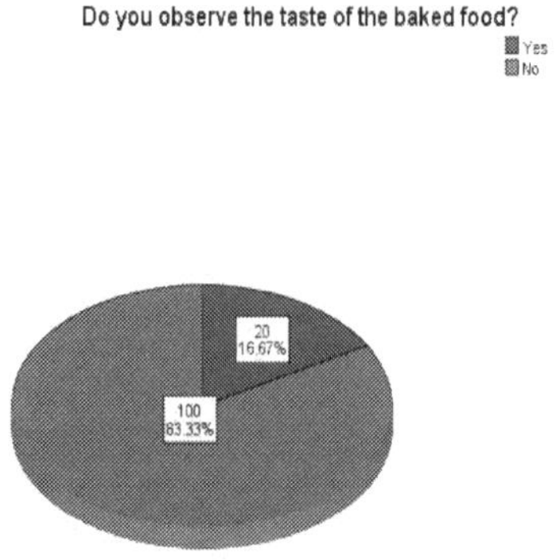

From the above table and pie chart, 83.33% parents said that they did not taste the baked meal whereas only 16.67% parents taste the baked food, hence the researcher can conclude that most of the parents were taking interest in the tasting of the baked meal distributing under MDMS to their children at Rampur District in Uttar Pradesh.

Do you observe MDMs as a citizen group?

		Frequency	%	Valid %	Cumulative %
Valid	No	120	100.0	100.0	100.0

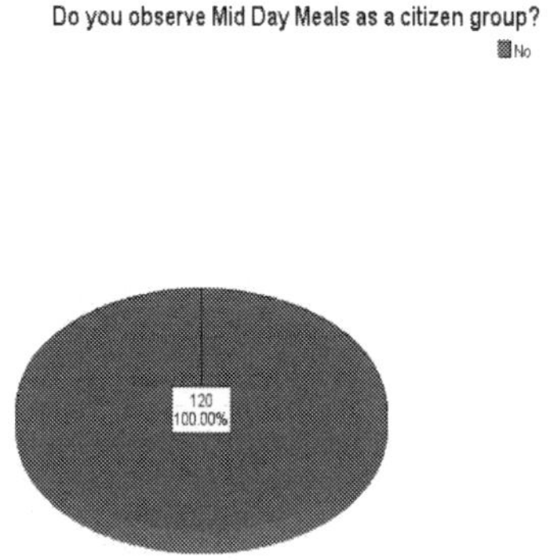

From the above table and pie chat, all the 100 % parents did not observe as the citizen group formed by the village people for the improvement of the scheme, hence the researcher can conclude that no parents were inspecting as the citizen group for the betterment of this MDMS at Rampur district in Uttar Pradesh.

Who do you complain about the MDM?

		Frequency	%	Valid %	Cumulative %
Valid	Yes	104	86.7	86.7	86.7
	Block level officer	16	13.3	13.3	100.0
	Total	120	100.0	100.0	

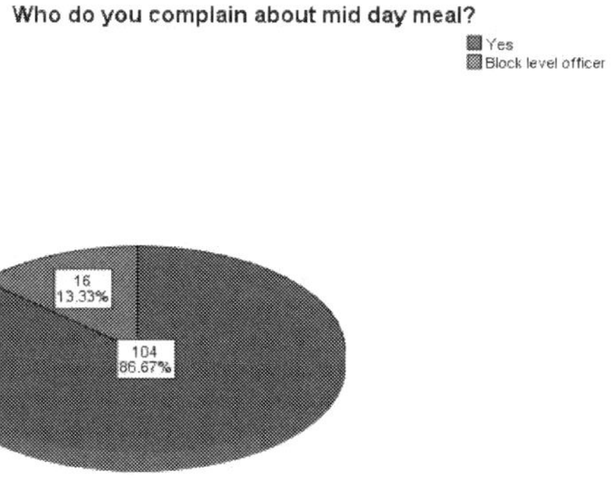

From the above table and pie chart, 86.67% parents do complain related with the MDM scheme and only 13.33% parents approached to the block level officer for complaining the issue related with the MDM scheme, hence the researcher can conclude that most of the parents are complaining about the issue related to the mid-day scheme at Rampur district in Uttar Pradesh.

Has the MDM Scheme improved your child's health and education?

		Frequency	%	Valid %	Cumulative %
Valid	Yes	62	51.7	51.7	51.7

	No	58	48.3	48.3	100.0
	Total	120	100.0	100.0	

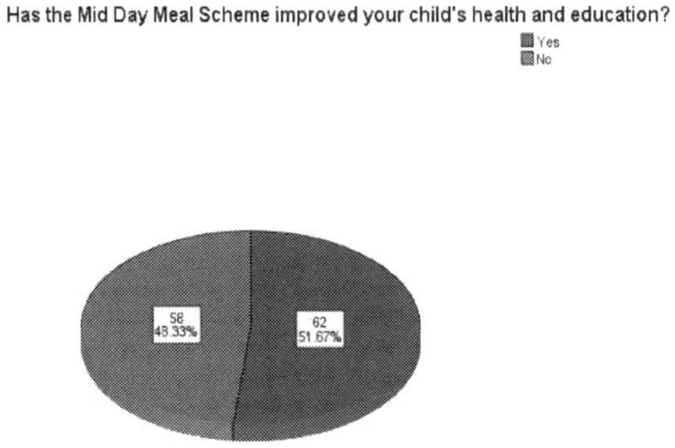

From the above table and pie chart, 51.67% parents said that their children's education and health improved whereas 48.33% were not accepting that their children's education and health improved, hence the researcher can conclude that, MDMS has improved the education and health among the children at Rampur district in Uttar Pradesh.

Do you inspect food grain supply process from Kotedar to Gram Pradhan and from Gram Pradhan to School administration under MDMS?

		Frequency	%	Valid %	Cumulative %
Valid	Yes	10	8.3	8.3	8.3
	No	110	91.7	91.7	100.0
	Total	120	100.0	100.0	

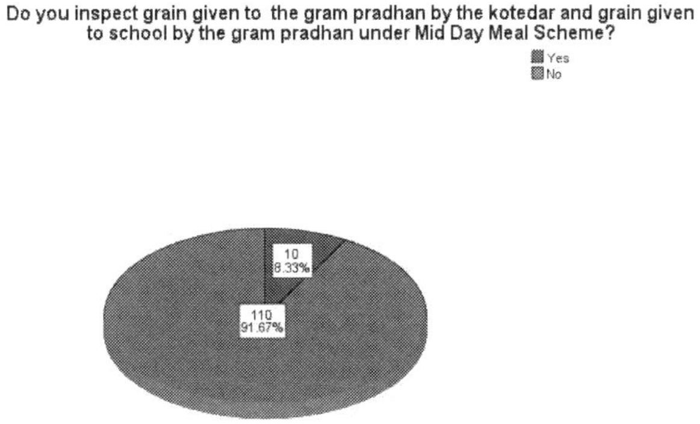

From the above table and pie chart, 91.67% parents said that they did not inspect the food grain supply process from the Kotedar to Gram Pradhan and from Gram Pradhan to the School Management whereas only 8.33% parents inspect the food grain supply process, hence the researcher can conclude that most of the parents do not inspect the food grain supply process from the Kotedar to Gram Pradhan and from Gram Pradhan to the School Management under MDMS at Rampur district in Uttar Pradesh. This shows that there is no check system mandatory by the parents for the food grain supply in this scheme.

For Parents: Second Stage Analysis: (Independent T Test)

This independent T test was applied for two independent groups where the researcher wants to know the significant difference between two groups. In this case the two groups were the two blocks of Rampur district that was Chamrauvaa and Shahabad and test parameter were Institutional efficiency, food delivery, corruption & mismanagement and implementation failure under MDMS.

The Null Hypothesis has been formulated as follows

H01p : There is no significant difference of opinion of parents between the Chamrauvaa and Shahabad block with respect to the institutional efficiency of MDMS at Rampur district in Uttar Pradesh.

H02p : There is no significant difference of opinion of parents between the Chamrauvaa and Shahabad block with respect to the food delivery of MDMS at Rampur district in Uttar Pradesh.

H03p : There is no significant difference of opinion of parents between the Chamrauvaa and Shahabad block with respect to the corruption & mismanagement under MDMS at Rampur district in Uttar Pradesh.

H04p : There is no significant difference of opinion of parents between the Chamrauvaa and Shahabad block with respect to the implementation failure of MDMS scheme at Rampur district in Uttar Pradesh.

Here the researcher has formulated the four null hypotheses for Parents (p) with respect to institutional efficiency, food delivery, corruption & mismanagement and implementation failure which was tested through the Independent T test as follows:

Descriptive Analysis:

Test Variable- Institutional Efficiency

Descriptive Statistics

	N	Min.	Max.	Mean	Std. Deviation
Institutional Efficiency	120	1.40	4.00	2.7000	1.01914
Valid N (listwise)	120				

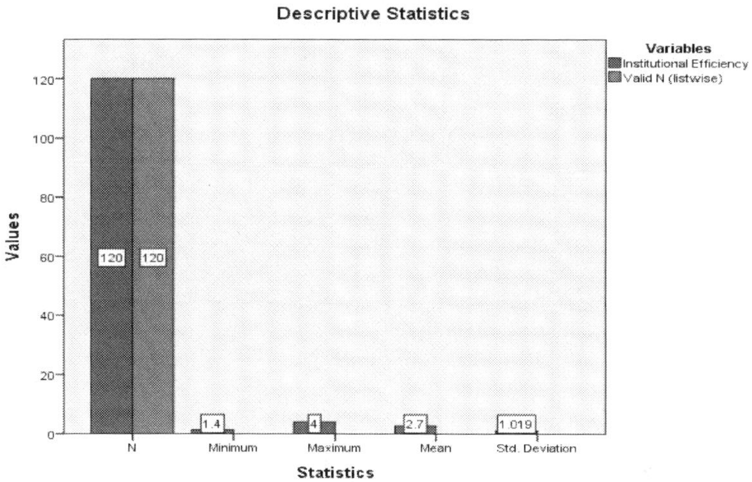

From the above descriptive statistics table and bar chart the mean score of institutional efficiency with respect to parents for Rampur district is 2.7000 which is above 2 and below 3 Likert scale rating which is near to neutral, therefore on the basis of parents opinion, the researcher can conclude that the opinion of parents with respect to institutional efficiency is neutral that means neither agreed nor disagreed about institutional efficiency or parents were not sure about the institutional efficiency at Rampur district in Uttar Pradesh.

T-Test Analysis (Comparison between two blocks Chamrauvaa and Shahabad at Rampur district in Uttar Pradesh:

H01p: There is no significant difference of opinion of parents between the Chamrauvaa and Shahabad block with respect to the institutional efficiency of MDM scheme at Rampur district in Uttar Pradesh.

Test Variable- Institutional Efficiency

Grouping Variable- Two Block Chamrauvaa & Shahabad

Group Statistics

	Block	N	**M**	SD	SEM
Institutional Efficiency	Chamrauvaa	60	**2.7667**	1.03771	.13397
	Shahabad	60	**2.6333**	1.00451	.12968

Where M= Mean, SD= Standard Deviation, SEM= Standard Error Mean

From the above group statistics table the mean score of institutional efficiency for Chamrauvaa block is 2.7667 which is above 2 and below 3 Likert scale rating which is near to neutral and for Shahabad block is 2.6333 which is again above 2 and below 3 Likert scale which is near to neutral, therefore on the basis of parents opinion, the researcher can conclude that the institutional efficiency at Chamrauvaa block is almost same as Shahabad block at Rampur district in Uttar Pradesh.

Independent T Test		t-test for Equality of Means						
		t	df	Sig.	MD	SED	95% Confidence Interval of the Difference	
							Lower	Upper
Institutional Efficiency	Equal variances assumed	.715	118	.476	.13333	.18645	-.23589	.50256
	Equal variances not assumed	.715	117.875	**.476**	.13333	.18645	-.23590	

In this above output table, the researcher gets results of the two tests- Levene's Test for Equality of Variance and t-test for Equality of Means. The table contains two sets of analysis, the first one assuming equal variances in the two groups and the second one assuming unequal variance.

Since the first Null Hypothesis was H01p: There is no significant difference of opinion of parents between the Chamrauvaa and Shahabad block with respect to the institutional efficiency of MDM scheme at Rampur district in Uttar Pradesh.

From the above table

The sig. value (2 tailed) 0.476 >0.05(commonly accepted level of significance), hence Accept Null hypothesis H01p, therefore the researcher can conclude that there is no significant difference of opinion of parents between the Chamrauvaa and Shahabad block with respect to the institutional efficiency of MDM scheme at Rampur district in Uttar Pradesh.

Test Variable- Food Delivery

Descriptive Statistics					
	N	Min.	Max.	Mean	Std. Deviation
Food Delivery	120	2.20	4.00	2.3467	.45632
Valid N (listwise)	120				

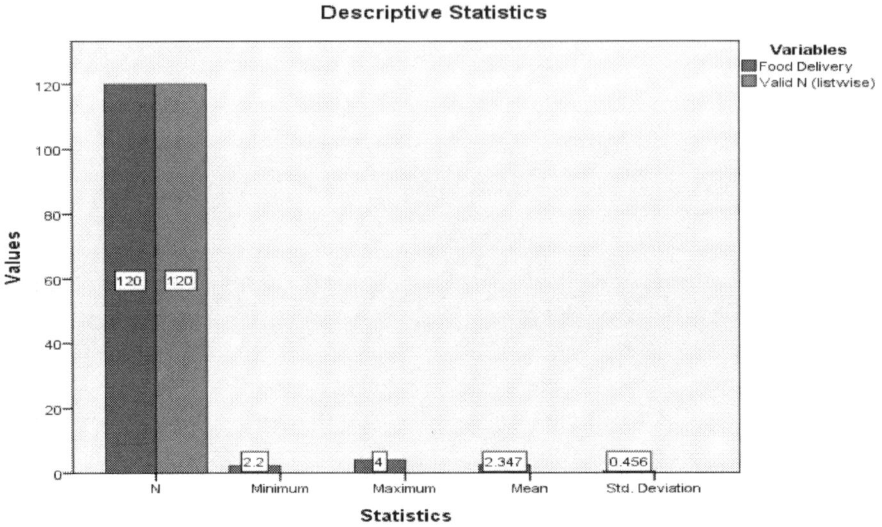

From the above descriptive statistics table and bar chart the mean score of food delivery with respect to parents for Rampur district is 2.347 which is above 2 and below 3 Likert scale rating which is near to disagree, therefore on the basis of parents opinion, the researcher can conclude that the opinion of parents with respect to food delivery is not satisfactory at Rampur district in Uttar Pradesh.

Test Variable- Food Delivery

Group Statistics

	Block	N	**M**	SD	SEM
Food Delivery	Chamrauvaa	60	**2.2000**	.00000	.00000
	Shahabad	60	**2.4933**	.61337	.07919

Where M=Mean, SD=Standard Deviation, SEM=Standard Error Mean

From the above group statistics table the mean score of Food Delivery for Chamrauvaa block is 2.2000 which is above 2 and below 3 Likert scale rating which is near to disagree and for Shahabad block is 2.4933 which is above 2 and below 3 Likert scale which is near to disagree, therefore the researcher can conclude that the parents opinion with respect to Food Delivery is more disagreeable for Chamrauvaa block in comparison to Shahabad block that means in the parents' opinion food delivery is better at Chamrauvaa block in comparison to Shahabad block under MDM scheme at Rampur district in Uttar Pradesh.

Independent T Test		t-test for Equality of Means						
							95% Confidence Interval	
		t	df	Sig.	MD	SED	Lower	Upper
Food Delivery	**Equal variances assumed**	-3.704	118	.000	-.29333	.07919	-.45014	-.13652
	Equal variances not assumed	-3.704	59.000	**.000**	-.29333	.07919	-.45178	-.13488

Where MD= Mean Difference, SED=Standard Error Difference

Since the second null Hypothesis was H02p: There is no significant difference of opinion of parents between the Chamrauvaa and Shahabad block with respect to the food Delivery under MDM scheme at Rampur district in Uttar Pradesh.

From the above table

The sig. value (2 tailed) 0.000 < 0.05(commonly accepted level of significance), hence Reject Null Hypothesis H02p, therefore the researcher can conclude that there is a significant difference of opinion of parents between the Chamrauvaa and Shahabad block with respect to the food Delivery under MDM scheme at Rampur district in Uttar Pradesh.

Test Variable- Corruption & Mismanagement

Descriptive Statistics

	N	Min.	Max.	Mean	Std. Deviation
Corruption & Mismanagement	120	2.40	4.60	2.6933	.50339
Valid N (listwise)	120				

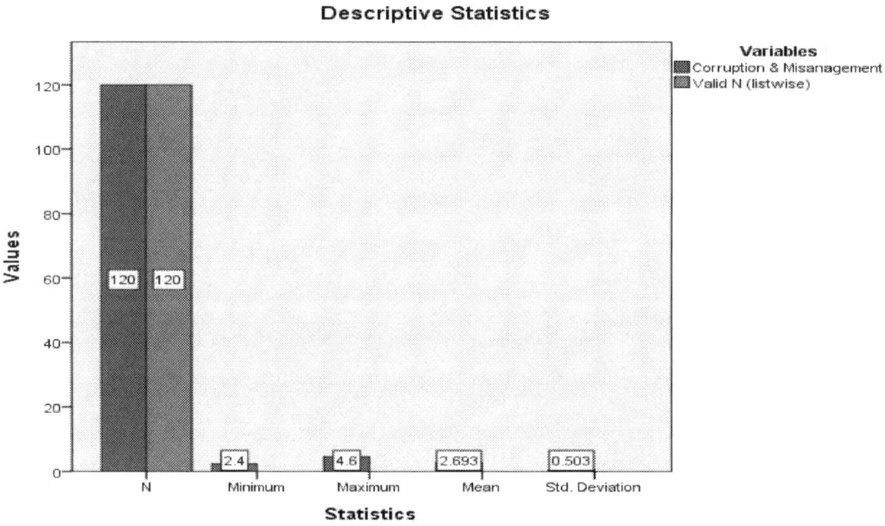

From the above descriptive statistics table and bar chart the mean score of corruption and mismanagement with respect to parents for Rampur district is 2.693 which is above 2 and below 3 Likert scale rating which is near to neutral, therefore on the basis of parents opinion, the researcher can conclude that the opinion of parents with respect to corruption and mismanagement is neutral at Rampur district in Uttar Pradesh.

Test Variable- Corruption & Mismanagement

Group Statistics

	Block	N	**M**	SD	SEM
Corruption & Mismanagement	Chamrauvaa	60	**2.5333**	.09508	.01227
	Shahabad	60	**2.8533**	.67081	.08660

Where M=Mean, SD=Standard Deviation, SEM=Standard Error Mean

From the above group statistics table the mean score of Corruption & Mismanagement for Chamrauvaa block is 2.5333 which is above 2 and below 3 Likert scale rating which is near to disagree and for Shahabad block is 2.8533 which is above 2 and below 3 Likert scale which is near to neutral, therefore the researcher can conclude that in parents opinion with respect to Corruption & Mismanagement, there is more disagreement in Chamrauvaa block than Shahabad block that means there is less corruption & mismanagement at Chamrauvaa block in comparison to Shahabad block under MDM scheme at Rampur district in Uttar Pradesh as per the parents opinion.

Independent T Test		t-test for Equality of Means						
		t	df	Sig.	MD	SED	95% Confidence Interval	
							Lower	Upper
Corruption & Mismanagement	Equal variances assumed	-3.659	118	.000	-.32000	.08747	-.49321	-.14679
	Equal variances not assumed	-3.659	61.369	**.001**	-.32000	.08747	-.49488	-.14512

Where MD= Mean Difference, SED=Standard Error Difference

Since the third null Hypothesis was H03p: There is no significant difference of opinion of parents between the Chamrauvaa and Shahabad block with respect to the Corruption & Mismanagement under MDM scheme at Rampur district in Uttar Pradesh.

From the above table

The sig. value (2 tailed) 0.001 < 0.05(commonly accepted level of significance), hence Reject Null Hypothesis H03p, therefore the researcher can conclude that there is a significant difference of opinion of parents between the Chamrauvaa and Shahabad block with respect to the Corruption & Mismanagement under MDM scheme at Rampur district in Uttar Pradesh.

Test Variable- Implementation Failure

Descriptive Statistics

	N	Min.	Max.	Mean	Std. Deviation
Implementation Failure	120	1.60	4.00	2.2967	.57452
Valid N (listwise)	120				

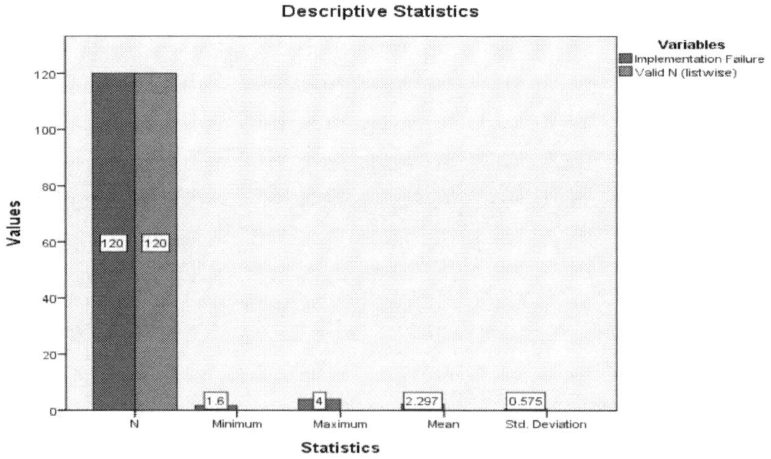

From the above descriptive statistics table and bar chart the mean score of implementation failure with respect to parents for Rampur district is 2.297 which is near to 2 Likert scale rating which is near to disagree, therefore, the researcher can conclude that there was no implementation failure at Rampur district in Uttar Pradesh as per parents opinion.

Test Variable- Implementation Failure

Group Statistics

	Block	N	**M**	SD	SEM
Implementation Failure	Chamrauvaa	60	**2.1333**	.30066	.03881
	Shahabad	60	**2.4600**	.72186	.09319

Where M=Mean, SD=Standard Deviation, SEM=Standard Error Mean

From the above group statistics table the mean score of Implementation Failure for Chamrauvaa block is 2.1333 which is above 2 and below 3 Likert scale rating which is near to disagree and for Shahabad block is 2.4600 which is above 2 and below 3 Likert scale which is near to disagree, therefore the researcher can conclude that the parents opinion with respect to Implementation Failure greater disagree for Chamrauvaa block in comparison to Shahabad block that means Implementation Failure is less at Chamrauvaa block in comparison to Shahabad block under MDM scheme at Rampur district in Uttar Pradesh.

Independent T Test		t-test for Equality of Means						
		t	df	Sig.	MD	SED	95% Confidence Interval	
							Lower	Upper
Implementation Failure	Equal variances assumed	-3.236	118	.002	-.32667	.10095	-.52658	-.12675

	Equal variances not assumed	-3.236	78.872	**.002**	-.32667	.10095	-.52761	-.12572

Where MD= Mean Difference, SED=Standard Error Difference

Since the fourth null Hypothesis was H04p: There is no significant difference of opinion of parents between the Chamrauvaa and Shahabad block with respect to the Implementation Failure under MDM scheme at Rampur district in Uttar Pradesh.

From the above table

The sig. (2 tailed) 0.002 < 0.05(commonly accepted level of significance), hence Reject H04p, Therefore the researcher can conclude that there is a significant difference of opinion of parents between the Chamrauvaa and Shahabad block with respect to the Implementation Failure under MDMS at Rampur district in Uttar Pradesh.

For Parents: Public Participation in MDMS:

The null hypothesis was formulated as

H05p: There is no significant difference of opinion of parents between the Chamrauvaa and Shahabad block with respect to the participation under MDM scheme at Rampur district in Uttar Pradesh.

H06p: There is no significant difference of opinion of parents between the Chamrauvaa and Shahabad block with respect to the Public Inaccessibility under MDM scheme at Rampur district in Uttar Pradesh.

Here the researcher has formulated two null hypothesis for Parents(p) with respect to participation and Public Inaccessibility which were tested through independent T test as follows:

Descriptive Analysis:

Test Variable- Public Participation

Descriptive Statistics

	N	Min.	Max.	Mean	Std. Deviation
Participation	120	2.00	4.20	3.7767	.57288
Valid N (listwise)	120				

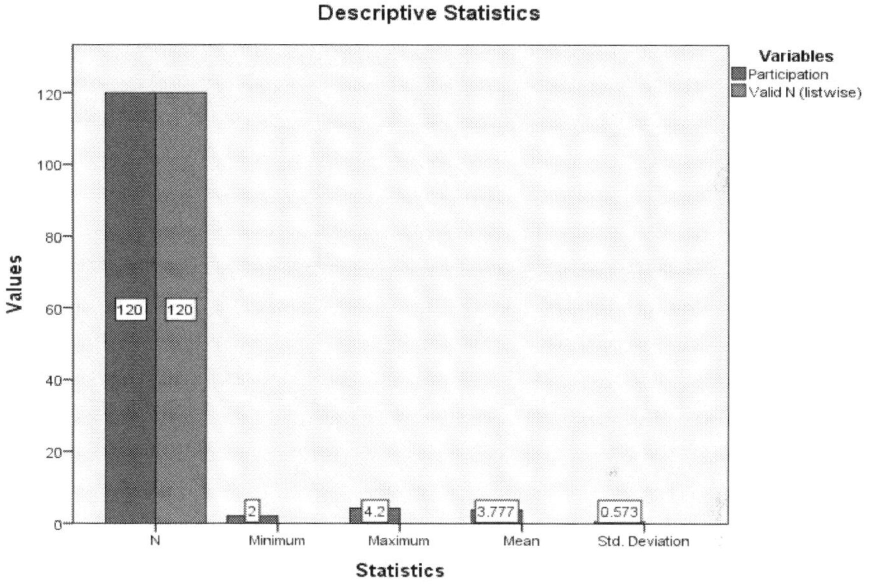

From the above descriptive statistics table and bar chart the mean score of participation with respect to parents for Rampur district is 3.777 which is above 3 and below 4 Likert scale rating which is near to agree, therefore on the basis of parents opinion, the researcher can conclude that the opinion of parents with respect to participation is satisfactory at Rampur district in Uttar Pradesh.

Test Variable- Participation

Group Statistics

	Block	N	**M**	SD	SEM
Participation	Chamrauvaa	60	**3.9000**	.43179	.05574
	Shahabad	60	**3.6533**	.66676	.08608

Where M=Mean, SD=Standard Deviation, SEM=Standard Error Mean

From the above group statistics table the mean score of participation for Chamrauvaa block is 3.9000 which is above 3 and below 4 Likert scale rating which is near to agree and for Shahabad block is 3.6533 which is again above 3 and below 4 Likert scale which is near to agree, therefore on the basis of parents opinion, the researcher can conclude that the participation under MDM scheme at Chamrauvaa block is better than Shahabad block at Rampur district in Uttar Pradesh.

Independent T Test		t-test for Equality of Means						
		t	df	**Sig.**	MD	SED	95% Confidence Interval	
							Lower	Upper
Participation	Equal variances assumed	2.405	118	.018	.24667	.10255	.04359	.44975
	Equal variances not assumed	2.405	101.085	**.018**	.24667	.10255	.04323	.45010

Where MD= Mean Difference, SED=Standard Error Difference

Since the fifth null Hypothesis was H05p: There is no significant difference of opinion of parents between the Chamrauvaa and Shahabad block with respect to the participation under MDM scheme at Rampur district in Uttar Pradesh.

From the above table

The sig. value (2 tailed) 0.018 < 0.05(commonly accepted level of significance), hence Reject Null hypothesis H05p, therefore the researcher can conclude that there is a significant difference of opinion of parents between the Chamrauvaa and Shahabad block with respect to the participation under MDM scheme at Rampur district in Uttar Pradesh.

Test Variable- Public Inaccessibility

Descriptive Statistics

	N	Min.	Max.	Mean	Std. Deviation
Public Inaccessibility	120	2.20	4.40	2.5767	.57170
Valid N (listwise)	120				

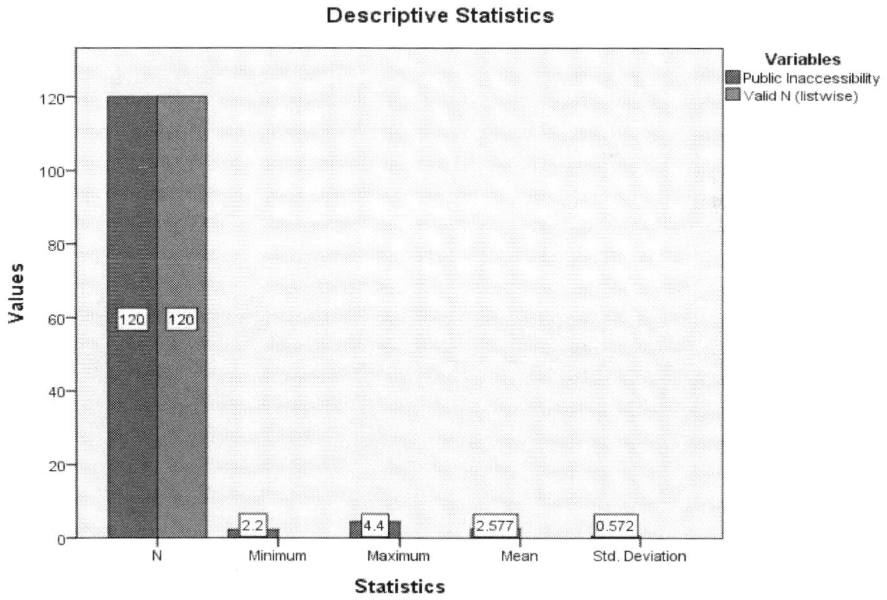

From the above descriptive statistics table and bar chart the mean score of public inaccessibility with respect to parents for Rampur district is 2.577 which is above 2 and below 3 likert scale rating which is near to disagree, therefore on the basis of parents opinion, the researcher can conclude that the opinion of parents with respect to public inaccessibility is not satisfactory that means public are accessible for mid-day scheme at Rampur district in Uttar Pradesh.

Test Variable- Public Inaccessibility

Group Statistics

	Block	N	**M**	SD	SEM
Public Inaccessibility	Chamrauvaa	60	**2.4000**	.20169	.02604
	Shahabad	60	**2.7533**	.74503	.09618

Where M=Mean, SD=Standard Deviation, SEM=Standard Error Mean

From the above group statistics table the mean score of Public Inaccessibility for Chamrauvaa block is 2.4000 which is above 2 and below 3 Likert scale rating which is near to disagree and for Shahabad block is 2.7533 which is above 2 and below 3 Likert scale which is near to neutral, therefore the researcher can conclude that the parents opinion with respect to Public Inaccessibility is more disagree for Chamrauvaa block in comparison to Shahabad block that means public accessibility is better at Chamrauvaa block in comparison to Shahabad block under MDM scheme at Rampur district in Uttar Pradesh.

Independent T Test	t-test for Equality of Means						
	t	df	Sig.	MD	SED	95% Confidence Interval	
						Lower	Upper

Public Inaccessibility	Equal variances assumed	-3.546	118	.001	-.35333	.09965	-.55066	-.15601
	Equal variances not assumed	-3.546	67.601	**.001**	-.35333	.09965	-.55219	-.15447

Where MD= Mean Difference, SED=Standard Error Difference

Since the sixth null Hypothesis was H06p: There is no significant difference of opinion of parents between the Chamrauvaa and Shahabad block with respect to the Public Inaccessibility under MDM scheme at Rampur district in Uttar Pradesh.

From the above table

The sig. (2 tailed) 0.001 < 0.05(commonly accepted level of significance), hence Reject H06p, Therefore the researcher can conclude that there is a significant difference of opinion of parents between the Chamrauvaa and Shahabad block with respect to the Public Inaccessibility under MDMS at Rampur district in Uttar Pradesh.

For Parents : Accountability in MDMS:

The Null Hypothesis was formulated as

H07p: There is no significant difference of opinion of parents between the Chamrauvaa and Shahabad block with respect to the management of funds under MDM scheme at Rampur district in Uttar Pradesh.

H08p: There is no significant difference of opinion of parents between the Chamrauvaa and Shahabad block with respect to the Monitoring and Supervision under MDM scheme at Rampur district in Uttar Pradesh.

Here the researcher has formulated the two Null hypotheses for Parents(p) with respect to management of funds and monitoring

& supervision which were tested through independent T test as follows:

Descriptive Analysis:

Test Variable- Management of Funds

Descriptive Statistics

	N	Min.	Max.	Mean	Std. Deviation
Management of Funds	120	1.40	2.60	1.5967	.26566
Valid N (listwise)	120				

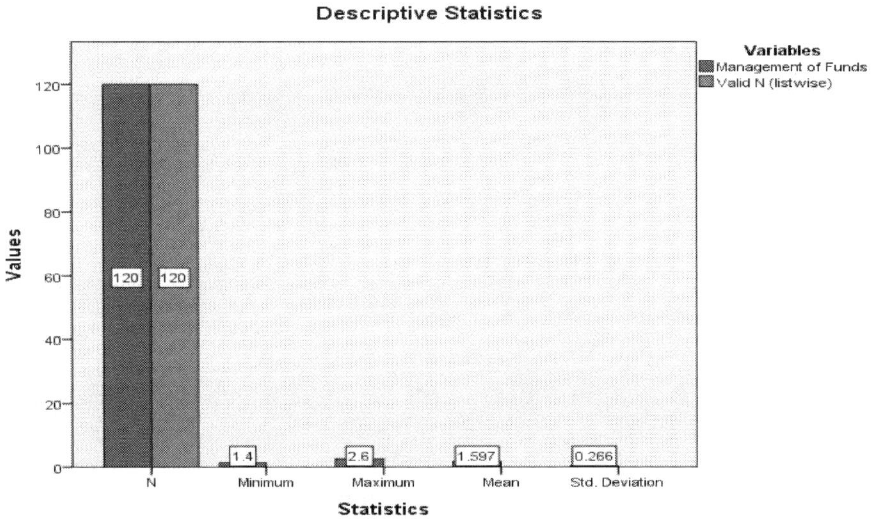

From the above descriptive statistics table and bar chart the mean score of management of funds with respect to parents for Rampur district is 1.597 which is above 1 and below 2 Likert scale rating which is near to disagree, therefore on the basis of parents opinion, the researcher can conclude that the opinion of parents with respect to management of funds is not satisfactory at Rampur district in Uttar Pradesh.

Test Variable- Management of Funds

Group Statistics

	Block	N	**M**	SD	SEM
Management of Funds	Chamrauvaa	60	**1.5333**	.15033	.01941
	Shahabad	60	**1.6600**	.33406	.04313

Where M=Mean, SD=Standard Deviation, SEM=Standard Error Mean

From the above group statistics table the mean score of Role of State for Chamrauvaa block is 1.5333 which is above 1 and below 2 Likert scale rating which is near to disagree and for Shahabad block is 1.6600 which is again above 1 and below 2 Likert scale which is near to disagree, therefore the researcher can conclude that the parents opinion with respect to management of funds is more proper for Chamrauvaa block in comparison to Shahabad block under MDM scheme at Rampur district in Uttar Pradesh.

Independent T Test		t-test for Equality of Means						
		t	df	Sig.	MD	SED	95% Confidence Interval	
							Lower	Upper
Management of Funds	Equal variances assumed	-2.678	118	.008	-.12667	.04729	-.22032	-.03302
	Equal variances not assumed	-2.678	81.955	**.009**	-.12667	.04729	-.22075	-.03259

Where MD= Mean Difference, SED=Standard Error Difference

Since the fourth null Hypothesis was H07p: There is no significant difference of opinion of parents between the Chamrauvaa and Shahabad block with respect to the management of funds under MDM scheme at Rampur district in Uttar Pradesh.

From the above table

The sig. value (2 tailed) 0.009 < 0.05(commonly accepted level of significance), hence Reject Null hypothesis H07p, therefore the researcher can conclude that there is a significant difference of opinion of parents between the Chamrauvaa and Shahabad block with respect to the management of funds under MDM scheme at Rampur district in Uttar Pradesh.

Descriptive Statistics

	N	Min.	Max.	Mean	Std. Deviation
Monitoring and Supervision	120	1.60	3.00	2.6733	.33197
Valid N (listwise)	120				

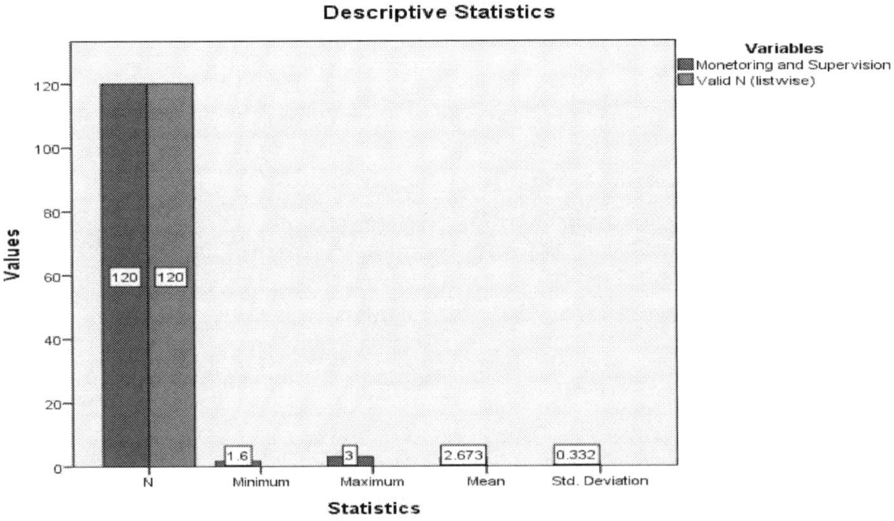

From the above descriptive statistics table and bar chart the mean score of monitoring and supervision with respect to parents for Rampur district is 2.673 which is above 2 and below 3 Likert scale rating which is near to neutral, therefore on the basis of parents opinion, the researcher can conclude that the opinion of parents with respect to monitoring and supervision is neutral for mid-day scheme at Rampur district in Uttar Pradesh.

Test Variable- Monitoring and Supervision

Group Statistics

	Block	N	**M**	SD	SEM
Monitoring and Supervision	Chamrauvaa	60	**2.7667**	.18102	.02337
	Shahabad	60	**2.5800**	.41448	.05351

Where M=Mean, SD=Standard Deviation, SEM=Standard Error Mean

From the above group statistics table the mean score of Monitoring and Supervision for Chamrauvaa block is 2.7667 which is above 2 and below 3 Likert scale rating which is near to neutral and for Shahabad block is 2.5800 which is again above 2 and below 3 Likert scale which is near to neutral, therefore on the basis of parents opinion, the researcher can conclude that the Monitoring and Supervision operation is better for Chamrauvaa block than Shahabad block under MDM scheme at Rampur district in Uttar Pradesh.

Independent T Test		t-test for Equality of Means						
		t	df	**Sig.**	MD	SED	95% Confidence Interval	
							Lower	Upper
Monitori-ng and	Equal variances assumed	3.197	118	.002	.18667	.05839	.07104	.30230

Supervis-ion	Equal variances not assumed	3.197	80.717	**.002**	.18667	.05839	.07048	.30285

Where MD= Mean Difference, SED=Standard Error Difference

Since the eight null Hypothesis was H08p: There is no significant difference of opinion of parents between the Chamrauvaa and Shahabad block with respect to the Monitoring and Supervision under MDM scheme at Rampur district in Uttar Pradesh.

From the above table

The sig. value (2 tailed) 0.002 < 0.05(commonly accepted level of significance), hence Reject Null hypothesis H08p, therefore the researcher can conclude that there is a significant difference of opinion of parents between the Chamrauvaa and Shahabad block with respect to the Monitoring and Supervision under MDMS at Rampur district in Uttar Pradesh.

For Teachers: Perception in MDMS:

First Stage Analysis: For Teachers (Frequency Test)

Whether the MDMS is playing a key role in the inner development of India?

		Frequency	%	Valid %	Cumulative %
Valid	Yes	12	100.0	100.0	100.0

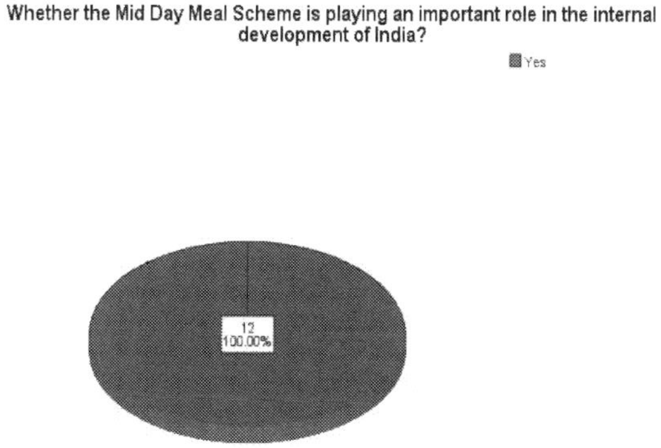

From the above table and pie chart, all the teachers said that mid-day scheme at Rampur district in Uttar Pradesh is playing an important role in the internal development of India, hence the researcher can conclude that the there is a relationship between the mid-day scheme and the internal development of India.

In the human framework, the MDMS is completing the concept of a welfare state?

		Frequency	%	Valid %	Cumulative %
Valid	Yes	12	100.0	100.0	100.0

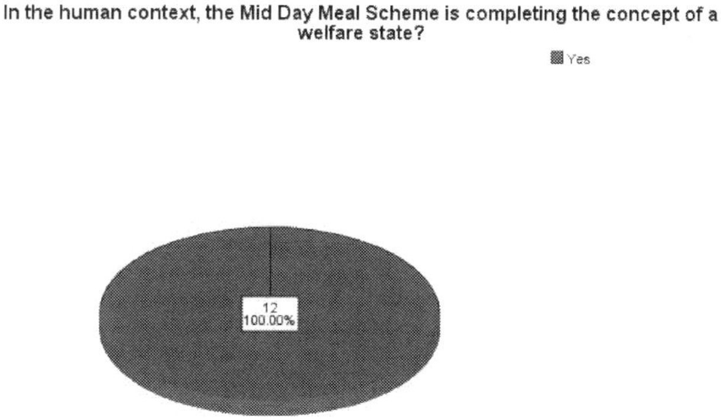

From the above table and pie chart, all the teachers said that MDM scheme is completing the concept of the welfare state in the human context; hence the researcher can conclude that the mid-day scheme playing an important role for the welfare state at Rampur district in Uttar Pradesh.

Is MDM Scheme Empowering Education and Health, 2 Fundamental Rights of Life?

		Frequency	%	Valid %	Cumulative %
Valid	Yes	12	100.0	100.0	100.0

Is Mid Day Meal Scheme Empowering Education and Health, 2 Fundamental Rights of Life?

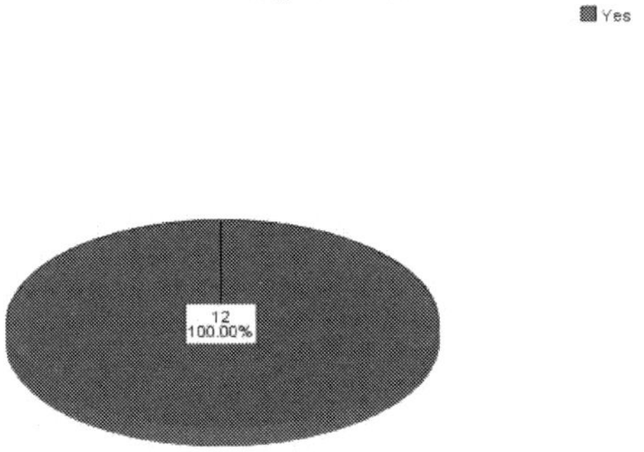

From the above table and pie chart, all the teachers said that MDM scheme is empowering the two fundamental rights, education, and health; hence the researcher can conclude that the mid-day scheme is empowering the education and health among the children at Rampur district in Uttar Pradesh.

Is the food given to the children in your school according to the weekly menu?

		Frequency	%	Valid %	Cumulative %
Valid	Yes	12	100.0	100.0	100.0

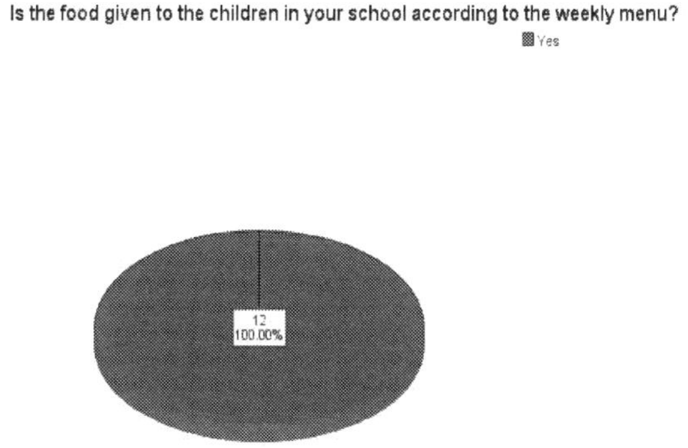

From the above table and pie chart, all the teachers said that food given to the children in the school are according to the weekly menu under MDM scheme; hence the researcher can conclude that food given to the children is according to the weekly menu at Rampur district in Uttar Pradesh.

Do Gram Pradhan or Villagers or Parents monitor the food being fed to the children in your school?

		Frequency	%	Valid %	Cumulative %
Valid	Yes	9	75.0	75.0	75.0
	No	3	25.0	25.0	100.0
	Total	12	100.0	100.0	

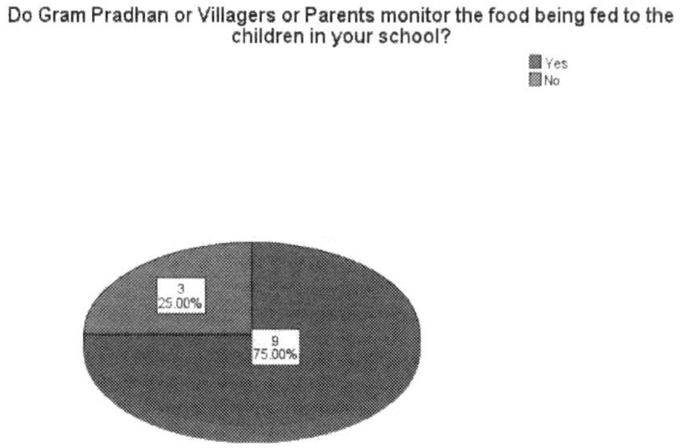

From the above table and pie chart, 75% teachers said that Gram Pradhan/Villagers/Parents monitor the food given to the children whereas 25% said that Gram Pradhan/Villagers/Parents don't monitor the meal distributed to the students, hence the researcher can conclude that most of the teachers agree that the food monitoring under MDM scheme is done by the Gram Pradhan/Villagers/Parents at Rampur district in Uttar Pradesh.

Whether the food given to the students in your school is complained by the Gram Pradhan or the Parents or the Guardians of the children?

		Frequency	%	Valid %	Cumulative %
Valid	Yes	3	25.0	25.0	25.0
	No	9	75.0	75.0	100.0
	Total	12	100.0	100.0	

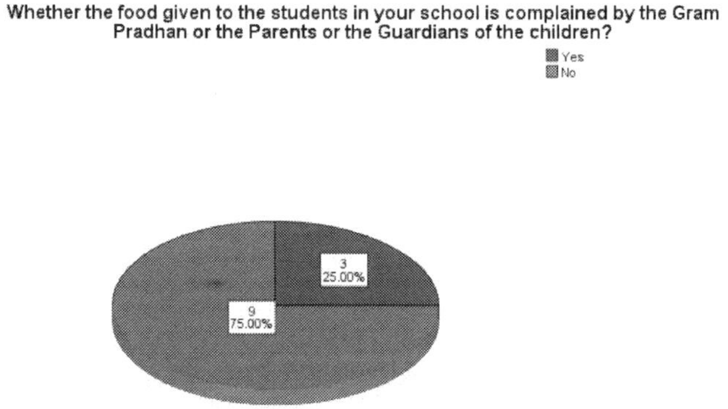

From the above table and pie chart, 75% teachers said that there was no complained lodged by the Gram Pradhan/ Parents/ Guardians related with the food given to the school children under MDM scheme whereas 25% teacher said that Gram Pradhan/ Parents/ Guardians were complaining about the food , hence the researcher can conclude that most of the teachers agree that there is no complaint lodged by the Gram Pradhan/ Parents/

Guardians for the food given to the kids under MDMS at Rampur district in Uttar Pradesh.

There is a decrease in communication, mutual relations among Gram Pradhan, Kotedar, Parents, and concerned officials.

		Frequency	%	Valid %	Cumulative %
Valid	Yes	12	100.0	100.0	100.0

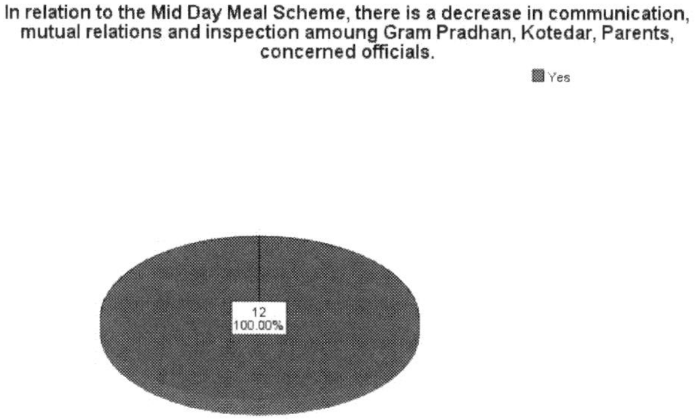

From the above table and pie chart, all the teachers said that there is a lack of communication, lack of mutual relationship and lack of inspection among the Gram Pradhan, Kotedar (supplier of food grain), Parents and Officer in charge of this MDM scheme, hence the researcher can conclude that there is no proper coordination between Gram Pradhan, Kotedar, Parents and school administration of this MDMS at Rampur district in Uttar Pradesh.

Does your school get grains timely?

		Frequency	%	Valid %	Cumulative %
Valid	Yes	9	75.0	75.0	75.0
	No	3	25.0	25.0	100.0
	Total	12	100.0	100.0	

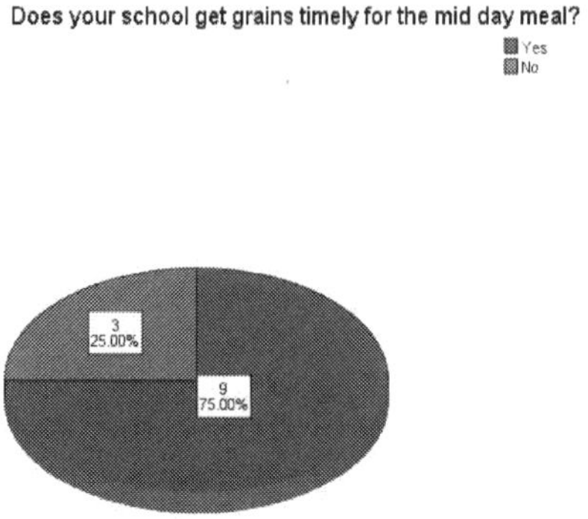

From the above table and pie chart, 75% teachers said that they got the food grains timely whereas 25% teachers said that they did not get food grain timely, hence the researcher can conclude that most of the teacher agreed that food grain was available on time for the students under the MDMS at Rampur district in Uttar Pradesh.

Is there a social audit of the MDMS?

		Frequency	%	Valid %	Cumulative %
Valid	No	12	100.0	100.0	100.0

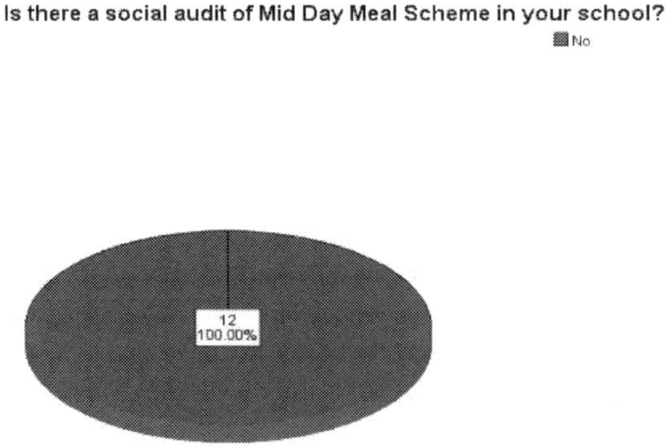

From the above table and pie chart, all the teachers said that there was no social audit of MDMS in their school, hence the researcher can conclude that social audit was lacking in the proper execution of the MDMS at Rampur district in Uttar Pradesh.

Does the MDMS be inspected by the Citizen Group?

		Frequency	%	Valid %	Cumulative %
Valid	Yes	3	25.0	25.0	25.0
	No	9	75.0	75.0	100.0
	Total	12	100.0	100.0	

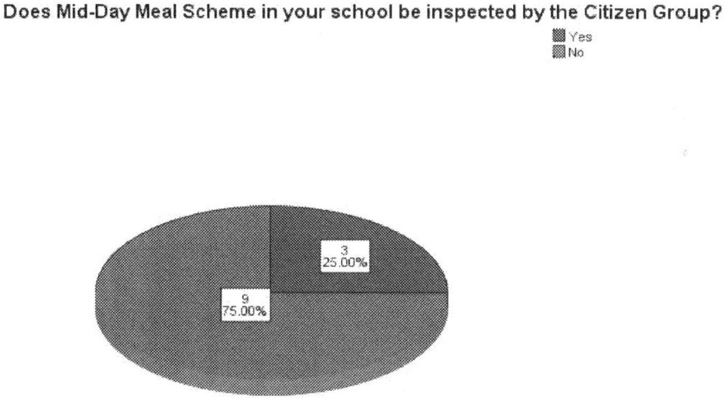

From the above table and pie chart, 75% teacher said that there was no inspection as the citizen group of the village people whereas 25% teacher said that inspection of the MDM was done by the citizen group, hence the researcher can conclude that most of the teacher agreed that inspection of the MDMS was lacking at Rampur district in Uttar Pradesh.

Do children in your school be seated separately on caste basis while serving food?

		Frequency	%	Valid %	Cumulative %
Valid	No	12	100.0	100.0	100.0

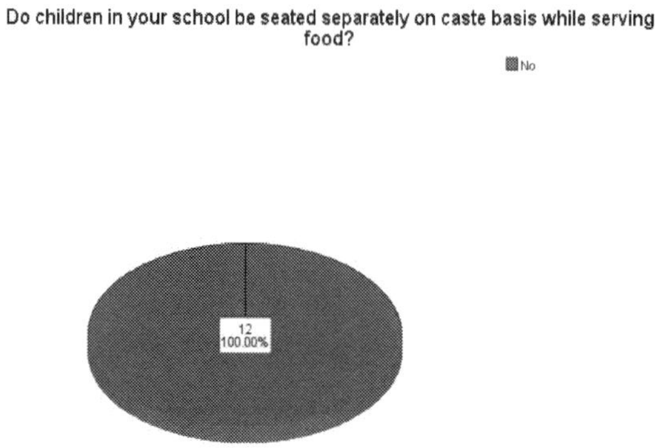

From the above table and pie chart, all the teachers said that no children were seated separately on the basis of caste while serving the food under the MDMS, hence the researcher can conclude that teacher did not differentiate the children on the basis of their caste while serving the food under this scheme at Rampur district in Uttar Pradesh.

Does the MDMS affect your local politics?

		Frequency	%	Valid %	Cumulative %
Valid	Yes	6	50.0	50.0	50.0
	No	6	50.0	50.0	100.0
	Total	12	100.0	100.0	

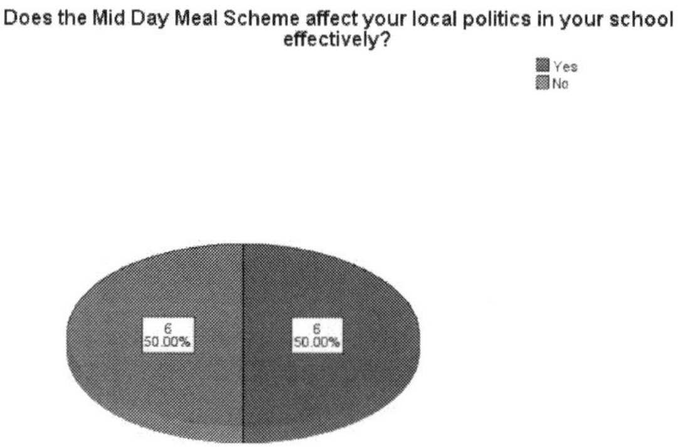

From the above table and pie chart, 50% teachers said that, MDMS affected the local village level politics whereas the same 50% teachers also said that, MDMS did not affect the local village level politics, hence the researcher can conclude that 50% teacher agreed and rest 50% teacher disagreed that the local level village politics affected the MDMS at Rampur district in Uttar Pradesh.

Does the MDMS be inspected daily by IVRS?

		Frequency	%	Valid %	Cumulative %
Valid	Yes	12	100.0	100.0	100.0

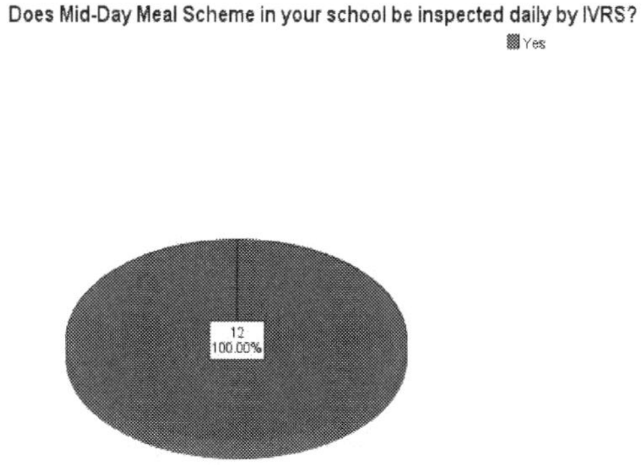

From the above table and pie chart, all the teachers said that there was a daily monitoring of the MDMS by IVRS (Interacting Voice Response System), hence the researcher can conclude that IVRS system was running in the school for the inspection and monitoring of the MDMS at Rampur district in Uttar Pradesh.

Do children get milk /fruits once a week?

		Frequency	%	Valid %	Cumulative %
Valid	Yes	12	100.0	100.0	100.0

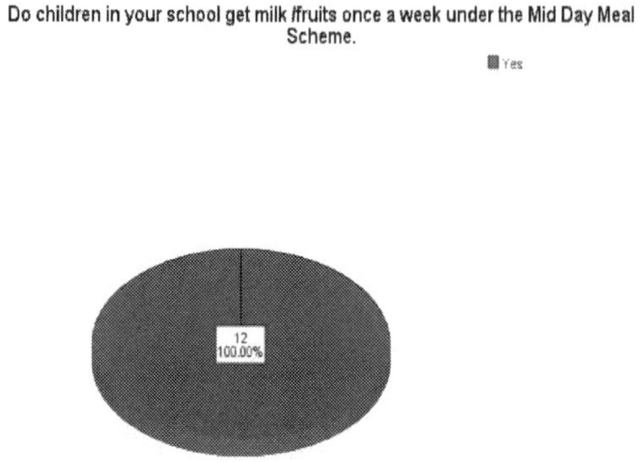

From the above table and pie chart, all the teachers said that children get the milk and fruits once in a week under MDM scheme; hence the research can conclude that milk and fruits are distributed to the children once in a week under this scheme as per the opinion of the teacher at Rampur district in Uttar Pradesh.

Are complaints of MDMS being resolved by the Gram Pradhan/ BSA?

		Frequency	%	Valid %	Cumulative %
Valid	Yes	9	75.0	75.0	75.0
	No	3	25.0	25.0	100.0
	Total	12	100.0	100.0	

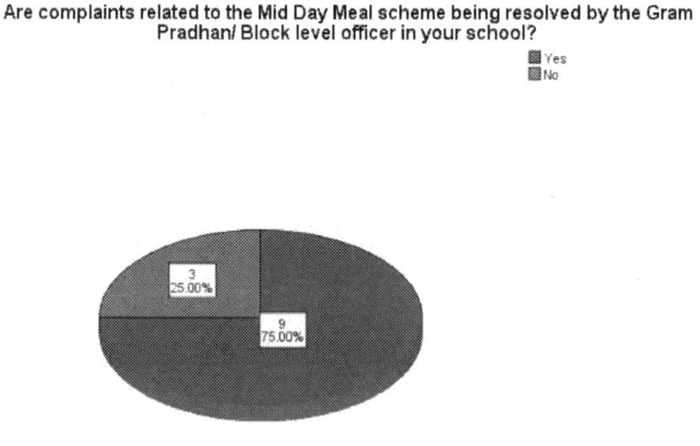

From the above table and pie chart, 75% teacher said that complaints of MDMS were resolved by the Gram Pradhan/ BSA for the school administration whereas 25% teachers said that complaints are not resolved by the Gram Pradhan/Block Level Officer, hence the researcher can conclude that most of the teacher are agree that complaints are resolved by the Gram Pradhan and BSA for the MDMS at Rampur district in Uttar Pradesh.

Do the money received by the cook and his colleagues on time?

		Frequency	%	Valid %	Cumulative %
Valid	Yes	6	50.0	50.0	50.0
	No	6	50.0	50.0	100.0
	Total	12	100.0	100.0	

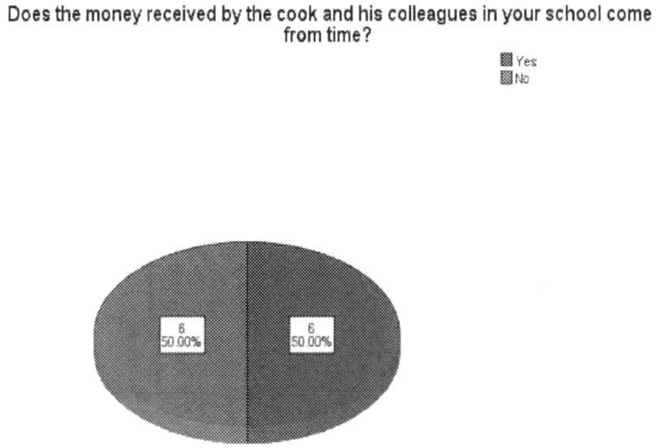

From the above table and pie chart, 50% teachers said that there was a timely payment to the cook and his assistant whereas same 50% teacher said that there was no timely payment to the cook and his assistant, hence the researcher conclude that 50% teachers agreed and rest 50% teachers disagreed regarding the payment issue to the cook and his assistant under the MDMS at Rampur district in Uttar Pradesh.

If payment is not being paid to the cook, what is the impact on the MDMS?

		Frequency	%	Valid %	Cumulative %
Valid	Bad	12	100.0	100.0	100.0

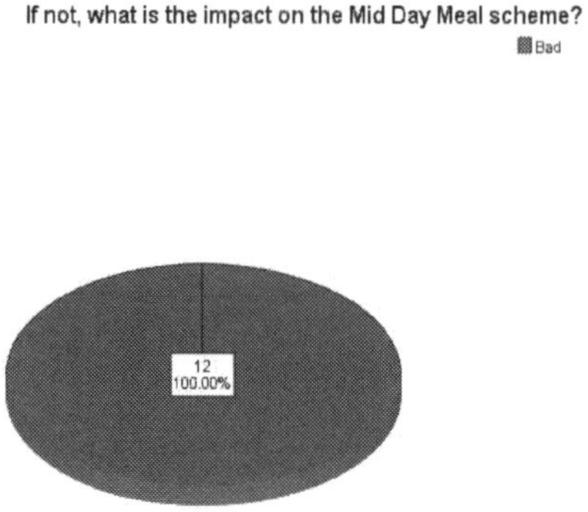

From the above table and pie chart, all the teacher said that if the payment was not being paid to the cook and his assistant then there will be an adverse effect on the MDMS, hence the researcher can conclude that there will be the adverse effect if the payment was not given to the cook and his assistant under the MDMS at Rampur district in Uttar Pradesh.

Second Stage Analysis: (Independent T Test)

The Null Hypothesis has been formulated as follows

H01t: There is no significant difference of opinion of teachers between the Chamrauvaa and Shahabad block with respect to the institutional efficiency of MDMS at Rampur district in Uttar Pradesh.

H02t: There is no significant difference of opinion of teachers between the Chamrauvaa and Shahabad block with respect to the food delivery of MDMS at Rampur district in Uttar Pradesh.

H03t: There is no significant difference of opinion of teachers between the Chamrauvaa and Shahabad block with respect to the corruption & mismanagement under MDMS at Rampur district in Uttar Pradesh.

H04t: There is no significant difference of opinion of teachers between the Chamrauvaa and Shahabad block with respect to the implementation failure of MDMS at Rampur district in Uttar Pradesh.

Here again four Null hypothesis was formulated for Teachers (t) with respect to four test parameters such as institutional efficiency, food delivery, corruption & mismanagement and implementation failure which were tested through the independent T test.

Descriptive Analysis:

Test Variable- Institutional Efficiency

Descriptive Statistics

	N	Min.	Max.	Mean	Std. Deviation
Institutional Efficiency	12	1.40	4.00	2.4333	.94900
Valid N (listwise)	12				

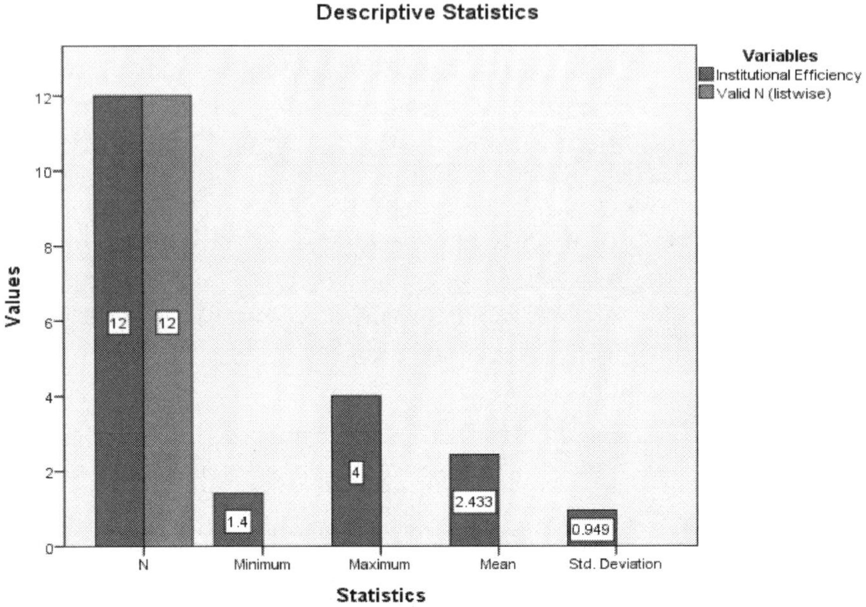

From the above descriptive statistics table and bar chart the mean score of institutional efficiency with respect to teachers for Rampur district is 2.433 which is above 2 and below 3 Likert scale rating which is near to disagree , therefore on the basis of teachers opinion, the researcher can conclude that the opinion of teachers with respect to institutional efficiency is to disagree at Rampur district in Uttar Pradesh.

Test Variable- Institutional Efficiency

Grouping Variable- Two Block Chamrauvaa & Shahabad

Group Statistics

	Block	N	**M**	SD	SEM
	Chamrauvaa	6	**2.7667**	1.12724	.46019

Institutional Efficiency	Shahabad	6	**2.1000**	.66633	.27203

Where M=Mean, SD=Standard Deviation, SEM=Standard Error Mean

From the above group statistics table the mean score of Institutional Efficiency for Chamrauvaa block is 2.7667 which is above 2 and below 3 Likert scale rating which is near to neutral and for Shahabad block is 2.1000 which is near to 2 Likert scale which is near to disagree, therefore the researcher can conclude that the Teachers opinion with respect to Institutional Efficiency is better for Chamrauvaa block in comparison to Shahabad block under MDM scheme at Rampur district in Uttar Pradesh.

Independent T- Test		t-test for Equality of Means						
		t	df	Sig.	MD	SED	95% Confidence Interval	
							Lower	Upper
Institutional Efficiency	Equal variances assumed	1.247	10	.241	.66667	.53458	-.52446	1.85779
	Equal variances not assumed	1.247	8.114	**.247**	.66667	.53458	-.56307	1.89641

Where MD= Mean Difference, SED=Standard Error Difference

Since the first null Hypothesis was H01: There is no significant difference of opinion of Teachers between the Chamrauvaa and Shahabad block with respect to the Institutional Efficiency under MDM scheme at Rampur district in Uttar Pradesh.

From the above table

The sig. value (2 tailed) 0.247 > 0.05(commonly accepted level of significance), hence Accept Null hypothesis H01, Therefore the researcher can conclude that there is no significant difference of opinion of Teachers between the Chamrauvaa and Shahabad block with respect to the Institutional Efficiency under MDM scheme at Rampur district in Uttar Pradesh.

Descriptive Statistics

	N	Min.	Max.	Mean	Std. Deviation
Food Delivery	12	2.20	4.00	2.9333	.81054
Valid N (listwise)	12				

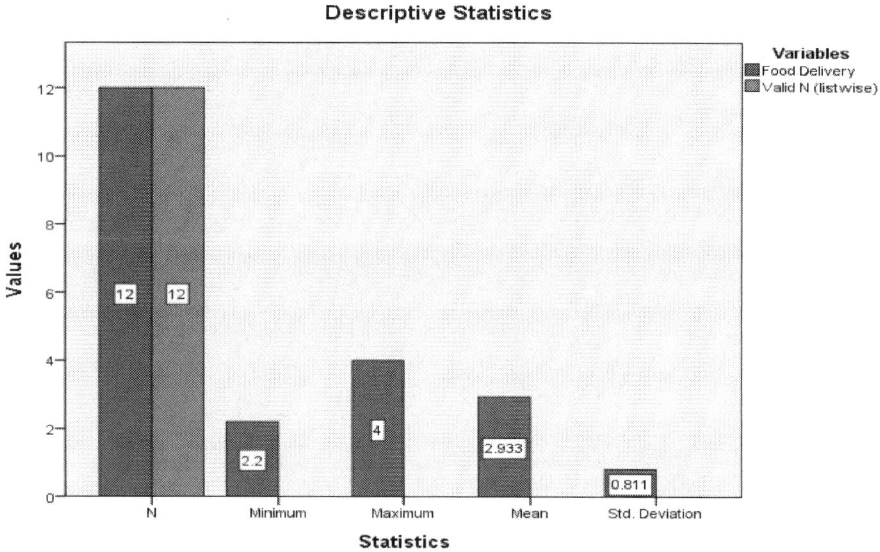

From the above descriptive statistics table and bar chart the mean score of food delivery with respect to teachers for Rampur district is 2.933 which is above 2 and below 3 Likert scale rating which is near to neutral, therefore on the basis of teachers opinion, the researcher can conclude that the opinion of teachers with respect to food delivery is at moderate level at Rampur district in Uttar Pradesh.

Group Statistics

	Block	N	**M**	SD	SEM
Food Delivery	Chamrauvaa	6	**2.2000**	.00000	.00000
	Shahabad	6	**3.6667**	.39328	.16055

Where M=Mean, SD=Standard Deviation, SEM=Standard Error Mean

From the above group statistics table the mean score of Food Delivery for Chamrauvaa block is 2.2000 which is above 2 and below 3 Likert scale rating which is near to disagree and for Shahabad block is 3.667 which is above 3 and below 4 Likert scale which is near to agree, therefore the researcher can conclude that the teachers opinion with respect to Food Delivery is more disagree for Chamrauvaa block in comparison to Shahabad block that means food delivery is not better at Chamrauvaa block in comparison to Shahabad block under MDM scheme at Rampur district in Uttar Pradesh.

Independent T Test		t-test for Equality of Means						
		t	df	Sig	MD	SED	95% Confidence Interval	
							Lower	Upper
Food Delivery	Equal variances assumed	-9.135	10	.000	-1.46667	.16055	-1.82440	-1.10893
	Equal variances not assumed	-9.135	5.000	**.000**	-1.46667	.16055	-1.87939	-1.05395

Where MD= Mean Difference, SED= Std. Error Difference

Since the second null Hypothesis was H02t: There is no significant difference of opinion of teachers between the Chamrauvaa and

Shahabad block with respect to the food Delivery under MDM scheme at Rampur district in Uttar Pradesh.

From the above table

The sig. value (2 tailed) 0.000 < 0.05(commonly accepted level of significance), hence Reject null hypothesis H02t, therefore the researcher can conclude that there is a significant difference of opinion of teachers between the Chamrauvaa and Shahabad block with respect to the food Delivery under MDM scheme at Rampur district in Uttar Pradesh.

Descriptive Statistics

	N	Min.	Max.	Mean	Std. Deviation
Corruption & Mismanagement	12	2.40	4.60	3.3333	.87939
Valid N (listwise)	12				

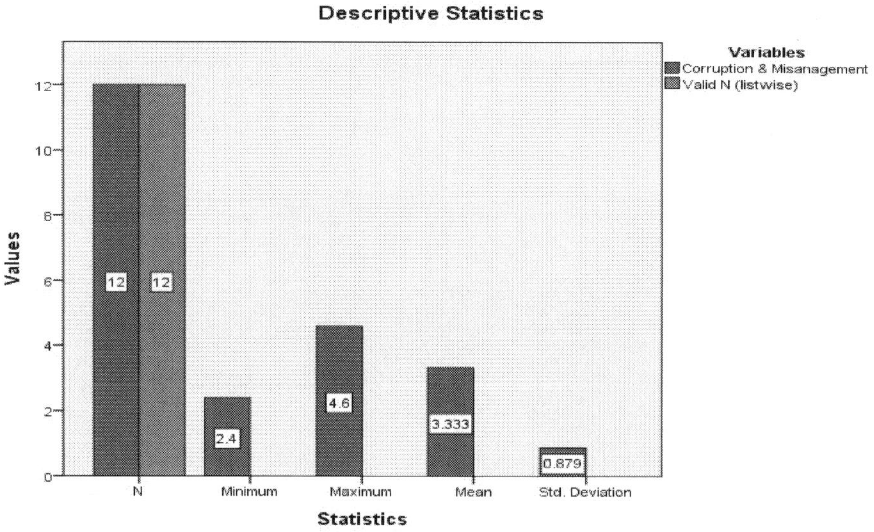

From the above descriptive statistics table and bar chart the mean score of corruption and mismanagement with respect to parents for Rampur district is 3.333 which is above 2 and below 3 Likert scale rating which is near to neutral, therefore on the basis of teachers opinion, the researcher can conclude that the opinion of teachers with respect to corruption and mismanagement is neutral at Rampur district in Uttar Pradesh.

Group Statistics

	Block	N	**M**	SD	SEM
Corruption & Mismanagement	Chamrauvaa	6	**2.5333**	.10328	.04216
	Shahabad	6	**4.1333**	.39328	.16055

Where M=Mean, SD=Standard Deviation, SEM=Standard Error Mean

From the above group statistics table the mean score of Corruption & Mismanagement for Chamrauvaa block is 2.5333 which is above 2 and below 3 Likert scale rating which is near to disagree and for Shahabad block is 4.1333 which is above 4 and below 5 Likert scale which is near to agree, therefore the researcher can conclude that the parents opinion with respect to Corruption & Mismanagement is more disagree for Chamrauvaa block in comparison to Shahabad block that means there is more corruption & mismanagement at Chamrauvaa block in comparison to Shahabad block under MDM scheme at Rampur district in Uttar Pradesh.

Independent T Test		t-test for Equality of Means						
		t	df	Sig.	MD	SED	95% Confidence Interval	
							Lower	Upper
Corruption & Mismanagement	Equal variances assumed	-9.639	10	.000	-1.60000	.16600	-1.96987	-1.23013

	Equal variances not assumed	-9.639	5.686	.000	-1.60000	.16600	-2.01168	-1.18832

Where MD= Mean Difference, SED=Standard Error Difference

Since the third null Hypothesis was H03t: There is no significant difference of opinion of teachers between the Chamrauvaa and Shahabad block with respect to the Corruption & Mismanagement under MDM scheme at Rampur district in Uttar Pradesh.

From the above table

The sig. value (2 tailed) 0.001 < 0.05(commonly accepted level of significance), hence Reject null hypothesis H03t, therefore the researcher can conclude that there is a significant difference of opinion of teachers between the Chamrauvaa and Shahabad block with respect to the Corruption & Mismanagement under MDM scheme at Rampur district in Uttar Pradesh.

Descriptive Statistics

	N	Min.	Max.	Mean	Std. Deviation
Implementation Failure	12	1.60	4.00	2.9500	.90303
Valid N (listwise)	12				

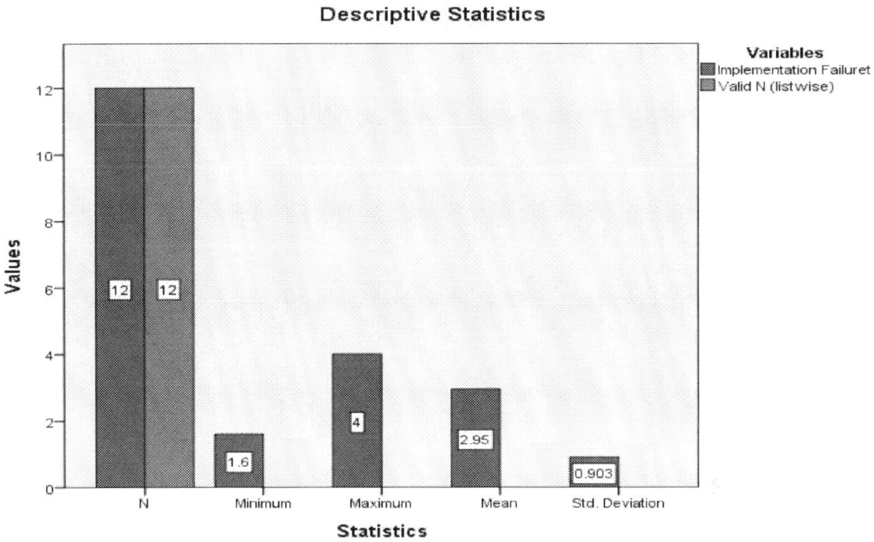

From the above descriptive statistics table and bar chart the mean score of implementation failure with respect to teachers for Rampur district is 2.9500 which is above 2 and below 3 likert scale rating which is near to neutral, therefore on the basis of teachers opinion, the researcher can conclude that the opinion of teachers with respect to implementation failure is at moderate level at Rampur district in Uttar Pradesh.

Group Statistics

	Block	N	**M**	SD	SEM
Implementation Failure	Chamrauvaa	6	**2.1333**	.32660	.13333
	Shahabad	6	**3.7667**	.29439	.12019

Where M=Mean, SD=Standard Deviation, SEM=Standard Error Mean

From the above group statistics table the mean score of Implementation Failure for Chamrauvaa block is 2.1333 which is above 2 and below 3 Likert scale rating which is near to disagree and for Shahabad block is 3.7667 which is above 3 and below 4

Likert scale which is near to agree, therefore the researcher can conclude that the teachers opinion with respect to Implementation Failure is more disagree for Chamrauvaa block in comparison to Shahabad block that means Implementation Failure is less at Chamrauvaa block in comparison to Shahabad block under MDM scheme at Rampur district in Uttar Pradesh.

Independent T Test		t-test for Equality of Means						
		t	df	Sig.	MD	SED	95% Confidence Interval	
							Lower	Upper
Implementation Failure	Equal variances assumed	-9.099	10	.000	-1.63333	.17951	-2.03330	-1.23337
	Equal variances not assumed	-9.099	9.894	.000	-1.63333	.17951	-2.03388	-1.23279

Where MD= Mean Difference, SED=Standard Error Difference

Since the fourth null Hypothesis was H04t: There is no significant difference of opinion of teachers between the Chamrauvaa and Shahabad block with respect to the Implementation Failure under MDMS at Rampur district in Uttar Pradesh.

From the above table

The sig. value (2 tailed) 0.000 < 0.05(commonly accepted level of significance), hence Reject null hypothesis H04t, therefore the researcher can conclude that there is a significant difference of opinion of teachers between the Chamrauvaa and Shahabad block with respect to the Implementation Failure under MDMS at Rampur district in Uttar Pradesh.

For Teachers: Public Participation in MDMS:

The Null Hypothesis is formulated as

H05t: There is no significant difference of opinion of Teachers between the Chamrauvaa and Shahabad block with respect to the Participation under MDM scheme at Rampur district in Uttar Pradesh.

H06t: There is no significant difference of opinion of teachers between the Chamrauvaa and Shahabad block with respect to the Public Inaccessibility under MDM scheme at Rampur district in Uttar Pradesh.

Here the researcher has formulated two null hypothesis for Teachers(t) with respect to participation and public inaccessibility which were tested through Independent T test as follows:

Descriptive Analysis:

Test Variable- Public Participation

Descriptive Statistics

	N	Min.	Max.	Mean	Std. Deviation
Participation	12	2.00	4.20	3.2833	.80208
Valid N (listwise)	12				

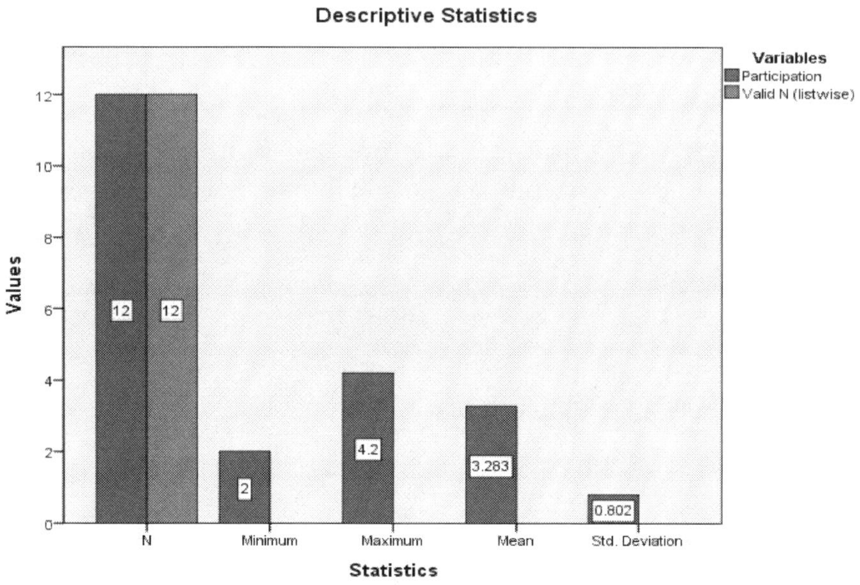

From the above descriptive statistics table and bar chart the mean score of participation with respect to teachers for Rampur district is 3.283 which is above 3 and below 4 Likert scale rating which is near to agree, therefore on the basis of teachers opinion, the researcher can conclude that the opinion of teachers with respect to participation is satisfactory at Rampur district in Uttar Pradesh.

Test Variable- Participation

Group Statistics

	Block	N	**M**	SD	SEM
Participation	Chamrauvaa	6	**3.9000**	.46904	.19149
	Shahabad	6	**2.6667**	.53166	.21705

Where M=Mean, SD=Standard Deviation, SEM=Standard Error Mean

From the above group statistics table the mean score of Participation for Chamrauvaa block is 3.9000 which is near to 4 Likert scale rating which is near to agree and for Shahabad block is 2.6667 which is above 2 and below 3 Likert scale which is near to neutral, therefore the researcher can conclude that the Teachers opinion with respect to Participation is more agree for Chamrauvaa block in comparison to Shahabad block that means people participation is better at Chamrauvaa block in comparison to Shahabad block under MDM scheme at Rampur district in Uttar Pradesh.

Independent T Test		t-test for Equality of Means						
		t	df	**Sig.**	MD	SED	95% Confidence Interval	
							Lower	Upper
Participation	Equal variances assumed	4.261	10	.002	1.23333	.28944	.58841	1.87825
	Equal variances not assumed	4.261	9.847	**.002**	1.23333	.28944	.58705	1.87962

Where MD= Mean Difference, SED=Standard Error Difference

Since the fifth null Hypothesis was H05t: There is no significant difference of opinion of Teachers between the Chamrauvaa and Shahabad block with respect to the Participation under MDM scheme at Rampur district in Uttar Pradesh.

From the above table

The sig. value (2 tailed) 0.002 < 0.05(commonly accepted level of significance), hence Reject null hypothesis H05t, therefore the researcher can conclude that there is a significant difference of opinion of Teachers between the Chamrauvaa and Shahabad block with respect to the Participation under MDM scheme at Rampur district in Uttar Pradesh.

Descriptive Statistics

	N	Min.	Max.	Mean	Std. Deviation
Public Inaccessibility	12	2.20	4.40	3.2833	.95521
Valid N (listwise)	12				

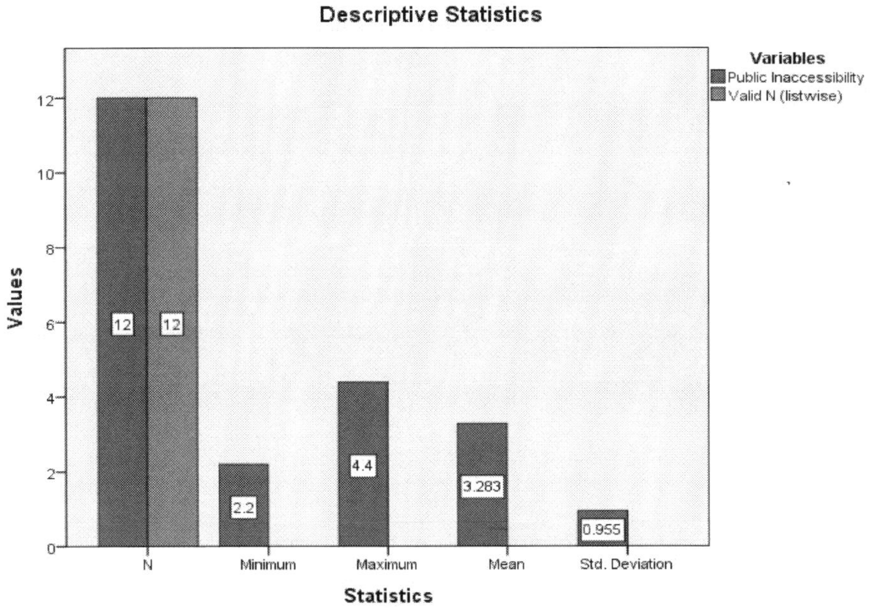

From the above descriptive statistics table and bar chart the mean score of public inaccessibility with respect to teachers for Rampur district is 3.283 which is above 2 and below 3 Likert scale rating which is near to neutral, therefore on the basis of teachers opinion, the researcher can conclude that the opinion of teachers with respect to public inaccessibility is at moderate level that means public are accessible at moderate level for mid-day scheme at Rampur district in Uttar Pradesh.

Test Variable- Public Inaccessibility

Group Statistics

	Block	N	**M**	SD	SEM
Public Inaccessibility	Chamrauvaa	6	**2.4000**	.21909	.08944
	Shahabad	6	**4.1667**	.29439	.12019

Where M=Mean, SD=Standard Deviation, SEM=Standard Error Mean

From the above group statistics table the mean score of Public Inaccessibility for Chamrauvaa block is 2.4000 which is near to 2 Likert scale rating which is near to disagree and for Shahabad block is 4.1667 which is near to 4 Likert scale which is near to agree, therefore the researcher can conclude that the Teachers opinion with respect to Public Inaccessibility is more disagree for Chamrauvaa block in comparison to Shahabad block that means people accessibility is better at Chamrauvaa block in comparison to Shahabad block under MDM scheme at Rampur district in Uttar Pradesh.

Independent T Test		t-test for Equality of Means						
		t	df	Sig.	MD	SED	95% Confidence Interval	
							Lower	Upper
Public Inaccessibility	Equal variances assumed	-11.792	10	.000	-1.76667	.14981	-2.10047	-1.43286
	Equal variances not assumed	-11.792	9.238	.000	-1.76667	.14981	-2.10424	-1.42909

Where MD= Mean Difference, SED=Standard Error Difference

Since the sixth null Hypothesis was H06t: There is no significant difference of opinion of teachers between the Chamrauvaa and

Shahabad block with respect to the Public Inaccessibility under MDM scheme at Rampur district in Uttar Pradesh.

From the above table

The sig. value (2 tailed) 0.000 < 0.05(commonly accepted level of significance), hence Reject null hypothesis H06t, therefore the researcher can conclude that there is a significant difference of opinion of teachers between the Chamrauvaa and Shahabad block with respect to the Public Inaccessibility under MDMS at Rampur district in Uttar Pradesh.

For Teachers: Accountability in MDMS:

The null hypothesis is formulated as

H07t: There is no significant difference of opinion of Teachers between the Chamrauvaa and Shahabad block with respect to the management of funds under MDM scheme at Rampur district in Uttar Pradesh.

H08t: There is no significant difference of opinion of Teachers between the Chamrauvaa and Shahabad block with respect to the monitoring and supervision under MDM scheme at Rampur district in Uttar Pradesh.

Here the researcher has formulated two null hypothesis for Teachers(t) with respect to management of funds and monitoring & supervision which were tested through Independent T rest as follows:

Test Variable- Management of Funds

Descriptive Statistics

	N	Min.	Max.	Mean	Std. Deviation

Management of Funds	12	1.40	2.60	1.8500	.44415
Valid N (listwise)	12				

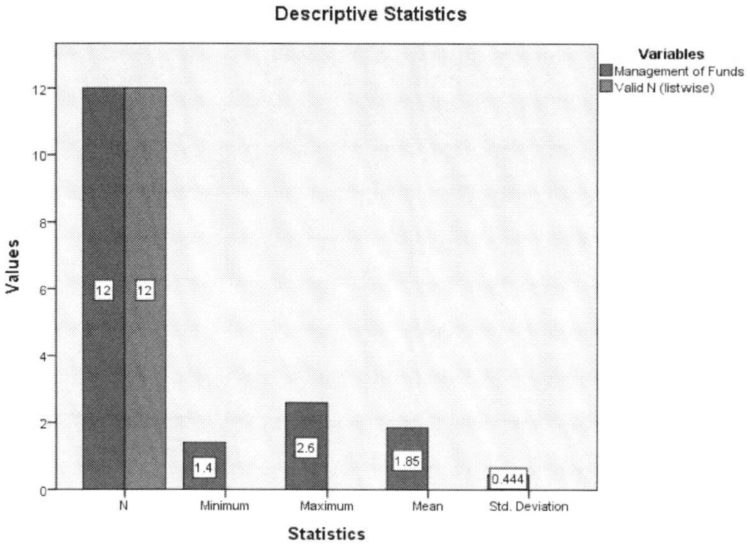

From the above descriptive statestics table and bar chart the mean score of management of funds with respect to teachers for Rampur district is 1.8500 which is above 1 and below 2 Likert scale rating which is near to disagree, therefore on the basis of teachers opinion, the researcher can conclude that the opinion of teachers with respect to management of funds is not satisfactory at Rampur district in Uttar Pradesh.

Test Variable- Management of Funds

Group Statistics

	Block	N	**M**	SD	SEM
Management of Funds	Chamrauvaa	6	**1.5333**	.16330	.06667
	Shahabad	6	**2.1667**	.40825	.16667

Where M=Mean, SD=Standard Deviation, SEM=Standard Error Mean

From the above group statistics table the mean score of management of funds for Chamrauvaa block is 1.5333 which is above 1 and below 2 Likert scale rating which is near to strongly disagree and for Shahabad block is 2.1667 which is near to 2 Likert scale which is near to disagree, therefore the researcher can conclude that the Teachers opinion with respect to management of funds is strongly disagreed for Chamrauvaa block in comparison to Shahabad block that means management of funds is less at Chamrauvaa block in comparison to Shahabad block under MDM scheme at Rampur district in Uttar Pradesh.

Independent T Test		t-test for Equality of Means						
		t	df	Sig.	MD	SED	95% Confidence Interval	
							Lower	Upper
Management of Funds	Equal variances assumed	-3.528	10	.005	-.63333	.17951	-1.03330	-.23337
	Equal variances not assumed	-3.528	6.560	**.011**	-.63333	.17951	-1.06364	-.20303

Where MD= Mean Difference, SED=Standard Error Difference

Since the seventh null Hypothesis was H07t: There is no significant difference of opinion of Teachers between the Chamrauvaa and Shahabad block with respect to the management of funds under MDM scheme at Rampur district in Uttar Pradesh.

From the above table

The sig. value (2 tailed) 0.001 < 0.05(commonly accepted level of significance), hence Reject null hypothesis H07t,tTherefore the researcher can conclude that there is a significant difference of opinion of Teachers between the Chamrauvaa and Shahabad block with respect to the management of funds under MDM scheme at Rampur district in Uttar Pradesh.

Descriptive Statistics

	N	Min.	Max.	Mean	Std. Deviation
Monitoring and Supervision	12	1.60	3.00	2.3000	.51522
Valid N (listwise)	12				

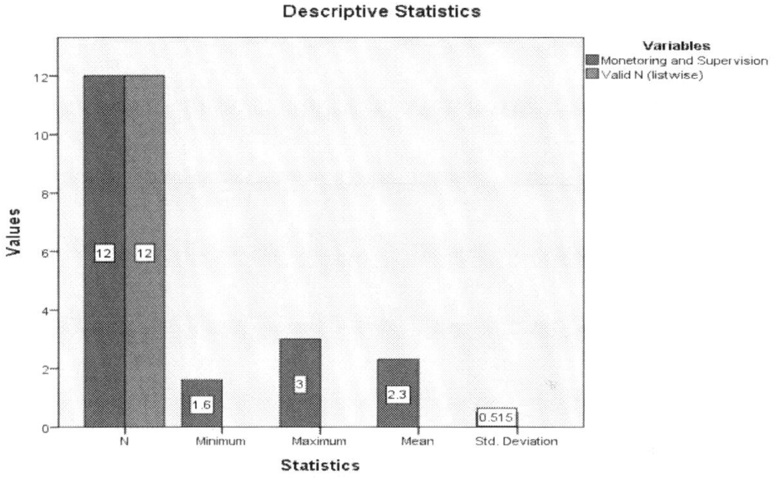

From the above descriptive statistics table and bar chart the mean score of monitoring and supervision with respect to teachers for Rampur district is 2.300 which is above 2 and below 3 Likert scale rating which is near to neutral, therefore on the basis of teachers opinion, the researcher can conclude that the opinion of teachers with respect to monitoring and supervision is neutral for mid-day scheme at Rampur district in Uttar Pradesh.

Test Variable- Monitoring and Supervision

Group Statistics

	Block	N	M	SD	SEM
Monitoring and Supervision	Chamrauvaa	6	**2.7667**	.19664	.08028
	Shahabad	6	**1.8333**	.15055	.06146

Where M=Mean, SD=Standard Deviation, SEM=Standard Error Mean

From the above group statistics table the mean score of monitoring and supervision for Chamrauvaa block is 2.7667 which is above 2 and below 3 Likert scale rating which is near to neutral and for Shahabad block is 1.8333 which is near to 2 Likert scale which is near to disagree, therefore the researcher can conclude that the Teachers opinion with respect to monitoring and supervision is more agree for Chamrauvaa block in comparison to Shahabad block that means monitoring and supervision operation is more at Chamrauvaa block in comparison to Shahabad block under MDM scheme at Rampur district in Uttar Pradesh.

Independent T test		t-test for Equality of Means						
		t	df	Sig.	MD	SED	95% Confidence Interval	
							Lower	Upper
Monitoring and Supervision	Equal variances assumed	9.231	10	.000	.93333	.10111	.70806	1.15861
	Equal variances not assumed	9.231	9.363	**.000**	.93333	.10111	.70596	1.16070

Where MD= Mean Difference, SED=Standard Error Difference

Since the eight null Hypothesis was H08t: There is no significant difference of opinion of Teachers between the Chamrauvaa and Shahabad block with respect to the monitoring and supervision under MDM scheme at Rampur district in Uttar Pradesh.

From the above table

The sig. value (2 tailed) 0.000 < 0.05(commonly accepted level of significance), hence Reject null hypothesis H08t, therefore the researcher can conclude that there is a significant difference of opinion of Teachers between the Chamrauvaa and Shahabad block with respect to the monitoring and supervision under MDMS at Rampur district in Uttar Pradesh.

For Gram Pradhans: Perception of MDMS:

First Stage Analysis: For Gram Pradhan (Frequency Test)

Is the MDMS being proven effective in making your village a welfare village?

		Frequency	%	Valid %	Cumulative %
Valid	Yes	6	100.0	100.0	100.0

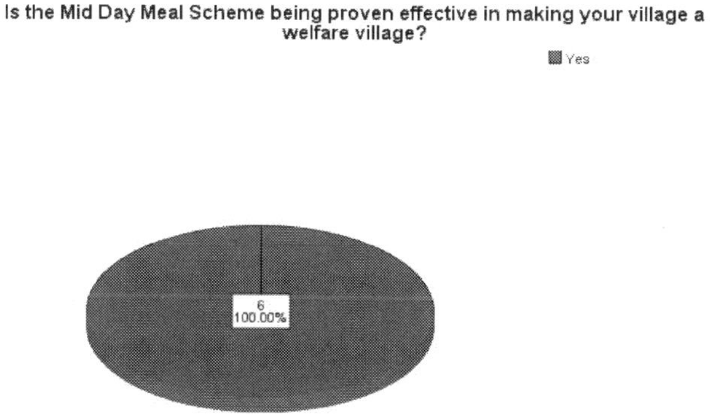

From the above table and pie chart, all the Gram Pradhan said that MDM scheme was proven effective in making the entire village a welfare village under; hence the researcher can conclude that Gram Pradhan agreed about the opinion that MDMS was effective for the welfare village concept at Rampur district in Uttar Pradesh.

Is the MDMS being proven helpful in the internal development of your village?

		Frequency	%	Valid %	Cumulative %
Valid	Yes	6	100.0	100.0	100.0

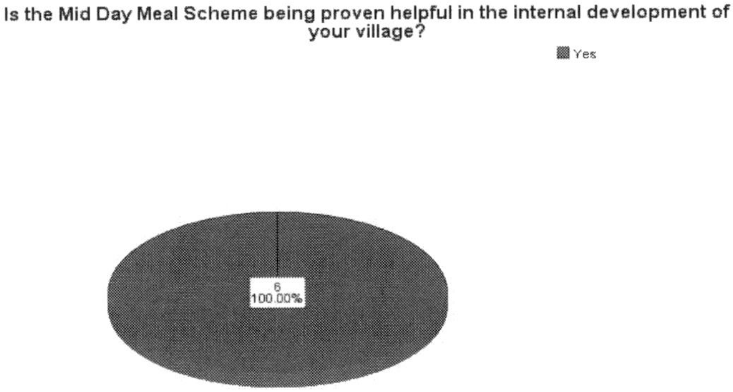

From the above table and pie chart, all the Gram Pradhan said that the MDMS was proven helpful in the internal development of the entire village , hence the researcher can conclude that Gram Pradhan agree about the opinion that MDM scheme is helpful in the internal development of the entire village at Rampur district in Uttar Pradesh.

Are the developments of the children of the underdeveloped category of your village through MDM Scheme?

		Frequency	%	Valid %	Cumulative %
Valid	Yes	6	100.0	100.0	100.0

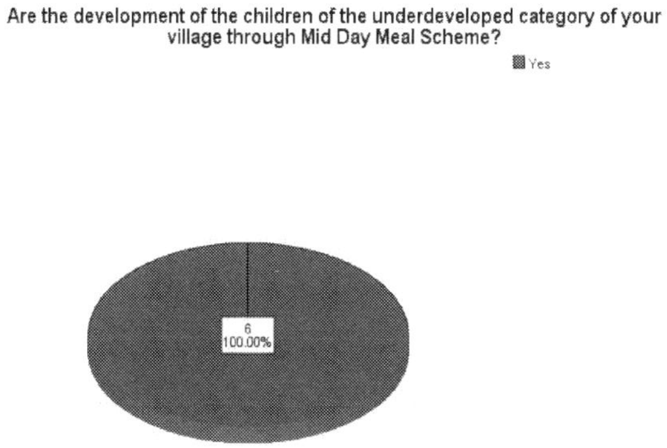

From the above table and pie chart, all the Gram Pradhan said that through the MDMS there was a proper development of the underdeveloped category children, hence the researcher can conclude that Gram Pradhan agree about the opinion that MDM scheme is helpful in the development of the underdeveloped children at Rampur district in Uttar Pradesh.

Is the MDMS fulfilling the right of children's health & education in your village?

		Frequency	%	Valid %	Cumulative %
Valid	Yes	6	100.0	100.0	100.0

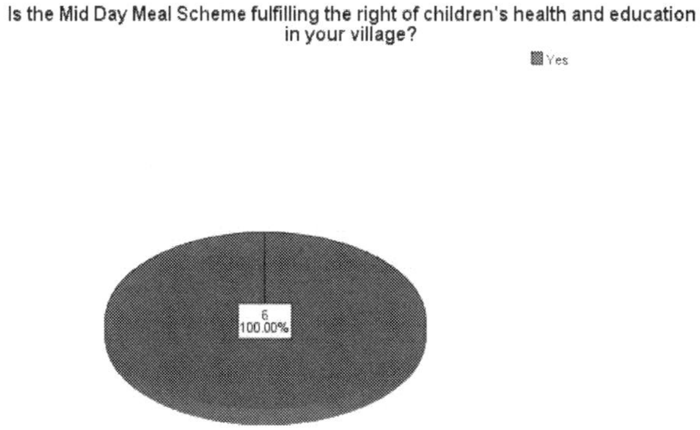

From the above table and pie chart, all the Gram Pradhan said that the MDMS was fulfilling the right of children's health and education in village, hence the researcher can conclude that Gram

Pradhan agreed about the opinion that MDMS was effective & fulfilling the concept of health and education among the children under the mid-day scheme for the entire village children at Rampur district in Uttar Pradesh.

Is the MDMS being affected by the local politics of the village?

		Frequency	%	Valid %	Cumulative %
Valid	No	6	100.0	100.0	100.0

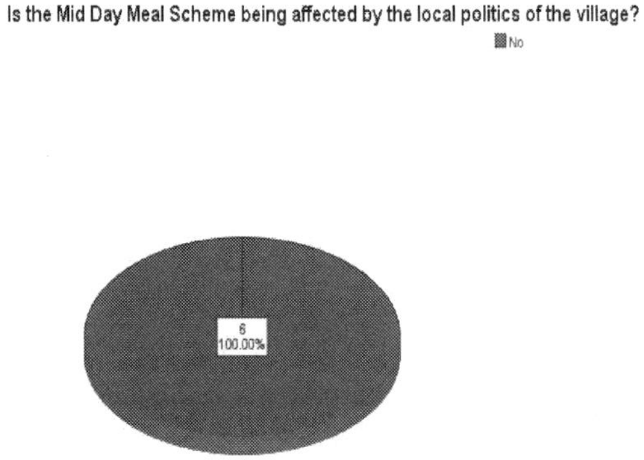

From the above table and pie chart, all the Gram Pradhan said that MDM scheme does not affect the local village level politics, hence the researcher can conclude that Gram Pradhan disagrees about the opinion that MDM scheme is affecting the village level politics at Rampur district in Uttar Pradesh.

Do you go to school from time to time and inspect food given to children under the MDMS?

		Frequency	%	Valid %	Cumulative %
Valid	Yes	6	100.0	100.0	100.0

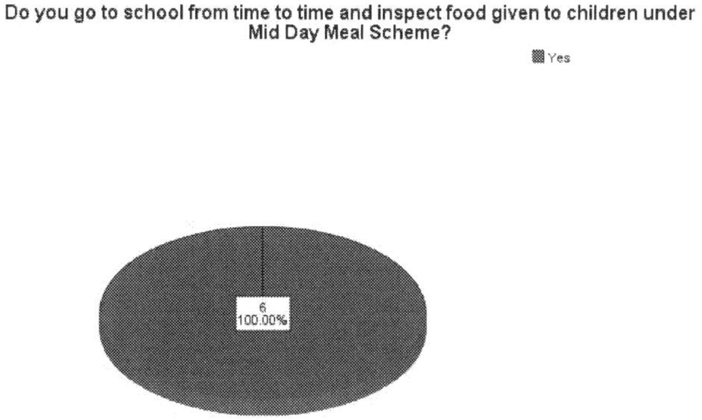

From the above table and pie chart, all the Gram Pradhan said that they inspected the food given to the children time to time, hence the researcher can conclude that Gram Pradhan was inspecting the meal quality time to time for the MDMS at Rampur district in Uttar Pradesh.

Do you check the documents of MDMS in the school?

		Frequency	%	Valid %	Cumulative %
Valid	Yes	6	100.0	100.0	100.0

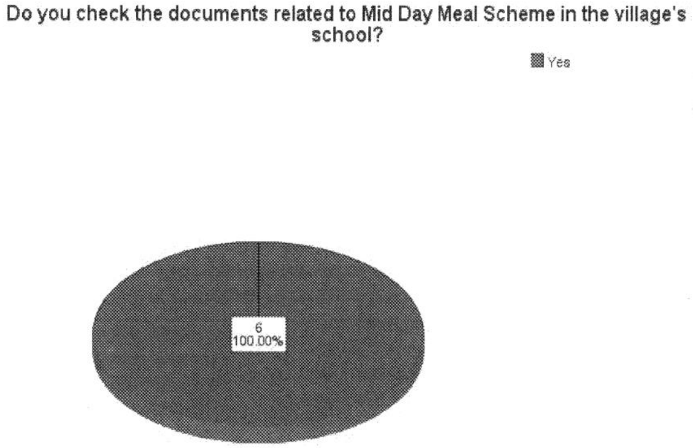

From the above table and pie chart, all the Gram Pradhan said that they checked the documents; hence the researcher can conclude that Gram Pradhan was checking the important documents of MDMS at Rampur district in Uttar Pradesh.

Did the funds received for the MDMS in your school on time?

		Frequency	%	Valid %	Cumulative %
Valid	Yes	6	100.0	100.0	100.0

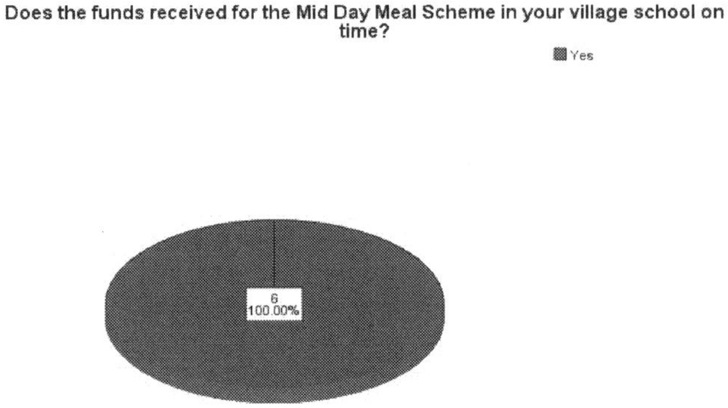

From the above table and pie chart, all the Gram Pradhan said that the funds received for the MDMS were on time for the better implementation of this scheme, hence the researcher can conclude that in the opinion of Gram Pradhan, the funds received timely for the MDMS at Rampur district in Uttar Pradesh.

If funds not received timely, then do you prepare children food with your own money?

		Frequency	%	Valid %	Cumulative %
Valid	Yes	6	100.0	100.0	100.0

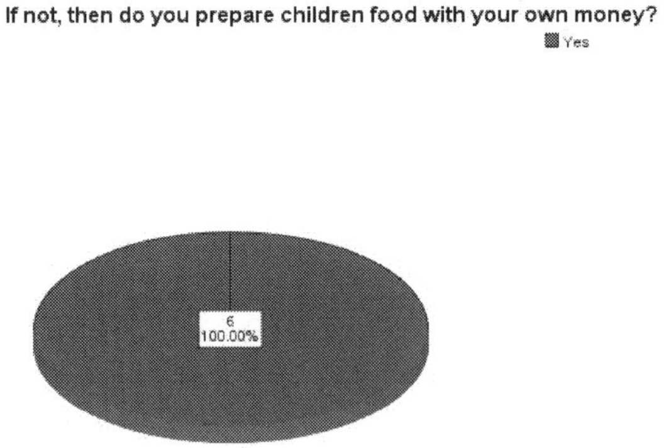

From the above table and pie chart, all the Gram Pradhan said that if funds were not received on time they prepared the children food with their own money, hence the researcher can conclude that in the opinion of Gram Pradhan, if funds were not received on time they prepare the children food with their own earn money under the MDMS at Rampur district in Uttar Pradesh.

Do you complain about the MDMS to any administrative officer?

		Frequency	%	Valid %	Cumulative %
Valid	Yes	6	100.0	100.0	100.0

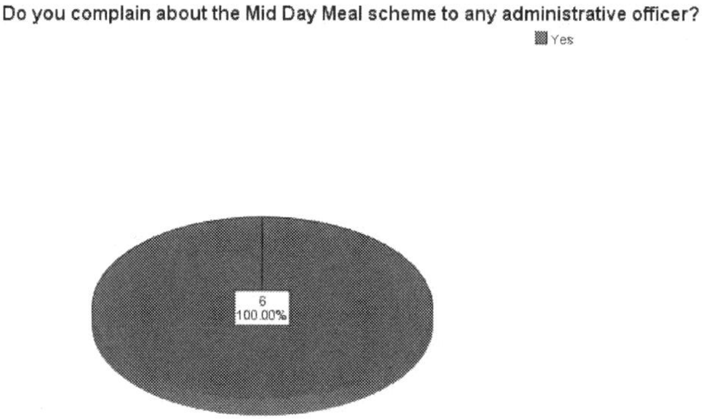

From the above table and pie chart, all the Gram Pradhan said that they complained about the MDMS to the BSA for the better implementation of this scheme, hence the researcher can conclude that in the opinion of Gram Pradhan, they always did genuine complaint related to the MDMS to the BSA at Rampur district in Uttar Pradesh.

Is the grievance related to the MDMS being prompt at the administrative level or delayed?

		Frequency	%	Valid %	Cumulative %
Valid	No	6	100.0	100.0	100.0

Is the grievance related to the Mid Day Meal Scheme being prompt at the administrative level or delayed?

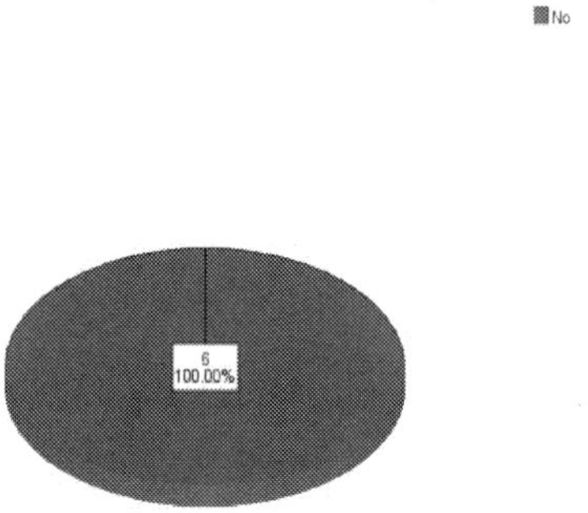

From the above table and pie chart, all the Gram Pradhan said that the grievance related to the MDMS was not being prompt at the administrative level (BSA Level) under this scheme, hence the researcher can conclude that in the opinion of Gram Pradhan, grievances were not handled by the administrative authority for the MDMS at Rampur district in Uttar Pradesh.

In the MDMS, the food being given to the children in your village's school is inspected by the people of the village.

		Frequency	%	Valid %	Cumulative %
Valid	No	6	100.0	100.0	100.0

In the Mid Day Meal Scheme, the food being given to the children in your village's school is inspected by the people of the village.

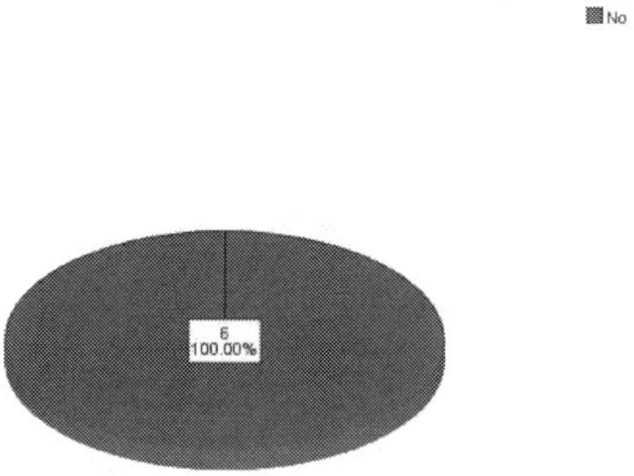

From the above table and pie chart, all the Gram Pradhan said that village people were no inspecting the food quality distributed to the children for the better implementation of this scheme, hence the researcher can conclude that in the opinion of Gram Pradhan, the village people were not monitoring the food quality given to the kids under the MDMS at Rampur district in Uttar Pradesh.

Does your village school maintain the standard of grain quality given by the Kotedar?

		Frequency	%	Valid %	Cumulative %
Valid	Yes	6	100.0	100.0	100.0

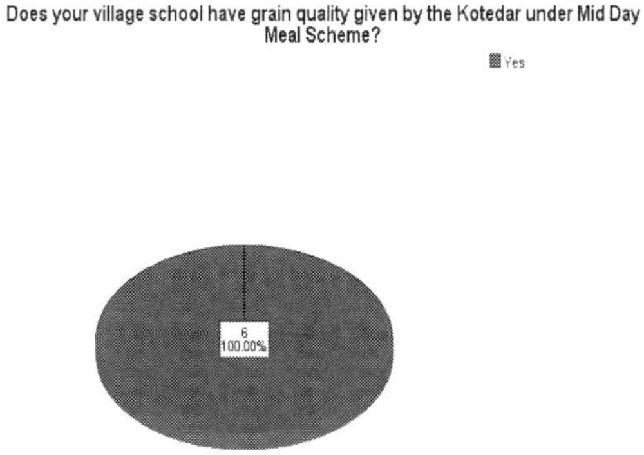

From the above table and pie chart, all the Gram Pradhan said that the village school maintain the standard of the food grain quality given by the kotedar under the MDM for the better implementation of this scheme, hence the researcher can conclude that in the opinion of Gram Pradhan, school administration maintain the standard of food grain quality under the MDMS at Rampur district in Uttar Pradesh.

Is the food grain under the MDMS in your village's school given on time by the Kotedar?

		Frequency	%	Valid %	Cumulative %
Valid	Yes	6	100.0	100.0	100.0

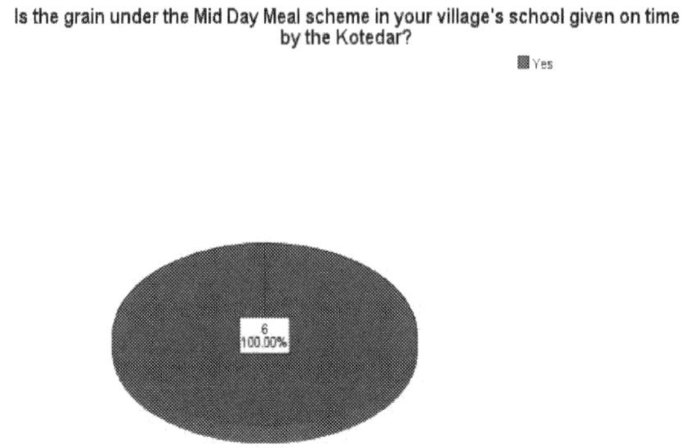

From the above table and pie chart, all the Gram Pradhan said that foodgrain received by the kotedar on time for the better implementation of this scheme; hence the researcher can conclude that in the opinion of Gram Pradhan, food grains provided by the kotedar on time under the MDMS at Rampur district in Uttar Pradesh.

Did MDMS inspect through a social audit?

	Frequency	%	Valid %	Cumulative %
Valid No	6	100.0	100.0	100.0

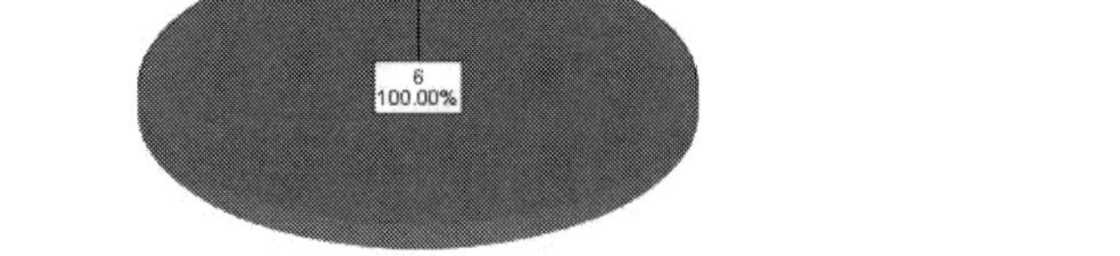

From the above table and pie chart, all the Gram Pradhan said that there was no inspection through the social audit for the better implementation; hence the researcher can conclude that in the opinion of Gram Pradhan, there was no social audit under MDMS at Rampur district in Uttar Pradesh.

For Gram Pradhans: Second Stage Analysis: (Independent T Test)

The Null Hypothesis has been formulated as follows

H01g: There is no significant difference of opinion of Gram Pradhans between the Chamrauvaa and Shahabad block with respect to the institutional efficiency of MDMS at Rampur district in Uttar Pradesh.

H02g: There is no significant difference of opinion of Gram Pradhans between the Chamrauvaa and Shahabad block with respect to the food delivery of MDMS at Rampur district in Uttar Pradesh.

H03g: There is no significant difference of opinion of Gram Pradhans between the Chamrauvaa and Shahabad block with respect to the corruption & mismanagement under MDMS at Rampur district in Uttar Pradesh.

H04g: There is no significant difference of opinion of Gram Pradhans between the Chamrauvaa and Shahabad block with respect to the implementation failure of MDMS at Rampur district in Uttar Pradesh.

Here again four null hypothesis was formulated for the Gram Pradhans (g) with respect to the four test parameters such as institutional efficiency, food delivery, corruption & mismanagement and implementation failure under MDMS for the two blocks Chamrauvaa and Shahabad at Rampur district in Uttar Pradesh.

Descriptive Analysis:

Test Variable- Institutional Efficiency

Descriptive Statistics

	N	Min.	Max.	Mean	Std. Deviation
Institutional Efficiency	6	1.60	3.60	2.4667	.74476
Valid N (listwise)	6				

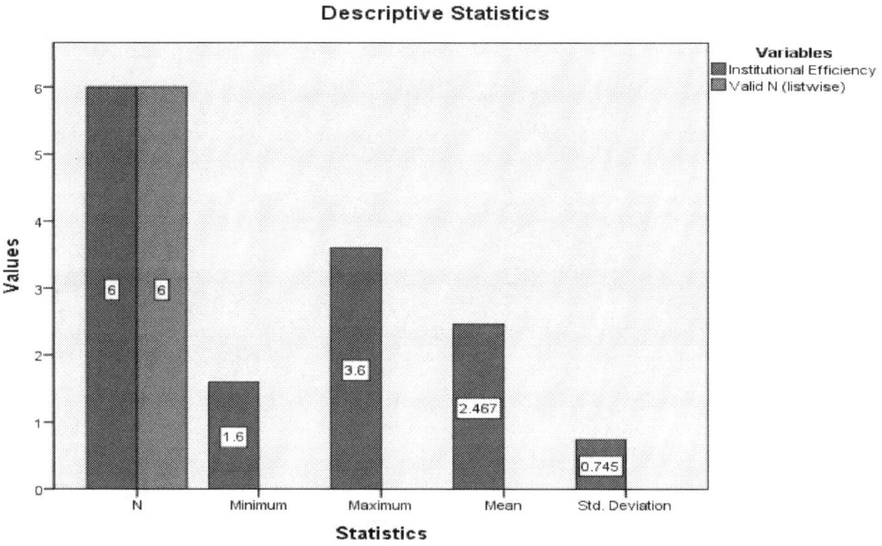

From the above descriptive statistics table and bar chart the mean score of institutional efficiency with respect to Gram Pradhans for Rampur district is 2.467 which is above 2 and below 3 Likert scale rating which is near to neutral, therefore on the basis of parents opinion, the researcher can conclude that the opinion of Gram Pradhans with respect to institutional efficiency is neutral at Rampur district in Uttar Pradesh.

Group Statistics

	Block	N	M	SD	SEM
Institutional Efficiency	Chamrauvaa	3	**3.0667**	.50332	.29059
	Shahabad	3	**1.8667**	.23094	.13333

Where M=Mean, SD=Standard Deviation, SEM=Standard Error Mean

From the above group statistics table the mean score of institutional efficiency for Chamrauvaa block is 3.0667 which is above 2 and below 3 Likert scale rating which is near to neutral and for Shahabad block is 1.8667 which is again above 1 and below 2 Likert scale which is near to disagree, therefore on the basis of Gram Pradhan's opinion, the researcher can conclude that the institutional efficiency at Chamrauvaa block is better than Shahabad block at Rampur district in Uttar Pradesh.

Independent T Test		t-test for Equality of Means						
		t	df	Sig.	MD	SED	95% Confidence Interval	
							Lower	Upper
Institutiona l Efficiency	Equal variances assumed	3.753	4	.020	1.200	.31972	.31231	2.08769
	Equal variances not assumed	3.753	2.806	**.037**	1.200	.31972	.14161	2.25839

Where MD= Mean Difference, SED=Standard Error Difference

Since the first Null Hypothesis was H01g: There is no significant difference of opinion of Gram Pradhans between the Chamrauvaa and Shahabad block with respect to the institutional efficiency of MDM scheme at Rampur district in Uttar Pradesh.

From the above table

The sig. value (2 tailed) 0.037 < 0.05(commonly accepted level of significance), hence Reject Null hypothesis H01g, therefore the researcher can conclude that there is a significant difference of opinion of Gram Pradhans between the Chamrauvaa and Shahabad block with respect to the institutional efficiency of MDMS at Rampur district in Uttar Pradesh.

Descriptive Statistics

	N	Min.	Max.	Mean	Std. Deviation
Food Delivery	6	2.20	4.00	2.9000	.80747
Valid N (listwise)	6				

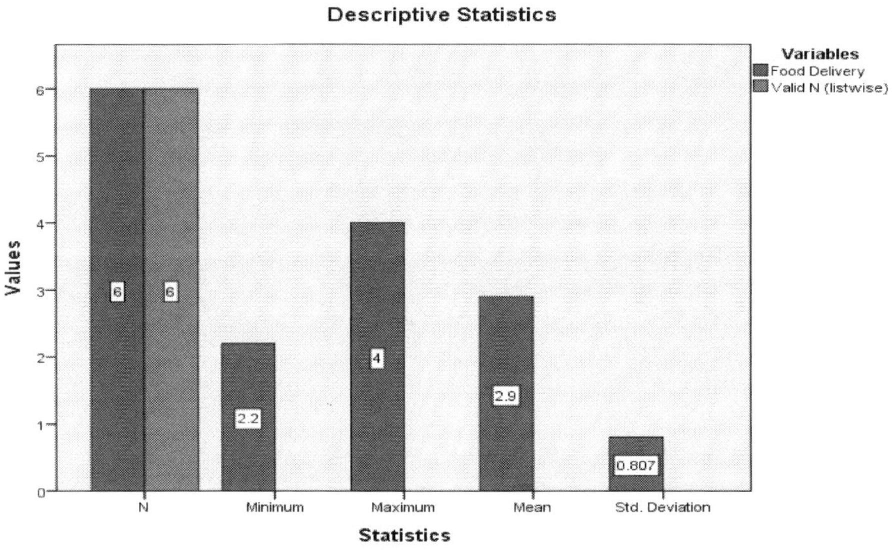

From the above descriptive statistics table and bar chart the mean score of food delivery with respect to Gram Pradhans for Rampur district is 2.9000 which is above 2 and below 3 Likert scale rating which is near to neutral, therefore on the basis of parents opinion, the researcher can conclude that the opinion of Gram Pradhans with respect to food delivery is at moderate level at Rampur district in Uttar Pradesh.

Group Statistics

	Block	N	**M**	SD	SEM
Food Delivery	Chamrauvaa	3	**2.2000**	.00000	.00000
	Shahabad	3	**3.6000**	.40000	.23094

Where M=Mean, SD=Standard Deviation, SEM=Standard Error Mean

From the above group statistics table the mean score of Food Delivery for Chamrauvaa block is 2.2000 which is above 2 and below 3 likert scale rating which is near to disagree and for Shahabad block is 3.6000 which is above 3 and below 4 likert scale which is near to agree, therefore the researcher can conclude that the Gram Pradhans opinion with respect to Food Delivery is more disagree for Chamrauvaa block in comparison to Shahabad block that means food delivery is not better at Chamrauvaa block in comparison to Shahabad block under MDM scheme at Rampur district in Uttar Pradesh.

Independent T Test		t-test for Equality of Means						
		t	df	Sig.	MD	SED	95% Confidence Interval	
							Lower	Upper
Food Delivery	Equal variances assumed	-6.062	4	.004	-1.40000	.23094	-2.04119	-.75881
	Equal variances not assumed	-6.062	2.000	**.026**	-1.40000	.23094	-2.39366	-.40634

Where MD= Mean Difference, SED=Standard Error Difference

Since the second null Hypothesis was H02g: There is no significant difference of opinion of Gram Pradhans between the Chamrauvaa and Shahabad block with respect to the food Delivery under MDM scheme at Rampur district in Uttar Pradesh.

From the above table

The sig. value (2 tailed) 0.026 < 0.05(commonly accepted level of significance), hence Reject Null hypothesis H02g, therefore the researcher can conclude that there is a significant difference of opinion of Gram Pradhans between the Chamrauvaa and Shahabad block with respect to the food Delivery under MDM scheme at Rampur district in Uttar Pradesh.

Descriptive Statistics

	N	Min.	Max.	Mean	Std. Deviation
Corruption & Mismanagement	6	2.40	4.60	3.3000	.90111
Valid N (listwise)	6				

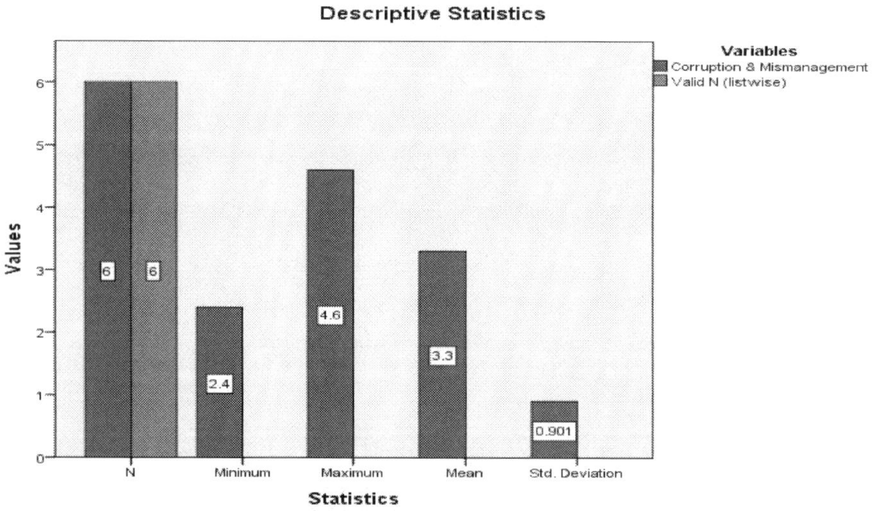

From the above descriptive statistics table and bar chart the mean score of corruption and mismanagement with respect to parents for Rampur district is 3.300 which is above 3 and below 4 likert scale rating which is near to neutral, therefore the researcher can conclude that the opinion of Gram Pradhans with respect to corruption and mismanagement is neutral at Rampur district in Uttar Pradesh.

Group Statistics

	Block	N	M	SD	SEM
Corruption & Mismanagement	Chamrauvaa	3	**2.5333**	.11547	.06667
	Shahabad	3	**4.0667**	.50332	.29059

Where M=Mean, SD=Standard Deviation, SEM=Standard Error Mean

From the above group statistics table the mean score of Corruption & Mismanagement for Chamrauvaa block is 2.5333 which is above 2 and below 3 Likert scale rating which is near to disagree and for Shahabad block is 4.0667 which is above 4 and below 4 Likert scale which is near to agree, therefore the researcher can conclude that the Gram Pradhans opinion with respect to Corruption & Mismanagement is more disagree for Chamrauvaa block in comparison to Shahabad block that means there is less corruption & mismanagement at Chamrauvaa block in comparison to Shahabad block under MDM scheme at Rampur district in Uttar Pradesh.

Independent T Test		t-test for Equality of Means						
		t	df	Sig.	MD	SED	95% Confidence Interval	
							Lower	Upper
Corruption & Mismanagement	Equal variances assumed	-5.143	4	.007	-1.53333	.29814	-2.36111	-.70556
	Equal variances not assumed	-5.143	2.210	**.029**	-1.53333	.29814	-2.70615	-.36052

Where MD= Mean Difference, SED=Standard Error Difference

Since the third null Hypothesis was H03g: There is no significant difference of opinion of Gram Pradhans between the Chamrauvaa and Shahabad block with respect to the Corruption & Mismanagement under MDM scheme at Rampur district in Uttar Pradesh.

From the above table

The sig. value (2 tailed) 0.029 < 0.05(commonly accepted level of significance), hence Reject Null hypothesis H03g, Therefore the researcher can conclude that there is a significant difference of opinion of Gram Pradhans between the Chamrauvaa and Shahabad block with respect to the Corruption & Mismanagement under MDM scheme at Rampur district in Uttar Pradesh.

Descriptive Statistics

	N	Min.	Max.	Mean	Std. Deviation
Implementation Failure	6	1.60	4.00	2.8333	.98319
Valid N (listwise)	6				

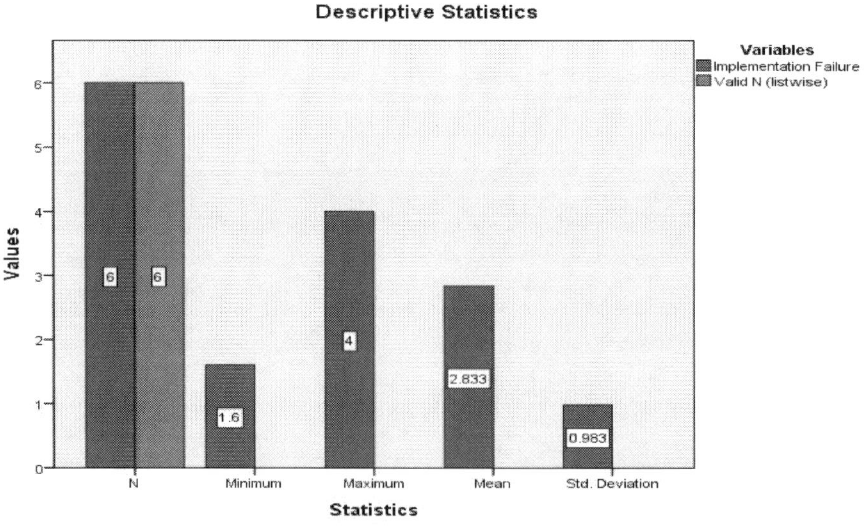

From the above descriptive statistics table and bar chart the mean score of implementation failure with respect to Gram Pradhans for Rampur district is 2.833 which is above 2 and below 3 Likert scale rating which is near to neutral, therefore on the basis of Gram Pradhan opinion, the researcher can conclude that the opinion of parents with respect to implementation failure is at moderate level at Rampur district in Uttar Pradesh.

Group Statistics

	Block	N	**M**	SD	SEM
Implementation Failure	Chamrauvaa	3	**2.0000**	.40000	.23094
	Shahabad	3	**3.6667**	.41633	.24037

Where M=Mean, SD=Standard Deviation, SEM=Standard Error Mean

From the above group statistics table the mean score of Implementation Failure for Chamrauvaa block is 2.000 which is above 2 and below 3 Likert scale rating which is near to disagree and for Shahabad block is 3.667 which is above 3 and below 4 Likert scale which is near to agree, therefore the researcher can conclude that the Gram Pradhans opinion with respect to Implementation Failure is more disagree for Chamrauvaa block in comparison to Shahabad block that means Implementation Failure is less at Chamrauvaa block in comparison to Shahabad block under MDM scheme at Rampur district in Uttar Pradesh.

Independent T Test		t-test for Equality of Means						
		t	df	Sig.	MD	SED	95% Confidence Interval	
							Lower	Upper
Implementation Failure	Equal variances assumed	-5.000	4	.007	-1.66667	.33333	-2.59215	-.74118

	Equal variances not assumed	-5.000	3.994	**.008**	-1.66667	.33333	-2.59273	-.74060

Where MD= Mean Difference, SED=Standard Error Difference

Since the fourth null Hypothesis was H04g: There is no significant difference of opinion of Gram Pradhans between the Chamrauvaa and Shahabad block with respect to the Implementation Failure under MDM scheme at Rampur district in Uttar Pradesh.

From the above table

The sig. value (2 tailed) 0.008 < 0.05(commonly accepted level of significance), hence Reject Null Hypothesis H04g, therefore the researcher can conclude that there is a significant difference of opinion of Gram Pradhans between the Chamrauvaa and Shahabad block with respect to the Implementation Failure under MDMS at Rampur district in Uttar Pradesh.

For Gram Pradhans: Public Participation under MDMS:

The null Hypothesis is formulated as

H05g : There is no significant difference of opinion of Gram Pradhans between the Chamrauvaa and Shahabad block with respect to the participation under MDMS at Rampur district in Uttar Pradesh.

H06g : There is no significant difference of opinion of Gram Pradhans between the Chamrauvaa and Shahabad block with respect to the Public Inaccessibility under MDMS at Rampur district in Uttar Pradesh.

Here again two Null Hypothesis was formulated for Gram Pradhan(g) with respect to two test parameters such as Participation and Public Inaccessibility which will be tested through independent T test for two blocks Chamrauvaa and Shahabad at Rampur district in Uttar Pradesh.

Descriptive Analysis:

Test Variable- Public Participation

Descriptive Statistics

	N	Min.	Max.	Mean	Std. Deviation
Participation	6	1.80	4.40	3.1333	1.04051
Valid N (listwise)	6				

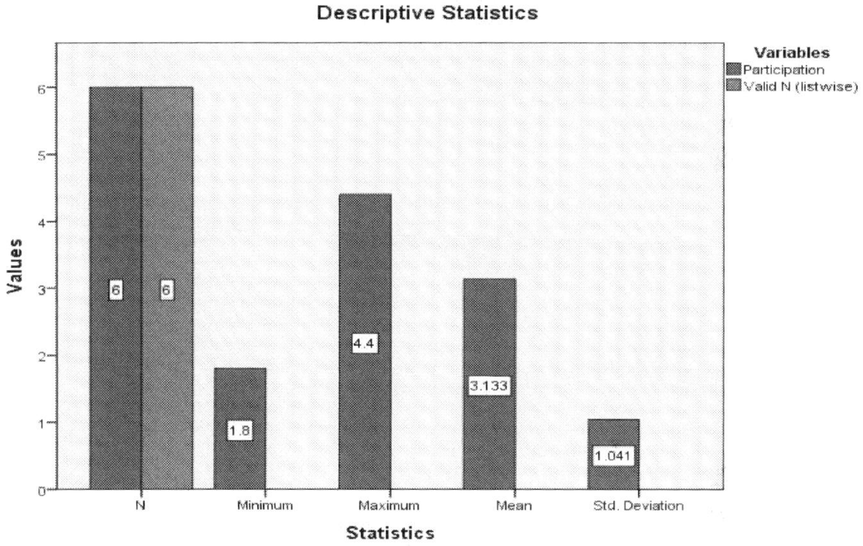

From the above descriptive statistics table and bar chart the mean score of participation with respect to Gram Pradhans for Rampur district is 3.133 which is above 3 and below 4 Likert scale rating which is near to neutral, therefore on the basis of parents opinion, the researcher can conclude that the opinion of Gram Pradhans with respect to participation is at moderate level at Rampur district in Uttar Pradesh.

Group Statistics

	Block	N	**M**	SD	SEM

Participation	Chamrauvaa	3	**3.9333**	.64291	.37118
	Shahabad	3	**2.3333**	.61101	.35277

Where M=Mean, SD=Standard Deviation, SEM=Standard Error Mean

From the above group statistics table the mean score of participation for Chamrauvaa block is 3.9333 which is above 3 and below 4 Likert scale rating which is near to agree and for Shahabad block is 2.3333 which is above 2 and below 3 Likert scale which is near to disagree, therefore on the basis of Gram Pradhan opinion, the researcher can conclude that the participation under MDM scheme at Chamrauvaa block is better than Shahabad block at Rampur district in Uttar Pradesh.

Independent T Test		t-test for Equality of Means						
		t	df	Sig.	MD	SED	95% Confidence Interval	
							Lower	Upper
Participation	Equal variances assumed	3.125	4	.035	1.60000	.51208	.17825	3.02175
	Equal variances not assumed	3.125	3.990	**.035**	1.60000	.51208	.17680	3.02320

Where MD= Mean Difference, SED=Standard Error Difference

Since the fifth null Hypothesis was H05g: There is no significant difference of opinion of Gram Pradhans between the Chamrauvaa and Shahabad block with respect to the participation under MDM scheme at Rampur district in Uttar Pradesh.

From the above table

The sig. value (2 tailed) 0.035 < 0.05(commonly accepted level of significance), hence Reject H05g, Therefore the researcher can conclude that there is a significant difference of opinion of Gram

Pradhans between the Chamrauvaa and Shahabad block with respect to the participation under MDM scheme at Rampur district in Uttar Pradesh.

Test Variable- Public Inaccessibility

Descriptive Statistics

	N	Min.	Max.	Mean	Std. Deviation
Public Inaccessibility	6	2.20	4.40	3.2333	1.01522
Valid N (listwise)	6				

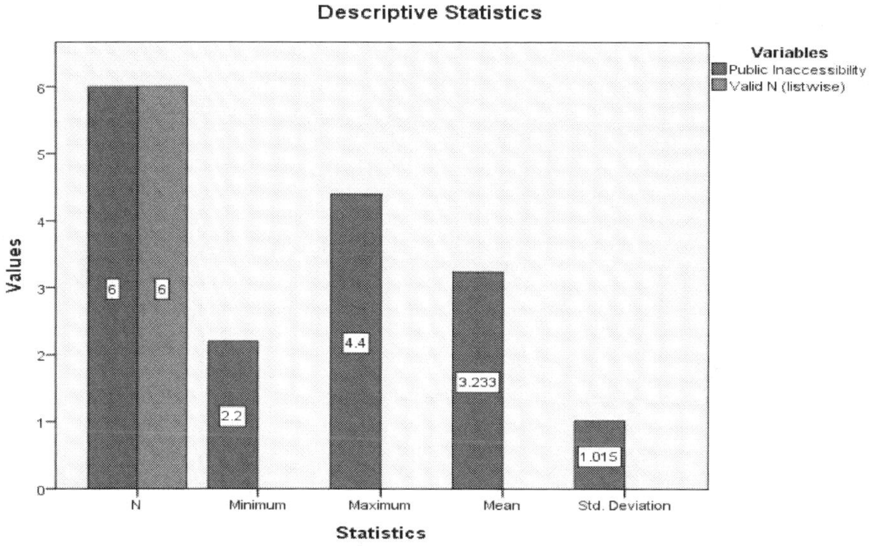

From the above descriptive statistics table and bar chart the mean score of public inaccessibility with respect to Gram Pradhans for Rampur district is 3.233 which is above 3 and below 4 Likert scale rating which is near to neutral, therefore on the basis of parents opinion, the researcher can conclude that the opinion of Gram Pradhans with respect to public inaccessibility is at moderate level that means public are at par accessible for mid-day scheme at Rampur district in Uttar Pradesh.

Group Statistics

	Block	N	**M**	SD	SEM
Public Inaccessibility	Chamrauvaa	3	**2.3333**	.23094	.13333
	Shahabad	3	**4.1333**	.30551	.17638

Where M=Mean, SD=Standard Deviation, SEM=Standard Error Mean

From the above group statistics table the mean score of Public Inaccessibility for Chamrauvaa block is 2.3333 which is above 2 and below 3 Likert scale rating which is near to disagree and for Shahabad block is 4.1333 which is above 4 and below 5 Likert scale which is near to agree, therefore the researcher can conclude that the Gram Pradhans opinion with respect to Public Inaccessibility is more disagree for Chamrauvaa block in comparison to Shahabad block that means public accessibility is better at Chamrauvaa block in comparison to Shahabad block under MDM scheme at Rampur district in Uttar Pradesh.

Independent T Test		t-test for Equality of Means						
		t	df	Sig.	MD	SED	95% Confidence Interval	
							Lower	Upper
Public Inaccessibility	Equal variances assumed	-8.141	4	.001	-1.80000	.22111	-2.41390	-1.18610
	Equal variances not assumed	-8.141	3.723	**.002**	-1.80000	.22111	-2.43233	-1.16767

Where MD= Mean Difference, SED=Standard Error Difference

Since the sixth null Hypothesis was H06g: There is no significant difference of opinion of Gram Pradhans between the Chamrauvaa and Shahabad block with respect to the Public Inaccessibility under MDM scheme at Rampur district in Uttar Pradesh.

From the above table

The sig. (2 tailed) 0.002 < 0.05(commonly accepted level of significance), hence Reject Null hypothesis H06g, therefore the researcher can conclude that there is a significant difference of opinion of Gram Pradhans between the Chamrauvaa and Shahabad block with respect to the Public Inaccessibility under MDM scheme at Rampur district in Uttar Pradesh.

For Gram Pradhan: Accountability in MDMS:

The Null Hypothesis is formulated as

H07g: There is no significant difference of opinion of Gram Pradhans between the Chamrauvaa and Shahabad block with respect to the Management of Funds under MDMS at Rampur district in Uttar Pradesh.

H08g: There is no significant difference of opinion of Gram Pradhans between the Chamrauvaa and Shahabad block with respect to the Monitoring and Supervision under MDMS scheme at Rampur district in Uttar Pradesh.

Here again two Null Hypothesis was formulated for Gram Pradhan (g) with respect to two test parameters such as Management of Funds and Monitoring and Supervision which will be tested through independent T test for two blocks Chamrauvaa and Shahabad at Rampur district in Uttar Pradesh.

Descriptive Analysis:

Test Variable- Management of Funds

Descriptive Statistics

	N	Min.	Max.	Mean	Std. Deviation

Management of Funds	6	1.40	2.60	1.9333	.46762
Valid N (listwise)	6				

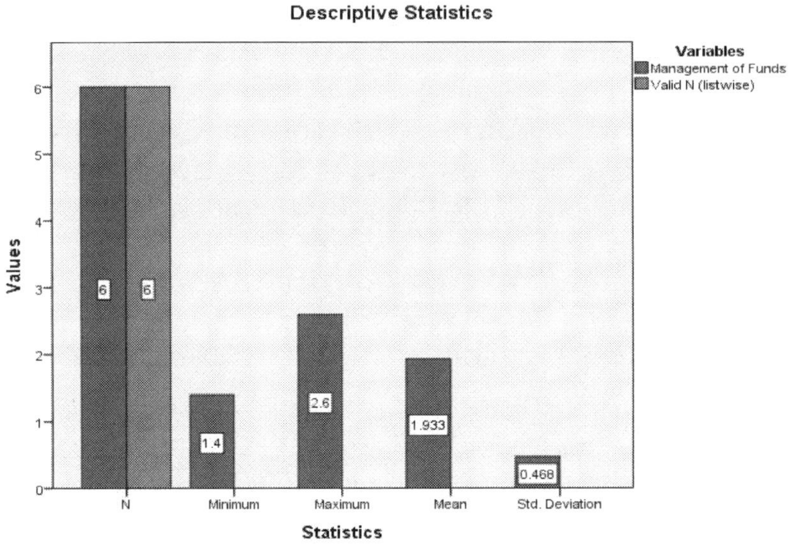

From the above descriptive statistics table and bar chart the mean score of management of funds with respect to parents for Rampur district is 1.933 which is above 1 and below 2 Likert scale rating which is near to disagree, therefore on the basis of parents opinion, the researcher can conclude that the opinion of Gram Pradhans with respect to management of funds is not satisfactory at Rampur district in Uttar Pradesh.

Group Statistics

	Block	N	**M**	SD	SEM
Management of Funds	Chamrauvaa	3	**2.2667**	.41633	.24037
	Shahabad	3	**1.6000**	.20000	.11547

Where M=Mean, SD=Standard Deviation, SEM=Standard Error Mean

From the above group statistics table the mean score of Role of State for Chamrauvaa block is 2.2667 which is above 1 and below 2 Likert scale rating which is near to disagree and for Shahabad block is 1.6600 which is again above 1 and below 2 Likert scale which is near to disagree, therefore the researcher can conclude that the Gram Pradhans opinion with respect to management of funds is more or less equally managed for Chamrauvaa block and Shahabad block under MDM scheme at Rampur district in Uttar Pradesh.

Independent T Test		t-test for Equality of Means						
		t	df	**Sig.**	MD	SED	95% Confidence Interval	
							Lower	Upper
Management of Funds	Equal variances assumed	2.500	4	.067	.66667	.26667	-.07372	1.40705
	Equal variances not assumed	2.500	2.876	**.091**	.66667	.26667	-.20299	1.53633

Where MD= Mean Difference, SED=Standard Error Difference

Since the fourth null Hypothesis was H07g: There is no significant difference of opinion of Gram Pradhans between the Chamrauvaa and Shahabad block with respect to the management of funds under MDM scheme at Rampur district in Uttar Pradesh.

From the above table

The sig. value (2 tailed) 0.091 > 0.05(commonly accepted level of significance), hence Accept Null hypothesis H07p,therefore the researcher can conclude that there is no significant difference of opinion of Gram Pradhans between the Chamrauvaa and Shahabad block with respect to the management of funds under the MDMS at Rampur district in Uttar Pradesh.

Descriptive Statistics

	N	Min.	Max.	Mean	Std. Deviation
Monitoring and Supervision	6	1.60	3.00	2.3000	.57619
Valid N (listwise)	6				

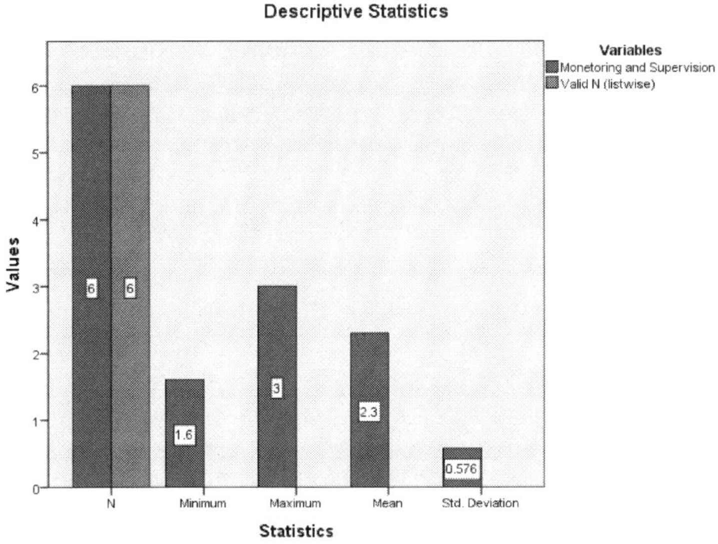

From the above descriptive statistics table and bar chart the mean score of monitoring and supervision with respect to parents for Rampur district is 2.300 which is above 2 and below 3 Likert scale rating which is near to disagree, therefore on the basis of Gram Pradhans opinion, the researcher can conclude that the opinion of Gram Pradhans with respect to monitoring and supervision is not properly managed for mid-day scheme at Rampur district in Uttar Pradesh.

Group Statistics

	Block	N	**M**	SD	SEM
	Chamrauvaa	3	**2.8000**	.20000	.11547

Monitoring and Supervision	Shahabad	3	**1.8000**	.20000	.11547

Where M=Mean, SD=Standard Deviation, SEM=Standard Error Mean

From the above group statistics table the mean score of Monetoring and Supervision for Chamrauvaa block is 2.800 which is above 2 and below 3 Likert scale rating which is near to neutral and for Shahabad block is 1.8000 which is again above 1 and below 2 Likert scale which is near to disagree, therefore on the basis of Gram Pradhan's opinion, the researcher can conclude that the Monetoring and Supervision operation is better for Chamrauvaa block than Shahabad block under MDM scheme at Rampur district in Uttar Pradesh.

Independent T Test		t-test for Equality of Means						
		t	df	Sig.	MD	SED	95% Confidence Interval	
							Lower	Upper
Monitoring and Supervision	Equal variances assumed	6.124	4	.004	1.00000	.16330	.54661	1.45339
	Equal variances not assumed	6.124	4.000	**.004**	1.00000	.16330	.54661	1.45339

Where MD= Mean Difference, SED=Standard Error Difference

Since the eight null Hypothesis was H08g: There is no significant difference of opinion of Gram Pradhans between the Chamrauvaa and Shahabad block with respect to the Monetoring and Supervision under MDMS at Rampur district in Uttar Pradesh.

From the above table

The sig. value (2 tailed) 0.004 < 0.05(commonly accepted level of significance), hence Reject Null hypothesis H08g, therefore the researcher can conclude that there is a significant difference of opinion of Gram Pradhans between the Chamrauvaa and Shahabad block with respect to the Monetoring and Supervision under MDMS at Rampur district in Uttar Pradesh.

Findings & Conclusion

From Students Point Of View

Most of the students were taking MDM every day and the MDMS was interesting amongst the students. 61.67% students stated that they got the MDM according to the weekly menu whereas 38.33% students said that they did not get MDM in accordance to the weekly menu. 53.33% students stated that they all are sitting collectively and additionally taking their MDM collectively whereas 46.67% students said that they do not take a seat collectively and do now not devour together in the school. 45% students said that they get the milk and fruits each and every week and most of the students do now not get the milk or fruits, due to the fact of most of the students are absent on that day in which there are a milk and fruit distribution day. 56.67% students bring their utensils from the home to devour the MDM in the school whereas 43.33% students said that they do no longer bring the utensils from the home due to the fact the faculty administration is imparting the utensils to the students. 18.33% students said that teachers first eat the food, 68.33% students said that teachers do not first eat the food under the MDMS in the school and 13.33 % students said that teacher sometimes first eat the food in the school.100% students stated that they do now not take the food at home and all the students take their MDM in the school. 60 % students said that the meals is prepared on the Wooden Stove whereas 40% students said that foods underneath MDMS are prepared on the Gas Stove and there may also be one reason that Woods are without problems handy in the village, therefore, the school administration is using the Wooden Stove for the preparation of MDM for their school. 63.33% students stated that their parents did not inspect the food providing in the MDMS from time to time whereas 36.67% students stated that their parents inspect the meals quality. There was Hand pump facility in their school under MDMS at Rampur district in Uttar Pradesh.

From Parents Point Of View

All the parents stated that their youth go to the school each and every day and the parents recognize the significance of the education in their children's lives. All the parents said that their kids got the MDM every day in the school and that this mid-day scheme is famous in the village amongst the students and parents. All the parents stated that their adolescents took the MDM in the school, not at home. 73.33 % parents stated that they did not look at the meals quality whereas only 26.67% mother and father look at the meals quality.68.33% mother and father stated that school administration is not providing the food in accordance to the weekly menu beneath MDMS whereas 31.67% parents said that the meals providing to their kids are in accordance to the weekly menu. 55% of mother and father were participating in the meeting of school management committee whereas 45 % of parents did not participate. 68.33 % parents said that the problems related with the MDM were no longer resolved in the school administration committee with the aid of the school administration whereas solely 31.67% parents said the problems raised through them were resolved and most of the parents were not satisfied through the working of the school administration committee for the execution of the MDMS. 66.67% parents stated that village politics did not have an effect whereas 33.33% parents said that village-level politics have an effect on the MDMS. 70% mother and father said that their teenagers are now not sitting on the basis of caste companies in the school while taking the MDM whereas solely 30% parents stated that their young people are sitting on the caste organizations in the school and most of the parents are at ease with the sitting arrangement at some stage in MDM due to the fact there is no caste biases by way of the school administration. 73.33% parents said that their kids do not carry the utensil from home for taking MDM in the faculty whereas only 26.67% mother and father said that their youngsters convey the utensils. 80% parents stated that the food grain quality was satisfactory whereas 20% parents look at the food grain quality. 83.33% parents said that they did not taste the baked meals whereas only 16.67% parent's style the baked meals and most of the parents are taking pastime in the tasting of the meals supplying under MDMS to their children. All the mother and father do no longer examine (inspect) the MDM as the citizen crew formed via the village people for the betterment of the MDMS.86.67% parents do whinge whereas only 13.33% parents approached the BSA for complaining the issue of this scheme. 51.67% parents stated that their children's education and fitness has multiplied whereas 48.33% are now not accepting that their children's education and health has improved. 91.67% mother and father stated that they do not look at the meals grain provide process from the Kotedar to Gram Pradhan and from Gram Pradhan to the School administration whereas solely 8.33% parents check out the food grain furnish process, consequently the researcher can conclude that most of the parents do no longer look into the food grain supply procedure from the Kotedar to Gram Pradhan and from Gram Pradhan to the School administration under the MDMS at Rampur district in Uttar Pradesh.

From Teachers Point Of View

All the teachers stated that MDMS was playing an important function in the internal improvement of India and there was a relationship between the MDMS and the inside development of India, This scheme was finishing the concept of welfare state in the human context, This scheme was empowering the two vital rights, education, and health, food given to the youth in the school are in accordance to the weekly menu. 75% of instructors said that Gram Pradhan/Villagers/Parents monitor the food given to the youngsters whereas 25% said that Gram Pradhan/Villagers/Parents don't screen the food given to the children. 75% teachers said that there is no complained lodged by the Gram Pradhan/ Parents/ Guardians related with the food given to the college adolescents whereas 25% teacher stated that Gram Pradhan/ Parents / Guardians are complaining about the meals given to their teenagers. All the teachers stated that there is a lack of communication, lack of mutual relationship and lack of inspection among the Gram Pradhan, Kotedar (dealer of food grain), Parents and BSA. 75% of teachers stated that they got the meals grains timely whereas 25% of teachers said that they did not get food grain timely. All the teachers stated that there was no social audit in their school. 75% of teachers said that there was no inspection of MDM by using the citizen crew of the village human beings whereas 25% teacher stated that inspection was finished through the citizen group. All the instructors stated that no teenagers are seated one at a time on the foundation of caste whilst serving the food. Half of teachers said that the MDMS impacts the local village level politics whereas other half of teachers additionally said the MDMS does now not have an effect on village level politics. All the teachers stated that there was daily monitoring by IVRS (Interacting Voice Response System). All the instructors stated that youngsters get the milk and fruits once in a week. 75% teacher stated that complaints were resolved by the Gram Pradhan/ Block Level Officer for the faculty administration whereas 25% teachers stated that complaints are no longer resolved by using the Gram Pradhan/Block Level Officer. 50% of teachers stated that there was timely payment to the cook and his assistant whereas 50% teachers said that there was no timely paymentto the cook and his assistant. All teachers said that if the payment is no longer being paid to the cook and his assistant then there will be an adverse effect on the MDMS at Rampur district in Uttar Pradesh.

From Gram Pradhans Point Of View

All the Gram Pradhans stated that the MDMS is demonstrated effective in making the whole village a welfare village, MDMS is established beneficial in the inside improvement of the entire village ,through the MDMS there is a applicable development of the underdeveloped class children, MDMS is pleasing the proper of children's fitness and training in village, MDMS does now not have an effect on the nearby village stage politics, all the Gram Pradhan stated that they look into the food given to the teenagers time to time underneath the MDMS, they test the documents associated to two the MDMS, therefore the researcher can conclude that Gram Pradhan two is checking the essential archives related with the MDMS, the fund acquired for the MDMS are on time for the better implementation of this scheme, if fund is now not obtained on time they put together the youth food with their very own money for the MDMS, they whinge associated to the MDMS to the authorities administrative officer such as BSA below the MDMS for the higher implementation of this scheme, the complaint related to the MDMS is now not being on the spot at the administrative level (BSA Level) beneath this scheme, there is no inspection of the food fine given to the adolescents with the aid of the village humans for the MDMS for the higher implementation of this scheme, village school hold the standard of the food grain first-class given with the aid of the kotedar below the MDM for the better implementation of this scheme, food grain acquired by way of the kotedar on time for the school for the MDMS for the better implementation of this scheme, there is no inspection done via the social audit for the MDMS for the better implementation for the MDMS at Rampur district in Uttar Pradesh.

From Bsa (Basic Siksha Adhikari)'S Point Of View

The BSA (Basic Siksha Adhikari) was providing the administrative help in the inspection of the MDMS in the schools, he was also getting the full aid at the authorities level for the inspection of this scheme, he has the maximum work load , the mid-day format was very desirable scheme amongst the children in the schools, the training and fitness of the teenagers is enhancing via the MDMS at the school degree , there was a local village politics between the Gram Pradhan and village humans in the easy execution of the scheme , there have to be any online monitoring device in the easy execution , there was a most paper work involved in the reporting , subsequently the researcher can conclude that MDM reporting system was complex and involve the heavy paper work for the smooth execution, government was imparting sufficient financial aid in the execution, teachers attendance was not regular, kitchen cook and his assistance's attendance was not regular, student's attendance was not regular, there was an ideal association for the food hygiene , food was oftentimes checked by way of the administration for the desirable execution, meals given to the youngsters was in accordance to the weekly menu, as a result the researcher can conclude that suited weekly menu gadget is following through the school administration for the better execution of the MDMS at Rampur District in Uttar Pradesh.

T-Test ANALYSIS for Two Blocks Chamrouaa and Shahabad of Rampur district in Uttar Pradesh

The researcher has no longer included the students and BSA in this T test study due to the fact the students are not comfy with the scaling kind questionnaire which is the vital requirement in the t-test analysis and since there is only one BSA has been appointed in a district and our study was only for one district that is Rampur and for T-test analysis there is a requirement of more than two sample size in a group therefore the researcher has not consider the BSA in the study of T-test analysis.

From Parents Point Of View

The researcher can conclude that the institutional effectivity at Chamrauvaa block is almost identical as Shahabad block and there is no significant difference of opinion of mother and father between the Chamrauvaa and Shahabad block with respect to the institutional effectivity of MDMS at Rampur district in Uttar Pradesh. The mother and father opinion with respect to Food Delivery is extra disagree for Chamrauvaa block in contrast to Shahabad block that skill meals transport is higher at Chamrauvaa block in assessment to Shahabad block and there is a extensive distinction of opinion of mother and father between the Chamrauvaa and Shahabad block with respect to the food Delivery under MDMS at Rampur district in Uttar Pradesh. the parents opinion with admire to Corruption & Mismanagement is more disagree for Chamrauvaa block in comparison to Shahabad block that skill there is much less corruption & mismanagement at Chamrauvaa block in contrast to Shahabad block and two there is a substantial difference of opinion of mother and father between the Chamrauvaa and Shahabad block with recognize to the Corruption & Mismanagement under MDMS at Rampur district in Uttar Pradesh. the parents opinion with respect to Implementation Failure is more disagree for Chamrauvaa block in assessment to Shahabad block that ability Implementation Failure is much less at Chamrauvaa block in evaluation to Shahabad block and there is a tremendous difference of opinion of parents between the Chamrauvaa and Shahabad block with appreciate to the Implementation Failure below MDMS at Rampur district in Uttar Pradesh. On the basis of parents opinion, the researcher can conclude that the participation below MDMS at Chamrauvaa block is better than Shahabad block and there is a sizable distinction of opinion of mother and father between the Chamrauvaa and Shahabad block with admire to the participation under MDMS at Rampur district in Uttar Pradesh. the parents opinion with recognize to Public Inaccessibility is extra disagree for Chamrauvaa block in contrast to Shahabad block that potential public accessibility is higher at Chamrauvaa block in comparison to Shahabad block and there is a massive distinction of opinion of parents between the Chamrauvaa and Shahabad block with appreciate to the Public Inaccessibility below MDMS at Rampur district in Uttar Pradesh. the parent's opinion with recognize to management of funds is greater suitable for Chamrauvaa block in evaluation to Shahabad block below MDMS and there is a vast difference of opinion of parents between the Chamrauvaa and Shahabad block with respect to the administration of funds underneath MDMS at Rampur district in Uttar Pradesh.

From Teachers Point Of View

The researcher can conclude that the Teachers opinion with appreciate to Institutional Efficiency is better for Chamrauvaa block in comparison to Shahabad block below MDMS and there is no full-size distinction of opinion of Teachers between the Chamrauvaa and Shahabad block with respect to the Institutional Efficiency underneath MDMS at Rampur district in Uttar Pradesh. the teachers opinion with respect to Food Delivery is more disagree for Chamrauvaa block in evaluation to Shahabad block that skill food delivery is now not higher at Chamrauvaa block in comparison to Shahabad block beneath MDMS and there is a tremendous difference of opinion of instructors between the

Chamrauvaa and Shahabad block with respect to the food Delivery under MDMS at Rampur district in Uttar Pradesh. the parents opinion with admire to Corruption & Mismanagement is extra disagree for Chamrauvaa block in comparison to Shahabad block that capacity there is greater corruption & mismanagement at Chamrauvaa block in contrast to Shahabad block and two there is a widespread distinction of opinion of instructors between the Chamrauvaa and Shahabad block with respect to the Corruption & Mismanagement under MDMS at Rampur district in Uttar Pradesh. the teachers opinion with recognize to Implementation Failure is extra disagree for Chamrauvaa block in evaluation to Shahabad block that capability Implementation Failure is much less at Chamrauvaa block in assessment to Shahabad block and two there is a giant distinction of opinion of teachers between the Chamrauvaa and Shahabad block with recognize to the Implementation Failure below MDMS at Rampur district in Uttar Pradesh. the Teachers opinion with admire to Participation is more agree for Chamrauvaa block in evaluation to Shahabad block that skill humans participation is better at Chamrauvaa block in evaluation to Shahabad block two and there is a giant distinction of opinion of Teachers between the Chamrauvaa and Shahabad block with respect to the Participation underneath MDMS at Rampur district in Uttar Pradesh. on the basis of teachers opinion, the researcher can conclude that the opinion of instructors with recognize to public inaccessibility is at average stage that capacity public are handy at reasonable degree for mid-day scheme and there is a tremendous distinction of opinion of teachers between the Chamrauvaa and Shahabad block with admire to the Public Inaccessibility below MDMS at Rampur district in Uttar Pradesh. the Teachers opinion with respect to administration of cash is strongly disagree for Chamrauvaa block in evaluation to Shahabad block that means management of money is less at Chamrauvaa block in assessment to Shahabad block and two there is a massive distinction of opinion of Teachers between the Chamrauvaa and Shahabad block with appreciate to the management of cash under MDMS at Rampur district in Uttar Pradesh. the Teachers opinion with admire to monitoring and supervision is more agree for Chamrauvaa block in contrast to Shahabad block that capability monitoring and supervision operation is extra at Chamrauvaa block in comparison to Shahabad block underneath MDMS and there is a good sized distinction of opinion of Teachers between the Chamrauvaa and Shahabad block with admire to the monitoring and supervision beneath MDMS at Rampur district in Uttar Pradesh.

From Gram Pradhan's Point Of View

The researcher can conclude that the institutional efficiency at Chamrauvaa block is better than Shahabad block and there is a huge distinction of opinion of Gram Pradhans between the Chamrauvaa and Shahabad block with recognize to the institutional efficiency of MDMS at Rampur district in Uttar Pradesh. the Gram Pradhans opinion with recognize to Food Delivery is extra disagree for Chamrauvaa block in comparison to Shahabad block that means meals delivery is no longer higher at Chamrauvaa block in contrast to Shahabad block and there is a good sized distinction of opinion of Gram Pradhans between the Chamrauvaa and Shahabad block with respect to the meals Delivery underneath MDMS at Rampur district in Uttar Pradesh. the Gram Pradhans opinion with respect to Corruption & Mismanagement is extra disagree for Chamrauvaa block in evaluation to Shahabad block that ability there is less corruption & mismanagement at Chamrauvaa block in comparison to Shahabad block and there is a significant distinction of opinion of Gram Pradhans between the Chamrauvaa and Shahabad block with respect to the Corruption & Mismanagement under MDMS at Rampur district in Uttar Pradesh. the Gram Pradhans opinion with respect to Implementation Failure is greater disagree for Chamrauvaa block in assessment to Shahabad block that means Implementation Failure is much less at Chamrauvaa block in contrast to Shahabad block and there is a sizable distinction of opinion of Gram Pradhans between the Chamrauvaa and Shahabad block with admire to the Implementation Failure under MDMS at Rampur district in Uttar Pradesh. on the foundation of Gram Pradhan opinion, the participation below MDMS at Chamrauvaa block is higher than Shahabad block and there is a widespread difference of opinion of Gram Pradhans between the Chamrauvaa and Shahabad block with admire to the participation under MDMS at Rampur district in Uttar Pradesh. the Gram Pradhans opinion with respect to Public Inaccessibility is more disagree for Chamrauvaa block in evaluation to Shahabad block that means public accessibility is better at Chamrauvaa block in evaluation to Shahabad block and there is a enormous difference of opinion of Gram Pradhans between the Chamrauvaa and Shahabad block with respect to the Public Inaccessibility beneath MDMS at Rampur district in Uttar Pradesh. the Gram Pradhans opinion with admire to management of funds is extra or less equally managed for Chamrauvaa block and Shahabad block and there is no big distinction of opinion of Gram Pradhans between the Chamrauvaa and Shahabad block with respect to the administration of cash below MDMS at Rampur district in Uttar Pradesh. On the basis of Gram Pradhans opinion, the researcher can conclude that the Monitoring and Supervision operation is better for Chamrauvaa block than Shahabad block and there is a great difference of opinion of Gram Pradhans between the Chamrauvaa and Shahabad block with respect to the Monitoring and Supervision below MDMS at Rampur district in Uttar Pradesh.

Chapter VII
Concluding Remarks

In Indian federal system, when the central government formulates development policies at the central level, it is the state governments or the local bodies implement as being the units of local administration. The state governments are expected to adopt certain development policies that are aimed at ensuring equality of opportunity for all regarding access to the basic necessities, education, health services, food, housing, employment, fair distribution of income and so on. On the other hand, they are also expected to create conditions, for realizing the fulfilment of the right to food by undertaking appropriate economic and social policies to correct the social injustices. In this context, the public sector and private sectors organizations coordinate, not only among themselves but also with other national and international Institutions as well as with the civil society to implement the scheme.

The MDM works as a decentralized programme, funded jointly with the aid of the Central and state governments. While the meals grain comes from Food Corporation of India through the state meals corporations, it is the School Management Committee (SMC) with the headmaster, Panchayati Raj Institutions (PRI) or different community representatives, and three fourths representation of mother and father of youngsters studying in that school, that is given the duty to buy pulses, vegetables, oil, spices, firewood, and so on as conversion cost. Parents are seen as the biggest stakeholder and that is why the programme shape furnished for the SMCs/Mothers' Committees to have a lead role in the administration and the accountability framework of the programme. Cooks paid Rs 1,000 a month and utensils furnished as section of the scheme come via programme funds. Non-governmental organizations (NGOs) are assigned the accountability to run the programme in a few schools.

Akshay Patra-like NGOs have also been assigned the responsibility in many states. Despite the reference to unsatisfactory implementation reported, studies have mounted the role of the MDM in growing school attendance rates. Government schools have the largest segment of poor kids coming from underprivileged households where food safety at home is an issue. The hot cooked meal, with all its limitations, does keep again kids in schools in large numbers. Studies have additionally indicated how many children, particularly in states with a very excessive proportion of poor families, come hungry to school. MDM does make a distinction in the lives of these children.

There are several other weaknesses of MDMS, both in implementation on the ground and in its concept and design .The MDMS has addressed to some extent the nutrition security of nutritionally deprived school children .But it does not cover children out of school .When we move away from an instrumentalist understanding of MDM as merely an instrument to get children into school and adopt a rights-based viewpoint that regards the nutrition security of the child as a human right, the need to expand the MDMS to cover out-of-school children becomes evident .

A key problem in implementation has to do with both the quantum of funds required and the flow of funds in the scheme . Until the revised norms of 2006 came into effect, the States, on their part, pleaded serious financial constraints in mobilizing the resources for cooking costs. Subsequent experience has shown that even the revised norms do not solve the resource problem completely .Even without ensuring legal minimum wages for cooks and helpers, the cooking costs have been going up.

Utilization certificates of meals grains/funds from the school should be taken by the block level officer on priority groundwork and be despatched to the district authority so that release of cash is expedited. All authorities or non-government or civil society has one common attraction to people that scheme is completely satisfactory and implementation of the scheme is having a trouble and need to be addressed. Together they all assume fixing the signs and symptoms of the hassle will solve the root cause, poverty, by means of putting higher monitoring, higher accountability and better administration by using the same government organisation which has a terrible record in imposing any policy. Monitoring of warm cooked meal to adolescents of major and higher essential classes in over 1,265,000 schools throughout India is a massive task, which desires manpower, infrastructure, and training. Which is really no longer feasible as the scheme is already marred by using corruption top to bottom and again kickback of money from the bottom to top. But for groups aiding Midday Meal scheme, this is a trivial project and can be accomplished with the aid of spending more money, this is exactly what the trouble is when humans strive to fix symptoms alternatively than stopping the scheme.

The policy of the MDMS is very important for primary education promotion especially in rural and backward areas where most people are under poverty. But it is determined that there is a large discrepancy in the implementation of MDM Scheme.

On the basis of the opinion given by the students, the researcher concluded that the students ate the MDM each day according to weekly menu and the scheme was popular amongst the students. Students were sitting together and also taking together. Most of the students did not get the milk or fruits, because most of the students were generally absent on milk or fruit distribution day. Students brought their utensils from the home for MDM. Teachers did not first eat the food provided in the school to the children .The meals prepared on the Wooden Stove because woods were easily accessible in the village. Our Guardian did not check the meals supplied and for drinking water, there was hand pump facility in the school.

Most of the parents stated that their children went to the school each day and the parents knew the importance of the education for their children. Children ate meal each and every day in the school and the scheme was very popular in the village among the students and parents. Children took the MDM at the school, not at home. Parents did not inspect the food quality. School administration was not providing the foods according to the weekly menu. Parents were taking part in the meeting of school management committee. Issues of the MDM were not resolved by the school administration. Children were not sitting on caste basis while taking the meal. Parents did not investigate the meal grain quality. Parents did not check the baked meals but were taking interest for checking the supplied food grains to their children. Parents complained the issue associated to the MDMS. As per the parents' opinion, their children's education and health improved through the MDMS. Parents did not check the MDMS food supply chain process at Rampur district in Uttar Pradesh.

According to them, Teachers presentated a balanced approach to implementation the mid-day scheme was playing an important role in the internal development of India. This was a useful welfare scheme. Food was given to the children on weekly menu basis. There was no complained lodged by the Gram Pradhans / Parents regarding the MDM. There was a lack of communication amongst the Gram Pradhan, Kotedar (supplier of meal grains), Parents and BSA. Teachers received the meal grains on time. There was no social audit of this scheme and no inspection of MDM scheme by the village people. There was daily monitoring by IVRS (Interacting Voice Response System). Complaints of the MDMS were resolved by the Gram Pradhans/BSA under the presence of the school administration. The payment to the cook and his assistant was probably on time and if the payment was not made to the cook and his assistant then this would be adverse effect on MDMS.

Gram Pradhans intimated a rosy picture of MDMS and glorified pradhan's role in it. The MDMS helped in the concept of making a village a welfare village, in the inner improvement of the whole village, a desirable development of the underdeveloped children and this scheme was popular in the proper education and health of the children. This scheme was not affected village politics. Gram Pradhan checked the food given to the kids , they also checked the documents related to the scheme, the fund received were on time, if fund was not received on time, then Gram Pradhan made the arrangement for the meal preparation with their own money.The Gram Pradhan complained the problem of this scheme to the BSA. There was no inspection of the food quality given to the kids; village school checked the standard of the food grain given by the Kotedar, food grain received by the Kotedar on time and there was no social audit for the MDMS at Rampur district in Uttar Pradesh.

BSA was getting the full Government administrative support. The mid-day format was very appealing amongst the kids, the education and fitness of the kids was improving by this scheme. BSA, *confessing* to the opinion of other said that the scheme much politisized at the local level. There must be an online monitoring of this scheme. There was a maximum paper work involved in the reporting of this scheme. Government was spending enough monetary support in this scheme. The teachers, cook, his assistant and student's attendance was not regular for the better implementation of this scheme. There was arrangement for the meals hygiene and the meals given to the kids were according to the weekly menu by the school administration at Rampur District in Uttar Pradesh. In the above discussion the students, parents, teachers, gram pradhans and BSA had given their individual opinion of mid-day scheme. Now in the next section we have discussed the comparative study of two blocks Chamrauvaa and Shahabad at Rampur district of Uttar Pradesh.

The researcher can conclude that the parent's opinion was equal for both the blocks Chamrauvaa and Shahabad for the Institutional efficiency of the MDM scheme. The opinion of parents with admire to Food Delivery under this scheme was better at Chamrauvaa block in comparison to Shahabad block. There was less corruption & mismanagement at Chamrauvaa block in comparison to Shahabad block. Implementation Failure under this scheme was less at Chamrauvaa block in comparison to Shahabad block. Participation of the people at Chamrauvaa block was higher than Shahabad block. Public accessibility was better at Chamrauvaa block in comparison to Shahabad block. The Management of cash was better for Chamrauvaa block in contrast to Shahabad block under MDMS at Rampur district in Uttar Pradesh.

The researcher can conclude that the Teachers opinion for the Institutional Efficiency was better for Chamrauvaa block in comparison to Shahabad block. Implementation Failure was less at Chamrauvaa block in comparison to Shahabad block. Public Participation was higher at Chamrauvaa block in comparison to Shahabad block. The public Inaccessibility was better at Chamrauvaa in comparison to Shahabad block. Management of funds was less at Chamrauvaa block in contrast to Shahabad block. Monitoring and Supervision operation was better at Chamrauvaa block in contrast to Shahabad block under MDMS at Rampur district in Uttar Pradesh.

The researcher can conclude that the Gram Pradhans opinion for the Institutional efficiency at Chamrauvaa block was better than Shahabad block. Food Delivery was not better for Chamrauvaa block in assessment to Shahabad block. Corruption & Mismanagement was less at Chamrauvaa block in comparison to

Shahabad block. Implementation Failure was less at Chamrauvaa block in contrast to Shahabad block. The public Participation was better at Chamrauvaa block than Shahabad block. Public Inaccessibility was better at Chamrauvaa block in contrast to Shahabad block. Management of cash was more or less equally managed for Chamrauvaa block and Shahabad block. Monitoring and Supervision operation was better for Chamrauvaa block than Shahabad block. From the combined opinion of the parents, teachers and Gram Pradhan, the researcher can finally conclude that the performance of the MDMS in the Chamrauvaa block was better than the Shahabad block at Rampur district in Uttar Pradesh.

Suggestions

Government bodies, parents, teacher and gram pradhan should ensure that there should be proper mid day meal distribution according to weekly menu with milk or fruit items and there should be a mandatory provision for the teachers to taste the food before its distribution to the children. Since the government is providing the gas connection to every village, hence the meals should be prepared on the Gas Stove. Though there was drinking water facility for the students but safe, clean, water cooler and water filter should be arranged for each school because health is the prime focus for the students for the quality education. There should be a mandatory provision for the parents to check the grains supplied, the food prepared and the quality & quanitity of the food distributed to their children under the mid day meal scheme at Rampur Disrtict in Uttar Pradesh.

Primary schools with all minimum required infrastructure facilities should be established in the neglected areas on priority basis. Central government should release budget to the states at the earliest. Facilities in the existing government schools should be expanded. To avoid the closure of unrecognized private schools for not fulfilling the prescribed recognition standards within three years, these schools must be helped to improve their facilities by resource support and providing linkages with financial institutions. To meet budgetary constraints, stress must be given on cost effectiveness and accountability at every level.

To meet the increasing demand of qualified and trained full time teachers, the teachers in required number must be recruited at the earliest. Pupil-teacher ratio must be maintained as per requirement. As more and more children move into the primary school age group, it becomes necessary to build more and more schools and recruit more teachers.

Primary schools need to be made aware of the provisions made for 25 percent reservation of seats for the economically and socially weaker and disadvantaged children and the role of school managing committees in this regard. The identification, selection and verification procedure of such children should be well defined and well informed. It should also be notified that how the whole process will be monitored.

Teachers' performance is the most crucial input in the field of education. Well qualified and highly motivated teachers are the key to effective implementation of the curriculum. They give impetus to the teaching-learning process.

It is the duty of the nodal ministry to evaluation the infrastructure development supposed for MDM scheme in the meetings of SMC and representatives of other nodal ministries which run the infrastructure improvement schemes have to be invited to these meetings. Steering-cum-monitoring committees ought to be made useful and active at district/block levels for high-quality implementation, convergence, and monitoring of the scheme.

Bibliography

(n.d.). Retrieved from http://upmdm.org/organization.html

Fennell, S. (2010). Educational Exclusion and Inclusive Development in Indi. University of Cambridge, 35, n.d.

Khera, R. (2013). MDMs: Looking Ahead. Economic & Political Weekly, 10.

(1956). Second Five Year Plan. New Delhi: Planning Commission, GOI.

(1960). Third Five-Year Plan. New Delhi: Planning Commission, GOI.

(1974). Fifth Five-Year Plan. New Delhi: Planning Commission, GOI.

(1983). Sixth Five-Year Plan,. New Delhi: Planning Commission, GOI.

Governance for Sustainable Human Development. (1997). UNDP.

(2006). National Guidelines of NP-NSPE. Government of India.

(2007). Eleventh Five year Plan. New Delhi: Planning Commission, GOI.

(2012). PAISA District Surveys: MDM Scheme.

(2012). Elementary School Feedingand Health Programme Transition strategy.

(2012). SWNMP Department, Secretariat, Chennai,.

SWNMP Department, Secretariat, Chennai, 19869/ NMP.1/2012-4 (April 14, 2012).

(2013, July 18). Retrieved from http://mdm.nic.in

Fifth Review Mission Uttar Pradesh . (2013-2014). 26-27.

Fifth Review Mission Uttar Pradesh . (2013-2014). 26.

(2014, January 24). Retrieved from http://mdm.nic.in/aboutus.html

(2014, January 24). Retrieved from http://mdm.nic.in

(2015, February 3). Retrieved from http://www.ihdindia.org

(2015, January 14). Retrieved from http://www.ohchr.org

(2015, July 1). Retrieved from www.cgshistory.weebly.com

(2015, December 21). Retrieved from www.cag.gov.in

(2015). Performance Audit of MDM Scheme. Comptroller and Auditor General of India.

(2016, March 18). Retrieved from http://www.un-ngls.org

(2016, March 18). Retrieved from http://www.who.int

(2016, March 18). Retrieved from www.educationengland.org.uk

(2016, March 18). Retrieved from www.hgsf-global.org

Annan, K. (1999). Preventing War and Disaster:Annual Report on the Work of the Organization. n.d.: n.d.

Caramani, D. (2014). Comparative Politics. 522.

Caramani, D. (2014). Comparative Politics. 523.

Caramani, D. (2014). Comparative Politics. 538-539.

Draze , J., & Goe, A. (2003). The future of MDM. EPW.

Evans, C. E., & Harpert, C. E. (2009). A history and review of school meal standards in the UK. Journal of Human Nutrition and Dietetics, 22, 89-99.

Gabriele, K. (2014). Is There an Asian Welfare State Model? East and South Asian Trajectories and Approaches to the Welfare State. Friedrich-Ebert-Stiftung (FES). Germany.

Gillard , D. (2003). Food for Thought: child nutrition, the school dinner and the food industry.

Goyal, D. (2013). The status of implementation of the MDMS.

Jain, J., & Shah, M. (2005). MDM in 70 most backward villages of Madhya Pradesh. SamajPragatiSahyog, Madhya Pradesh.

Julia, B. (2005). Assessment of programme implementation and its impact in Udaipur district. SevaMandir,U daipur,Rajasthan.

Kanbur, R. (2010). Journal of the Asia Pacific Economy.

Khera. (2005). The campaign for the implementation of the Supreme Court order.

Khera, R. (2013). MDMs: Looking Ahead. Economic & Political Weekly, 17(32), 10.

Kuhnle, S. (2004). The Developmental Welfare State in Scandinavia: Lessons for the Developing World. Social Policy and Development Programme, 17.

Lal, M. (n.d.). Education-The Inclusive Growth Strategy for the economically and socially disadvantaged in the Society.

Masayuki, F. (2000). The Welfare State, the Middle Class, and the Welfare Society. Review of Population and Social Policy, 9, 1-23.

Mathur, B. (2005). Situation Analysis of MDM Programme in Rajasthan. University of Rajasthan and UNICEF.

(n.d.). Retrieved from www.yojana.gov.in

(n.d.). Retrieved from http://timesofindia.indiatimes.com

Poppendieck, J. (2010). Free for all: Fixing School Food in America. University of Cal ifornia Press, Berkeley os Angeles London.

Powell, M. (2004). Welfare Regimes and the Welfare Mix. European Journal of Political Research, 43, 83-105.

Rajendran, M. M. (1981). Profile of the Child in India: Policies and Programmes. Ministry of Social Welfare, Government of India, New Delhi.

Sakhder, M. M. (1980). Theory of Welfare State (J.S. Bains & R,B Jain ed.). New Delhi: Radiant Publishers.

Savagaon, G. (n.d.). Elementary Education and Inclusive Development in India. 1(6).

Sen, A. (2005). Cooked MDM programme in West Bengal-A study in Birbhum district. PratichiTrust,West Bengal.

Sen, A., & Draze , J. (2000). Development as Freedom. New Delhi: Oxford University Press.

Sen, A., & Draze , J. (2013). An Uncertain Glory:India and Its Contradictions. New Delhi: Thomson Press India.

Sikligar, P. C. (2011). Mid Day Meal Scheme and School Education: Planning Implementation and Effectiveness. New Delhi: Concept Publishing Company Pvt. Ltd.

Sinha, D. (2008). Social Audit of MDM Scheme in AP. Economic & Political Weekly, 1-7.

(n.d.). The review report of 5th joint review mission on MDM scheme in Uttar Pradesh.

Verma, R. (2013, May-June). MDM - Not a Sufficient Deal. International Journal of Advances in Management and Economics, 2(3), 55-63.

Made in the USA
Monee, IL
12 November 2026

4f04d354-a4a5-4071-84c7-de59e73697abR01